ABOUT THE EDITOR

Anne Dempsey is an author, writer and journalist. Journalisti-
cally, her interests lie in the area of health, family relationships,
business and property. She is the author of *What Are You Doing
the Rest of Your Life?* and *The Retirement Book*, two explorations
of retirement in Ireland, and is co-author (with Alice Leahy) of
Not Just a Bed for the Night, a study into Irish homelessness. She
is a trainer in media relations and in health promotion and is a
qualified counsellor with her own practice. She has a daughter
and son, and lives with her husband in Greystones, County
Wicklow.

THE THIRD AGE HANDBOOK

A Guide for Older People in Ireland

Anne Dempsey

The Liffey Press

Published by
The Liffey Press
Ashbrook House, 10 Main Street,
Raheny, Dublin 5, Ireland
www.theliffeypress.com

A catalogue record of this book is
available from the British Library.

ISBN 1-904148-50-6

The author and publishers gratefully acknowledge the
financial support of the Department of Health and Children.

Printed in Spain by GraphyCems.

CONTENTS

About the Contributors .... *vii*

Acknowledgements...*ix*

**Introduction: The Challenge and Potential of the
Third Age** 1
Anne Dempsey

CHAPTER 1: **From Work to Retirement** 19
Eamon Donnelly

*In Focus: The Federation of Active
Retirement Associations*...47

CHAPTER 2: **People Helping People** 53
Clare McGuinness

In Focus: Become a Samaritan? 63

CHAPTER 3: **Never Too Old to Learn** 75
Berni Brady

In Focus: The University of the Third Age 87

CHAPTER 4: **Arts and Leisure** 95
Ann Leahy

In Focus: Getting into History 109

CHAPTER 5: **Fit for Life**... 117
Anne Dempsey

*In Focus: Managing Change and
Getting Fit*...119

CHAPTER 6: In Sickness and in Health 143
Janet Convery and Anne Dempsey

In Focus: Don't Let the Blues Hang Around......... 172

In Focus: Talking with Your Doctor...................... 183

**CHAPTER 7: Home Sweet Home: Living
Independently** 201
Janet Convery and Anne Dempsey

*In Focus: Keeping you and your Home
Safe from Crime*... 204

*In Focus: Staying at Home with Support:
Home Care Grants*... 213

CHAPTER 8: Life and Death 227
Anne Dempsey

In Focus: The Paper Trail.................................... 228

CHAPTER 9: Changing Ageist Attitudes? 241
Paul Murray

In Focus: Senior Citizens Parliament................... 244

CHAPTER 10: The Spiritual Dimension 259
Catherine McCann

Appendix 1: United Nations Principles for Older Persons 277

Appendix 2: List of Organisations... 281

Index 295

ABOUT THE CONTRIBUTORS

Berni Brady has been Director of AONTAS, the National Association of Adult Education, since 1993. Before taking up her position in AONTAS, Berni directed the Dublin Adult Literacy Scheme for 13 years.

Janet Convery is currently Director of Services for Older People in the East Coast Area Health Board and is very involved in policy, planning and service. Janet worked as a social worker and as family support co-ordinator for the Eastern Health Board for 10 years before taking up a full-time lecturing post at Trinity College Dublin, where she had taught part-time for several years.

Eamon Donnelly is a consultant and course leader for the Retirement Planning Council of Ireland.

Anne Leahy works at Age & Opportunity, the Irish national agency working to challenge negative attitudes to ageing and older people, and to promote greater participation by older people in society.

Catherine McCann is a counsellor, author and gardener. Her Shekina Sculpture Garden in Glenmalure, County Wicklow, is open to the public on selected days from May to September (Tel: 01-2838711).

Clare McGuinness is Executive Officer with Volunteering Ireland.

Paul Murray is Head of Communications at Age Action Ireland.

ACKNOWLEDGEMENTS

My name on the cover is not a true representation of author-ship. First of all, publisher David Givens had the vision that the time was right for this book. Second, thanks must go to the main contributors Berni Brady, Janet Convery, Eamon Donnelly, Ann Leahy, Catherine McCann, Clare McGuinness and Paul Murray, with appreciation also to Seamus Cashman and Mary Harkin.

Thirdly, I received help from Jim Collier, Kevin Cronin, Gordon Lennox, Neville Murphy, Michael O'Halloran and Judy Taylor. Finally, I salute the skills of editor Brian Langan with whom it has been a pleasure to work.

Anne Dempsey
November 2004.

for Dave

Introduction

THE CHALLENGE AND POTENTIAL OF THE THIRD AGE

Anne Dempsey

"Grow old along with me!
The best is yet to be,
The last of life, for which the first was made"
— Robert Browning

BEING YOU

Lillian Willoughby from Philadelphia went to prison for a week in autumn 2004 convicted of obstructing a US federal building as a protest against the war in Iraq. She was 89 years old. Whatever you think of her politics, the wheelchair-bound activist is proof that the spirit doesn't necessarily fade with age and infirmity.

Lillian may not conform to our idea of the typical octogenarian, and that's part of the point of this book. Nobody does. While the older population is often categorised in terms of their health status, attitudes or roles ("granny mugged at knife point"; "granddad completes marathon in under three hours"), this will always be a crude measurement at best. The over-60s in Ireland and elsewhere today are not a homogenous gathering. Examine any random group of older Irish public figures — take, for example, actor Anna Manahan, cardiologist Maurice

Nelligan, singer Sonny Knowles, broadcaster Andy O'Mahony, poet Brendan Kennelly, entrepreneur Anthony O'Reilly, writer Maeve Binchy, politician Mary O'Rourke, architect Sam Stephenson . . . we could go on. What these people have in common is that they are all over 60, but after that they probably differ widely from each other in terms of interests, politics, hobbies and attitudes.

You will probably find that many over-60s in your own circle may be relatively dissimilar from each other — apart from that date on the calendar which places them among our older population.

So if you are an older person in Ireland today, one of the most important things to know about yourself is that you are as unique as you have always been, and the passing of the years has not diminished this. You have the same rights and responsibilities, and probably your own mix of prejudices, attitudes and fears as does everyone else. You are an individual first, with your own preferences, beliefs, experiences, flaws and values.

So who exactly is old? One tongue-in-cheek definition is that an older person is someone five years older than you are. Old age is a constantly moveable feast for those involved, and Joe, a County Wicklow voluntary worker aged 68, is not alone in talking about the work he does with the "old folk" — in which group he does not include himself. The meaning of "old" changed considerably over the last century. In 1900 many a worker was worn out at 40 and dead by 50. Now our lifespan has the potential to be equally divided between years in work, and years post-work to include new life choices — though having sufficient health and finances to enjoy these is obviously relevant.

THIRD AGE — NOT GOOD NEWS FOR ALL CONCERNED

Another reason not to lump all older people together is that the experience of being old varies considerably between people in older age groups. An Inquiry into the Third Age established in 1989 by the Carnegie UK Trust defined third agers as those people who may have completed their second age of conventional work and child-rearing and can now look forward to two or more decades of healthy, active life before their fourth age of dependency and possibly disability arrives. However, there are widespread disparities between people in their third age, with some enjoying its potential, others quite the reverse. For many, the post-work decades are spoiled by lack of money, indifferent health, or poor skills, with some people experiencing multiple disadvantages.

When this author asked a cross-section of professionals working with older people what the issues were, most chose to stress bad news — the economic deprivation of many older people in Ireland today, their poor health status, their loneliness, their isolation (particularly in rural Ireland), poor housing — and the inadequate level of services in response to these comprehensive needs.

So, in summary, how people fare in the third age may depend on the life they have had up to this point. For those with good health, up-to-date skills and reasonable finances, the third age can be a fulfilling and rewarding time. But for those who are sick, poor, lonely, or carry a heavy burden of caring, it can be a time of stress and unhappiness.

Young-Old and Old-Old

There are also differences between the "young-old" and the "old-old". While we can't be definitive about this — because many octogenarians are still going strong and some sixty-somethings can stultify — people in their 60s tend to be more active and spry than people in their 80s. They are more likely to be living in their own home and still swimming in the mainstream of life. Theirs is the classic third age of our title; their main child-rearing years are behind them. Twenty years on, even the healthiest of them will probably be somewhat more dependent, in poorer health and have withdrawn somewhat from the hurly-burly. Of course, they can still be contributing members of society. No matter what our age, we can continue to be loved and loving spouses, partners, friends, parents, aunts and uncles, godparents, grandparents, great-grandparents — still able to enjoy life and to give to it.

CHANGES IN RETIREMENT PATTERNS

However, even the traditional definition of the third age is in the process of movement, review and redefinition and while it still fits for many, change is afoot. For a start, present and future trends in occupational pension provision mean that in the future many third agers may need to work beyond age 65, thus lessening some leisure years. In the past, law and practice resulting in compulsory retirement was considered ageist in some quarters, though, in truth, many were glad to receive their presentation and go. In future we may see the ending — or blurring of the age 65 retirement watershed, not as a result of employer appreciation of the contribution of older staff, but because such staff members need to work for longer to build up their pension fund. So less leisure, more work.

Only one in two workers have their own pension, according to the Pensions Board, and the government hopes to increase this proportion to seven out of ten over the next few years. In the past, employers were not obliged to provide their staff with a pension, and many firms avoided the significant expense involved in running an occupational scheme. Since September 2003, employers must give all employees not covered by an occupational scheme access to a standard Personal Retirement Savings Account, a portable pension with low minimum contribution levels.

CHANGES IN FAMILY TRENDS

Also, that second plank of the third age — i.e. a time after active child-rearing — is also under siege because of the kipper gen-eration. A "kipper" is someone who continues to live on in the parental home after becoming adult because they are unready or unable financially to set up their own home. The acronym stands for Kids In Parents' Pockets Eroding Retirement Savings. There are 6.8 million kippers in the UK, with less than one in two paying rent.

While we have no comparable figures on Irish kipperdom, our high cost of house purchase/rental would support the view that there are a lot of kippers out there. Describing their role as "eroding retirement savings" is probably a step too far. How-ever, having an adult son and daughter continuing to live at home when they want to go and you want them to go can keep parents in a parenting limbo. "I've heard of the generation gap, and I'm longing for it," says Sean, aged 58, wistfully. Two of his five adult children still live at home, and both for their sake — and for his, he wishes they were on their way.

CHANGES IN GRANDPARENTHOOD

Many third agers are grandparents. The rise in dual career families and the high cost of childcare means that some grand-parents are very hands-on, collecting grandchildren from crèche or school or minding them full-time during the week. Also, Ireland's prosperity since the 1990s which practically ended emigration and caused return migration means that the grandchildren are more likely to be close by rather than being reared in New York, Norwich or New South Wales as was the case a generation ago.

But — again in a change from the past — a significant sec-tion of middle-aged and older parents in Ireland today don't have any grandchildren. Late marriage, late parenthood and a move away from parenthood among today's thirtysomethings means that their parents still await grandchildren, and this can be a sadness. "When your children have children it can lead to more closeness and more mutual understanding between parents and their adult children. Also, knowing that the line is continuing can give a deep gratification and satisfaction, while grandchildren themselves can bring a lot of joy to grandparents and vice versa," says one counselling psychologist.

"Grandchildren give the older couple a second chance. The man may have been too busy in earlier life building up his career to spend a lot of time with his own children when they were small. Now he has time and he can revel in being a grandparent. This new flowering can make him closer to his own children, particularly his sons, and being grandparents together can bring the older couple closer and remind them of their younger selves."

WHAT PRICE AGEISM?

As well as giving within the family as parents and grandparents, many older people still contribute to public life at local, community and national level through volunteering, lending their expertise, mentoring, campaigning and helping out. These people are not a "problem" but an asset to the society they live in, continuing to give rather than take in cash and in kind.

In earlier and still simpler societies older people live on in the extended family and may be accorded respect due to their perceived wisdom and experience. More recently it was thought in some western societies that what was best as one aged was to gradually disengage from life. Older communities perhaps somewhat stereotypically portrayed in communities in Florida, USA, are examples of this. It could be argued that this separation has ghettoised older people, and helped the spread of ageism, a prejudice against older people because they are old.

So while active, independent lives are the reality for many older people, this is often not acknowledged, and our society now holds many, often unconscious, negative attitudes to ageing. The Employment Equality Act 1998 prohibits workplace discrimination on nine grounds including age, while the Equal Status Act 2000 prohibits discrimination in the provision of goods, services, accommodation and education on the same grounds. Cases of workplace discrimination on age grounds are typically concerned with recruitment and access to promotion.

AGEIST BEHAVIOUR, ATTITUDES AND LANGUAGE

But ageist behaviour is not confined to the workplace. Ageist behaviour involves talking down to older people, according less weight to their opinions, needs and beliefs, and taking their health and welfare needs less seriously. If you doubt this, consider the term "bed blockers" currently applied to older long-stay hospital patients and allegedly used by hospital management to save money — never mind what is best for the patients concerned. Concerned professionals also talk of long waiting lists for hip and cataract replacement, and question whether older people have equal access to health care. An example often cited is that the Breast Check service stops health screening at age 65, the very time that incidence of breast cancer begins to escalate. Another example of health ageism is when a physical or depressive illness in an older person is put down to their age and seen as an integral part of growing old, rather than being viewed as a disease or ailment needing treatment.

Ageist attitudes may include seeing most older people as physically and intellectually diminished, viewing a lower standing of living for them as acceptable, seeing paid work as the only work of value — therefore believing that retired people are no longer productive — and equating physical beauty solely with youth.

Ageist language includes referring to older people as "the elderly", which simultaneously creates a distance and herds older people together as one group.

Ageism permeates many aspects of society, including government, statutory bodies, voluntary groups, the general public and older people themselves. Ageist behaviour, attitudes and language can be thought of as institutionalised when we marginalise older people in our laws and policies, overlook them as spokespersons, deny them a voice around decision-making tables, and accept as normal the withdrawing of older (more wrinkly?) faces and voices from our media as presenters or commentators. Sheila, an attractive older woman still holding down a responsible job, speaks for many when she says: "Walking down the street, I have begun feeling invisible, eyes slide over me, sometimes I'm just not seen any more."

CREATING THE STEREOTYPE

Ageism is fuelled by the creation of stereotypes. A stereotype is a generalisation which gives to a particular group characteristics which are simplistic and unrepresentative. Stereotypes are often used to justify discrimination.

Stereotyping older people damages us all. First, it can allow us waste or overlook the resources, skills and experiences which they offer for their own and others' benefit. Secondly it allows us to patronise them and discriminate against them, thereby creating a less just society. Most of all, it allows us to deny the reality that one day we will grow old and it can create a self-fulfilling prophecy — the kind of life I fear I may have when I grow older is more likely to happen unless stereotypical attitudes are challenged now.

As an older person, ageism can damage you to the extent that you internalise society's negative stereotype. If you are constantly absorbing and experiencing the message that you are marginalised, different, less, you can begin to believe it, even unconsciously. These images can become part of your world-view; you begin to see yourselves as others see you, and so are diminished. Also, your confidence can be eroded, your potential limited to the extent that you allow these internalised messages impose a pressure to conform to a particular stereotype — which is then perpetuated.

Ageism makes poor economic sense. For example, if a fifty-something job hunter has difficulty finding work because of age, they may be forced to apply for unemployment benefit or allowance, thus becoming recipients rather than contributors. Each time this happens, a potential worker is being deprived of a right to work, to contribute, to pay taxes, to a fair share of consumer spend. Shunting people too rapidly through the third age will logically increase the dependent population. Seen in this light, ageism is wasteful — and costly.

Why is society ageist? Research would indicate that we stereotype older people because we fear older age. We fear the loss of physical and mental ability, attractiveness, earning power, status and independence. We seek to distance ourselves from what we fear might be our own future when we are older. And so we create what we fear.

DEMOGRAPHIC TIME BOMB OR EXPLOSIVE OPPORTUNITY?

In 1926, when the Central Statistics Office analysis began, Irishmen had a life expectancy of 57.4 years while women could expect to live 57.9 years. Life expectancy for babies born in 2002 is 75.1 for males and 80.3 for females. If you've already survived the first and second ages, longevity is greater. The reasons are improved maternal and infant survival rates, cleaner living conditions and the conquering of diseases like TB. Today, men at 65 can expect to live a further 12–15 years, while today's 65-year-old woman may live on average another 19 years.

Typically, as discussed, the rise in older population is described quite negatively, rather than welcoming an increase in all of our life spans. Some of this ageism may stem from earlier ideas about old age which need updating. Speaking during 2004 Active Age Week, Robin Webster, chief executive of Age Action, said: "Alongside the ageing of the population, we are witnessing a profound transformation in the experience and meaning of old age today. Retirement is no longer the straightforward entry point to old age that it once was, and, therefore, it is increasingly anachronistic as a definition of older people. At the same time, with increased longevity, older people are living longer and healthier old ages, and as a result the threshold of frailty is being pushed back. These changes in age structure, health and patterns of employment are transforming the nature of old age. They are thereby posing sharp questions about both the traditional passive roles expected of older people and the extent to which policy makers and major economic and political institutions have adjusted to socio-demographic change. In essence the question at issue is what is the place of older citizens in European society today."

TACKLING AGEISM

Good questions. How to answer them? Looking more honestly and accurately at older people today may cause us to debate the reasons for and consequences of our pervasive ageism. Hopefully this will lead to a reframing in which we can accept and appreciate that we are an ageing society, a situation needing response rather than reaction.

Tackling ageism in an ageing society is vital given that policy issues will be influenced by attitudes. The disengagement theory as described above could be replaced by the reconstruction theory, one committed to changing negative stereotypes and providing adequate support systems as needed.

A BROAD-BASED APPROACH

This would mean developing a positive ageing strategy across a range of government departments from finance to health, social welfare, environment and local government, supported by well-researched studies on ageing. There is evidence that some of these developments are already taking place. We now have our first Minister of State responsible for services for older people, who chairs an interdepartmental group on older people. Also, some employers are re-evaluating the importance of retaining older workers in the face of skill shortages.

In 2004, a summer school on ageing and health in west Dublin brought together anthropologists, technicians, designers, health promoters and others to look at ageing from the point of view of health economics, social gerontology (the study of older people), geriatric medicine and human rights — taking a broader view than is often the case. In discussing the value to all age groups of such a conference, Professor Desmond O'Neill, gerontologist, borrowed an apt quotation: "If we design for the old, we include the young; if we design for the young, we exclude the old," he said.

Also in 2004, University College Cork introduced the country's first masters in gerontology. This MA takes a holistic approach to ageing and seeks to promote understanding by examining the psychological, social, educational, health and caring aspects of the ageing process.

The 2002 Equality Authority report *Implementing Equality for Older People* contained 72 specific recommendations intended to form the basis of a comprehensive strategy for equality for older people in Irish society. Many recommendations — such as "age proofing", age awareness training and increased consultation with older people — involve little or no cost.

More recently the National Economic and Social Forum (NESF) called for increased participation in age awareness training across all government departments, improved co-ordination between government departments on policy issues affecting older people, legislation on entitlements to health and social services, and removal of barriers that inhibit older people in continuing to work beyond specific age thresholds should they so choose. Such barriers include existing employment legislation, eligibility for further education grants and age limits on motor insurance.

In November 2004, the Equality Authority (with the National Council on Ageing and Older People and the Health Board Executive), launched a public awareness campaign "Say No to Ageism". Their poster, which portrays some of the strictures, such as parking and speeding, that civil life imposes on us all, has the slogan "Life will always have limits. Age shouldn't be one of them. Say No to Ageism."

In the past, policy-making regarding older people tended to be sited mainly in the Department of Health and Children, logical if older people were seen primarily as "patients". However, health, income levels and housing remain key issues, especially since the group increasing at the fastest rate in the western world is the "old-old", those aged 85 and over. This group will need policies which optimise their health and well-being, giving care as and when necessary. In this context, finding ways to keep people at home, not as a cheap option, but with all the necessary supports, as piloted by a number of health boards, deserves more attention. As a model of care, these schemes seem to offer value for money and may meet the needs of some older people, either by postponing or avoiding the need for nursing home care.

We may also need to look at offering nursing home residents as much autonomy as possible. US studies show that residents' well-being may be related to their feelings of control and self-determination. In one study, a group of residents was encouraged to make day-to-day choices about what they ate, visiting times, the films they saw, interests and outings. Another group in the same home was given far less control over their lives. Eighteen months later, the first group was demonstrably happier, more alert and active than the second group, and only half as many of the first group had died as in the second group.

As stated, we often confuse the negative effects of disease in later life with the ageing process itself, and many major diseases such as heart disease, stroke and some cancers can be prevented or managed more effectively. Understanding your genetic inheritance, looking after your physical and emotional health, taking exercise, and good nutrition will all help the individual live longer. In this context, men may need particular attention and support, as a number of studies indicate that older men living alone do less well in older age, with the isolation of living in some parts of rural Ireland a real concern.

CHALLENGING THE STEREOTYPE

Never before in the history of humankind have so many of us lived so long. Or so hopefully. Taking a new look at the life trajectories of older people shows not an inevitable downward curve but a flow that stops, shifts, rests then moves on again. The traditional long-accepted vision of old age as inevitable decline is up for grabs, as older people add not only years to the life, but life to the years. Because you *can* teach old dogs new tricks. It used to be thought that the ageing process inevitably brings about intellectual decline. Some of these conclusions were based on cross-sectional tests: testing a group of 40-year-olds and a group of 70-year-olds and finding that the 40-year-olds scored higher. However, other researchers began to question this method as not comparing like with like. Longitudinal studies which assess someone at 40 then again at 70 came up with different results. These indicated that there can be less difference than was thought in cognitive functioning as people age. Some current studies suggest that a decline in mental abilities may not begin until people are in their early 70s.

Obviously, some people can and do become confused, forgetful, withdrawn in old age, but this can also be due to illness, depression and isolation rather than intellectual impairment. For example, it has been found that reminiscence therapy (which encourages people to think about their life and memories) has been used successfully in care settings such as nursing homes to bring apparently withdrawn, confused older people back to cogency and social connectedness.

GREY POWER

Because they are living longer, older people are much more numerous. At the beginning of the twentieth century, only one in 25 Europeans was aged over 65. Today there are half a million over-65s in Ireland, comprising almost one in ten of the population. By 2040, the number of over 65s is projected to grow to 1.25 million. Move on another 10 years to 2050 and it is predicted that the over-65s will have grown to 24 per cent, or almost one in four. By this time, over-65s will outnumber children under 15 for the first time, and that life after 65 will be twice as long as childhood.

As this older sector grows numerically and as a proportion of the population, their political clout becomes a force to be reckoned with. Older people tend to vote and to believe that their vote matters, and there is a range of issues which directly concern them such as pension rights, health care, employment, age discrimination, as well as general concern for human rights, the environment and other issues — and the time to pursue these.

While many older people in Ireland campaign actively on a range of issues, relatively few seem to speak up on the subject of ageism itself. Looking across to America gives a model of how things could be in the future as numbers of older people continue to increase. The American Association of Retired Persons (AARP), set up in 1958 has become a highly effective lobbying organisation. The AARP has 17 million members, representing half of all American's over-50s. The AARP has influenced the cost of health care, certain prescription drugs, the adequacy of pensions, and brought mandatory retirement ages and some aspects of age discrimination to public attention. The AARP demonstrates the power of the older consumer.

GREY CONSUMERS

Large numbers of competent older people is a consumer challenge and an opportunity. The manufacturers and service providers who will benefit are having to reconsider the older consumer to ensure that their spending power, rights, choices, and access are recognised. Already older consumers are being wooed. Universities are actively courting more mature student. The holiday trade is shifting away from Club 18–30 as the only travel model. Sea cruises are a growing market.

So as an older consumer you may influence the development of new ranges of products and the adaptation of many existing ones. Much of the country's facilities are designed for young people, but as green Ireland expands to include grey, so goods and services will similarly have to change. This could mean, for example, more large print books and magazines, more matinee performances, more accessible packaging for many consumer goods (surely long overdue) and clearer instructions to accompany many new technical and computerised implements. An older population has implications for customer care in other ways. There should be market opportunities for mail order and internet shopping, giving more choices to immobile or housebound people.

KEEPING PEOPLE IN THE THIRD AGE

As a society we have a choice. While society has a clear responsibility to support people in their first and fourth age — the dependent young and the dependent old-old — there is more of a choice about people in their third age. Either they can be regarded simply as an addition to the burden of dependence, or they can be enabled with changes in attitude and policy to make a major and important contribution to society and the economy. In short, the longer people can maintain their independence and postpone their fourth age, the better for everyone.

At a policy level, positive ageing means developing and implementing policies that integrate rather than segregate older people. We need a national positive ageing strategy to respond to the needs and potential of our ageing population. This reconstruction theory has a healthy degree of self-interest. It says that the more active and involved older adults are, the longer they are likely to stay in the third age.

A helpful and inclusive attitude towards old age is that we are all growing older all the time, that our bodies are constantly changing and developing, that our ideas and attitudes are constantly forming and reforming as we move from childhood to adolescence to adulthood to middle age and older age and that we hold within us our younger and our older selves.

AN INDIVIDUAL JOURNEY

This introduction began with an exploration of the uniqueness of each person and ends with a look at how each of us can achieve the potential of older age. The development theorist Erik Erikson believes that late adulthood is characterised by the last of the eight life stages, which stage he calls "integrity versus despair". He sees it as a time for looking back and taking stock. If this backward glance reveals a picture of a life more-or-less well spent, the older adult will be satisfied: integrity. But if earlier stages of life remain unresolved or poorly resolved, then the older person may feel doubtful, gloomy, and question their self-worth; in other words, despair. While Erikson's work has been influential, some have questioned the starkness of his belief. The reworking of Erikson's final stage by psychologist Robert Peck seems to offer more scope for us all. Peck describes the tasks that older people face as:

A. Differentiation versus role preoccupation;

B. Body transcendence versus body preoccupation; and

C. Ego transference versus ego preoccupation.

Task A — differentiation versus role preoccupation — is about redefining our worth in terms of something other than work roles. While losing the identity of work is a loss for some (though not all), third agers can move through this change to a place of acceptance in which they redefine themselves and their worth in a broader and ultimately more helpful way, and so begin to see themselves for who they are rather than just for what they do.

Task B — body transcendence versus body preoccupation — is about coping with declining health and well-being, giving in gracefully to the pull of years (invariably sagging and downward!) without losing some essential part of self. In fact, some older people will say that as the physical body declines, so the spirit can grow and flourish. Coming to terms with loss of looks is difficult in a society that is so youth-oriented, and the rise in popularity of cosmetic surgery shows how many still struggle with this reality.

The third task is about the realisation that death (transcendence) is inevitable, but it is balanced by the realisation that we may have contributed to the future in our own way through living our lives. Parents can also know they have contributed to the future through their children and grandchildren.

FINALLY

At the beginning of life, we are faced with many doors, offering
different experiences, opportunities, gifts to develop, journeys
to take. Unfortunately, we cannot go through them all. The path
that we chose as our younger selves meant the opening of some
doors and inevitably the closing of others. This is largely due to
the career choices we make, which for most people means turning back on other possibilities in terms of career-related learning or developing other facets of ourselves. Until now. One of the
joys of middle age and beyond is the chance to go back, to open
some of those closed doors and to explore what is beyond them.

We may be in for surprises. We may find gifts — for painting, enjoying music, being a campaigner — we did not have a
chance to realise earlier. We may find destinations that we
didn't have the time or money to visit or discover until now. We
may find learning — for new classes, new ideas, new challenges we felt we were not able for, or sold ourselves short on
before. Hopefully we will also find a new meeting with our
spiritual, questing, hopeful and reflective selves — a meeting
we might not have been ready for until now.

Chapter 1

FROM WORK TO RETIREMENT

Eamon Donnelly

"Don't think of retiring from the world until the world will be sorry that you retire. I hate a fellow whom pride or cowardice or laziness drive into a corner, and who does nothing when he is there but sit and growl. Let him come out as I do, and bark." — Samuel Johnson

INTRODUCTION

The transition to retirement is like all journeys — it benefits from careful planning well in advance of the starting date. It is also essential to know what you want to achieve both on the journey and when you reach your destination.

One thing you can be sure of is that this transition from a life dominated by work to one in which you will have more choices to make over the basics of living is being undertaken by more people than ever before. You will not be alone! We are at the beginning of what is being called the "Silver Century". Increasing numbers of older people will be the century's major demographic change. The proportion of those aged 60 and over will rise significantly in our society and in all western countries. Longevity will continue to increase — 11 per cent of our population is over 65, and this will grow to 17 per cent in 2025, rising steadily to 25 per cent — one in four. Conversely, retirement is occurring at an earlier age; at present the retirement age is probably closer to 60 than 65 for the majority of retirees. However, this statistic too may change as pension provision changes.

So a new world awaits us all, a world in which opportunities co-exist with challenges in a way that no previous age has experienced. The purpose of this chapter is to outline the paths that you can take in coping with the transition from work to retirement and also to suggest how to create a different life in the third age to that lived by our predecessors.

In doing this, I have drawn heavily on the experiences of the Retirement Planning Council of Ireland, which has provided retirement planning to thousands of people over the last 30 years. They can be contacted at 27–29 Lower Pembroke St., Dublin 2; Tel: 01-6613139; Website: www.rpc.ie.

MAKING ADJUSTMENTS

Retirement is not just a one-off event; it is a process, and like all processes, it involves change. Let me illustrate through a number of true case histories using fictitious names.

The Obsessive Worker

John Brown was the owner of a small family business which he started 30 years ago. It grew quite successfully, necessitating long hours and increasing travel around the country and abroad. John enjoyed the thrill of building up an enterprise which he could pass to his children in due course. He would, he thought, continue to be involved, as they would need his guidance. However, with the demands for more sophisticated ways of operating a bigger entity, by his late fifties John found himself somewhat out of his depth. A limited education did not equip him for the world of technology and regulatory compliance. In addition, his children had no interest in following him into the business.

And so John became sidelined in his own business. He had no interests outside work and faced a number of very painful years in learning to adapt to a life without it. He discovered, too late, that all his social life was business-centred and that he should have pursued some outside hobbies and pastimes. His wife had her own life — of necessity — and he was not part of it. The adjustment was difficult and included a bout of depression.

The Financial Optimist

Bill Murphy was never too worried about money. He had a good job and he and his wife Mary were confident that they could live on their occupational pensions plus the state pension. After all, he had been in continuous employment all his life, albeit with four different firms, and his wife had returned to work part-time after the children left the nest.

In addition, since he moved to his last firm 10 years ago, he had put money into an additional voluntary contribution plan (AVC) on a regular basis at 10 per cent of his salary. So everything would be all right and there was no real need to be concerned when he was offered retirement at age 63.

What a shock they got when they discovered that the accumulated pensions would give him only about one third of his current income. In addition, his AVCs had been hit by the collapse in the investment market and would not contribute in any real way to his shortfall in income.

Too late, he discovered that he should have undertaken a regular review — ideally on a yearly basis — of his pension investments, particularly since most of his monies were related to service with previous firms when his salary was significantly lower. It was now too late to correct the pension shortfall and so their lifestyle in retirement would have to be significantly more constrained than what they had come to enjoy. It was possible that they might have to sell their house, or some equity in it, or get another job (or jobs).

The Lonely Ex-worker

Jane Moore worked in a professional firm for 40 years. She was loyal, punctual and the centre of the social club. She organised every event that the partnership required and, as a singleton, was always ready to make up the numbers at short notice.

Retirement came, along with various dinners, lunches and other "au revoir" occasions. But in fact they were "adieu" events. Jane found that her social life had suddenly disappeared with her job. Her contacts were in the business community and primarily in her office. She realised, too late, that she had no real friends or networks outside of the firm and it took quite an adjustment, and a lot of work, to create a new social environment for herself.

So what have these stories got in common and what can they teach us? The main lesson is the need to plan for every aspect of your retirement. To help you decide how you feel about the future, complete the following exercise:

What will you do with the rest of your life?

Score the following from 1–12:

___   *Spend more time with spouse/partner/children/family*

___   *Make more time for myself*

___   *Expand social life/time with friends*

___   *Learn something new*

___   *Go to school/college*

___   *Do some community/voluntary work*

___   *Take up sport/keep fit*

___   *Expand an existing hobby*

___   *Take up a new hobby*

___   *Earn money*

___   *Travel*

___   *Move house*

___   *Other.*

Examine how you scored yourself and use it as a guide to put some structure on your retirement. Now consider the following.

THE CHANGES IN LIFE?

Most retirees face three key changes. The illustrations above show how these changes are gradual in some cases and immediate in others. The three areas that change in retirement are:

- *Money*

- *Time/Routine*

- *Relationships.*

This chapter will focus primarily on the first of these changes, money; we will touch on the others later in the chapter and they are dealt with in more detail in subsequent chapters.

MONEY

This will change overnight. The key question to ask is, "What will I have, after tax, to replace my salary?"

In retirement, income can come from a variety of sources — from your company pension or personal pension if self-employed, from any other investments, from state social insurance and from any paid employment you take up.

Assessing Your Income in Retirement

It is helpful well in advance of retirement to assess your income and expenditure now and compare it with income and expenditure after the actual date of retirement. For example, while your income may drop when you're retired, your outgoings, and tax liability may decrease also. The golden rule with tax is to make sure you are legally claiming the maximum and paying the minimum, and if necessary take advice on this.

The following list is a guide for this exercise.

Budgeting for Retirement

	Before Retirement	In Retirement
Income		
Pension		
Job(s)		
Savings		
Rental		
Social Welfare		
Other		
Total		
Expenses		
Mortgage/Rent		
Home insurance		
Electricity/Gas		
Telephone		
TV Licence/Cable		
Food		
Credit Cards		
Travel/Transport		
Life Assurance		
Pension		
Subscriptions		
Health Costs		
Car Tax/Insurance		
Petrol		
Other		
Total		

So while your income may be less, your expenses may have decreased also. Comparing like with like is vital when calculating projected retirement income.

YOUR PENSION

For most people retirement income is provided by a company pension, or a combination of occupational and state pension. Do you have a company pension? How is it calculated? What is it going to be after tax? Will it increase in the years ahead? Can you still make AVCs and if so how much? Do you have the option of creating an approved retirement fund (ARF)? What are the issues surrounding this? Will your spouse have a pension if anything happens to you? Are there any pensions due to you from previous employments and if so how much are they worth? Do you have access to tax-free cash in lieu of pension? What will you do with it?

These are just some of the principal questions to ask your pension trustees or financial adviser, preferably well in advance of retirement date. The following should help you find some of the answers.

How Pension Schemes Work

A pension scheme is quite simply an arrangement that provides for payments to be made to you on retirement from paid work, or to your dependants in the event of death. Occupational pension schemes is the name given to employer-sponsored schemes for employees that have been approved by the Revenue Commissioners under various Finance and Income Tax Acts. Under the Family Law Acts, the definition is widened to include pensions for the self-employed, annuities and buyout policies and any sort of pension promise, whether or not it is funded.

The Pensions Act 1990 recognises two distinct types of scheme:

- *A Defined Benefit Scheme*, in which the pensions and other benefits are clearly stated in the rules of the scheme and promised to members and their dependants;

- *A Defined Contribution Scheme* (also known as a Money Purchase Scheme), where the benefits payable are determined solely by reference to the contributions paid into the scheme and the investment return earned on those contributions. So there is no specific promise or guarantee of particular benefit levels, except perhaps on death.

Even where the main pension scheme is a defined benefit scheme, a scheme or section of a scheme designed to accept additional voluntary contributions (AVCs) will often be set up on a defined contribution basis. The pensions of self-employed people and those in non-pensionable employment are always defined contribution schemes. Personal Retirement Savings Accounts (PRSAs) are also defined contribution arrangements.

Defined Benefit Scheme

How does a defined benefit scheme work? An employer setting up a defined benefit scheme intends to promise the scheme members a specific amount of benefit to be paid on their retirement. In the old days, this might have been a fixed amount of annual or weekly pension, or perhaps a set amount of pension for every year spent in service. Later, the promised pension came to be defined as something based on pay and service combined, so the common pattern of defined benefits that we see today emerged. Modern defined benefit promises are usually expressed as a fraction or percentage of pay taken at or near retirement age, and multiplied by the completed service of the member.

For example, a common formula nowadays would promise one-sixtieth of final pensionable pay for each year of pensionable service. This is usually intended to fix the maximum pension promised at 40/60, or two-thirds, of final salary.

Because the benefit to be paid is fixed in this way, and because it is not possible to predict what the amount of final salary is going to be, it follows that we cannot know in advance what the promised benefit is going to cost. Defined benefit schemes are now becoming less common.

Pay As You Go

For some employers, such arrangements are not a problem. They simply pay their pensioners out of their current income and make no attempt to provide any provision in advance of retirement. Typically, this approach, called "pay as you go", is taken by government, by local authorities and by some other public sector employers who, at least in theory, cannot go bankrupt.

Advance Funding

For most employers and staff, however, this approach is not attractive. Employees are not happy with the idea that their security in retirement must depend on the employer being (a) still in existence and (b) making enough profit to pay their pensions. These employers put away money during their employees' working lives, to provide a fund from which the promised benefits can be paid in the future, with some of the money contributed by the members themselves. In that case, the rate of contribution is usually also defined. The employer then pays the balance of the cost.

The recommended rate of payment is decided by an actuary, who makes various assumptions as to what will happen in the future to the members (how long they will live, survival by dependants and so on), their future rates of pay and the investment returns that the fund will be able to earn. These assumptions are reviewed from time to time in the light of actual experience and a new rate of contribution recommended, if appropriate.

Defined Contribution Scheme

As has been said, the defined contribution scheme promises only that a certain level of contribution will be paid and the pensions to come from the scheme are not defined or promised. Generally, the employer's contribution is decided in advance, supplemented by employee contributions.

There are many variations on the way an employer's contribution may be established and the following are examples taken from schemes actually in operation:

- A fixed pension contribution, with the cost of death benefits and possibly also disability benefits paid in addition;

- A fixed overall contribution rate, with death and disability costs charged as a first charge against that contribution, the balance going to pension provision.

- Different rates of contribution at different starting ages — the older the employee when the scheme starts, the higher the contribution made by the employer. There are variations on this also — contributions that increase with the member's age, or with service completed.

Contributions can be at any suitable level but there are a number of conditions. The employer must make a substantial contribution to the cost of benefits in any particular year. The Revenue requirement can be satisfied if the employer pays the running costs and about 10 per cent of the benefit costs.

The benefits likely to be generated by both employer and employee contributions combined will not exceed the maximum limits which the Revenue impose on an employee by reference to salary and completed service at retirement.

Employee contributions themselves are limited to an overall maximum percentage of gross pay, including any contributions required by the rules of the scheme. The maximum allowable employee contribution, originally 15 per cent for all, is now

age-related: 15 per cent for those under age 30; 20 per cent between 30 and 39; 25 per cent for those aged 40–49; and 30 per
cent for those aged 50 or over. Employer contributions are
made in addition, as long as the overall benefit limits are not
breached. An earnings "cap" of €254,000 applies to contributions by employees.

Once contributions are received by the pension scheme
trustees, they are invested through an insurance company or
other investment manager. They are usually invested sepa-
rately for each individual member, so that the member's share
of the fund can be easily tracked.

How Pension Funds are Invested

Exactly how pension funds are invested depends on a number
of things, including how close the member may be to retirement age. For example, if the member was quite close to retirement, appropriate investment would be in assets whose
value was not likely to reduce. A younger member might invest
in more volatile assets, in the hope of making substantial capital
gains before he needs to consolidate in the run-up to retirement. The assets of pension funds build up without any tax being paid on investment income or capital gains. Under normal
circumstances, therefore, they should accumulate faster than an
investment fund that has to pay tax.

The annual report of the trustees of each pension scheme
will contain information on how the assets are invested, the
name of the investment manager and how he is paid. It will also
include information on the investment policies followed by the
trustees during the scheme year and on any changes made to
those policies. The report should give details of any significant
financial developments (such as large movements of money in
or out of the scheme) and comment on the performance of the
investments during the year.

Other information that must be given, if it applies, is whether there is what is called a concentration of investment — that is, whether more than 5 per cent of the assets are invested in a particular asset or asset type. If there is significant "self-investment" (this means investment in employer-related assets or property) it must also be reported.

When You Retire

When you retire in a defined contribution scheme, the total fund accumulated in your name becomes available to the trustees to provide benefits. If retiring at normal pension date, having completed at least 20 years' service, the maximum lump sum you can receive is 1.5 times the annual salary, with the balance of the fund applied to buy a pension for yourself and for any dependants. The amount of pension available after the lump sum has been taken will be dictated by (a) the value of the accumulated fund and (b) the state of annuity rates at the time of retirement. Neither of these can be predicted in advance.

So you have various choices at the point of retirement to provide for your dependants. Some people set up a pension only on their own lives. Others ensure that part of the capital available at retirement age is used to buy an extra pension which will be paid to a spouse or other dependant on the death of the member after retirement. The available capital can be used to tailor the benefits to fit your individual circumstances.

At any stage in a defined contribution scheme, the best that can be done is to make a reasonable estimate of what might be available. Such an estimate would be based on assumptions regarding future fund performance and annuity rates. It is important to review these regularly, to measure actual performance against the assumptions. That way, you may be in a position to make changes to the rate of contribution if needed.

If you die in service, the fund that has accumulated for your pension will form part of the overall death benefit provided by the scheme. Death benefits may be paid as tax-free lump sums within certain limits, with any balance going to purchase pensions.

Risks and Options

So there are advantages and disadvantages to the defined contribution scheme — increasingly the pension type of the future. First, it places a great many things firmly under your control. Benefits do not have to be taken in any prescribed pattern, even though the maximum levels of benefit are laid down by the Revenue Commissioners. Thus, you can decide on the distribution of benefits, between personal pension, lump sum, dependants' pensions and cost-of-living increases.

As well as this flexibility, defined contribution schemes have the great benefit of allowing you to trace the build-up of your fund, so that you know its exact capital value as it accumulates over the years.

However, you will not be able to estimate with any accuracy how that fund will translate into a pension until you are quite close to retirement age. There are other risks involved. You may be taking an investment risk — i.e. the possibility that the returns on money invested could be poor and cannot be guaranteed in advance, in most circumstances. If poor investment returns are experienced, it follows that the capital available at retirement age would be less than you might expect or wish for.

Personal Retirement Savings Accounts (PRSAs)

Personal Retirement Savings Accounts (PRSAs) were introduced through the Pensions Amendment Act 2002 as part of the government strategy to increase national pension coverage. PRSAs are new and flexible pension products designed to encourage more people to make adequate pension provision. PRSAs are owned by the individual, regardless of their employment status, transferable from job to job and available from a variety of providers.

Their introduction has arisen because of official concern that many people were not making adequate pension provision for themselves. The hope is that a pension product which offers low cost, flexibility, portability and easy access will encourage more employees to save towards their long-term financial security.

This new type of Pension Savings Plan can provide a pension fund to follow you through your career. In operation it is somewhat similar to a pension plan for a self-employed person, except that PRSA holders can, in certain circumstances, contribute to the PRSA fund from their salary, and an employer may also pay contributions to the PRSA.

There are two types. The standard type can offer investments only into pooled funds and is subject to maximum charges of one per cent asset value and/or five per cent of contributions. The non-standard type is not subject to any maximum charge, it allows greater flexibility in the investment options available and is generally regarded as a more sophisticated product in terms of investment advice and services. However, the non-standard PRSA comes at higher cost to the investor, and the investment needs of many people may be met by the standard PRSA.

Older people should check out the two types with particular care as, at higher contribution levels, some non-standard PRSAs appear to offer better value at retirement than their standard equivalent.

The first PRSAs were approved in February 2003. There are currently approximately 50 products available, the majority of these non-standard, offered by up to a dozen approved providers — predominantly life assurance companies. Before choosing, compare a number of different products to see which is right for you and consider taking advice from an independent financial consultant.

Since 15 September 2003, employers have been obliged to offer some pension access to all employees, and those not providing an occupational pension scheme must provide access to at least one standard PRSA.

When you contribute towards a PRSA, your contributions are invested on your behalf in an investment fund which would typically be a unit-linked investment fund run by a life assurance company. Most PRSAs offer you a choice of investment funds and you can switch between funds as you wish.

Every PRSA must have a "Default Investment Strategy" which has been approved by the Pensions Board. This Strategy will ensure that your fund will have a higher equity content in the early years while you are still a long way from retirement, moving to a high fixed interest securities content as you approach retirement. In other words, the Default Investment Strategy ensures that the fund has an investment risk which is appropriate to your age. You can override the Default Investment Strategy and switch funds at any time if you so wish.

There are many investment options available to you through your PRSA. Most people will choose a mixed fund called a Managed Fund which invests in a broad mix of stocks and shares, properties, fixed interest securities (government gilts) and cash. The mix of assets in the fund is decided by the professional investment fund managers. You can also choose from a wide range of funds through many fund managers which invest at home and/or abroad.

So, in summary, these are the benefits of a PRSA:

- Tax-efficient method of saving towards retirement.

- Full income tax relief on contributions. If you are a top rate tax payer, for every €1 that you contribute towards your PRSA, the government will give you back 42 cents.

- Designed with the older saver in mind. If you are over age 50, you can claim full tax relief on a contribution of 30 per cent of your income. (The maximum income from which you can make PRSA contributions in any one year is €254,000.)

- Contributions allowed to grow in special investment funds without being subject to tax.

- At retirement, 25 per cent of accumulated fund can be drawn out as a tax-free lump sum with the balance being drawn down as normal income.

Tax Treatment

Funding in advance for pensions is encouraged by the government, which gives favourable tax treatment to pension funds in both defined benefit and defined contribution schemes. Both employers and scheme members receive tax relief on their contributions as they pay them. In addition, employer contributions are not treated as employee earnings for tax purposes. Most important of all, the pension fund pays no tax on the investment income that it makes in the shape of dividend income and capital gains, all designed to encourage employers to contribute to pension schemes. In return, except for some limited benefits paid in cash on retirement or death, most of what is paid out as benefits from pension schemes is taxed under the PAYE system.

To qualify for this tax treatment, a scheme must be approved by the Revenue Commissioners, who police the maximum benefits that can be provided. It must be set up under a trust, which has the effect of legally separating the assets of the pension scheme from those of the employer.

Apart from retirement pensions, defined benefit schemes usually include the option for the retiring employee to exchange some of his or her pension for a lump sum. Lump sum benefits for dependants on death are common features. Many schemes also provide pensions payable to spouses and/or other dependants.

If You Are Self-Employed

Retirement Annuity Contracts or Personal Pension Plans are primarily for the self-employed, but are also designed for people who are not members of pension schemes in their places of employment. The investment position under these contracts is fairly straightforward. The person paying the pension premiums can choose the insurance company that is to manage or invest them.

So what's involved? In the first place, you must decide what kind of investment vehicle you want. Selecting a unit-linked fund will open up a greater variety of choices. Some insurance companies offer a wide range of funds in which the money may be invested — and the choice rests with the individual who pays the premiums. Other insurance companies offer not only a range of funds within their own management but also the services of other investment managers, including investment banks. Once the manager is selected, you can then choose whether to go for a "mixed" fund, in which the manager is investing in different kinds of assets, including ordinary shares, government and other fixed interest stocks and possibly property. There can be further choice available when it comes to ordinary shares (equity) investment, as the manager may offer a range of funds that invest in different markets, such as the UK, the United States, Japan, and so on.

There is often considerable freedom to switch between these funds as time goes on, so that control of the investment remains with the premium payer. Funds can now be moved freely from one investment manager to another, though there may be some costs incurred when this is done.

INCOME FROM INVESTMENTS

Have you any investments or savings? Include these in your budget when calculating your income in retirement. Give some thought too to how you would invest any lump sump from your pension plan. The critical questions to answer are:

1. Do you need an income from it?

2. Do you want capital growth?

3. What is your attitude to risk?

4. Over what period can you afford to invest?

5. Do you know a dependable adviser?

Remember the higher the return, the higher the risk!

Investing Your Lump Sum

The lump sum you receive on retirement may represent the largest cheque ever written in your name, rather like winning your own personal lottery. It follows that you need good advice on how to invest this nest egg (or indeed any large sum of money, such as an inheritance). There are many institutions eager for your money, all wanting to convince you that they offer the best return. In terms of mainstream investment schemes, you have four institutions to choose from — banks, building societies, post office and insurance companies — with each institution offering a number of schemes and products.

In deciding how to invest, you have to consider what is right for you. For many investors, there is a balance to be struck between security, availability, convenience and familiarity. Security is usually the most important consideration and many retired people will balance rate of return with measure of risk. Availability is also important, and it may not be desirable to lock all your money away in a long-term scheme. Convenience and familiarity are linked — most people have built up a relationship over the years with local institutions which they may want to maintain.

Where should you go for advice? Your employers may be helpful if they have experience in the banking/insurance/ investment field. Examining the products offered by the other institutions and comparing like with like is also a good idea. The Golden Pages have names of brokers dealing specifically with pension investments, but unless you have a personal recommendation for someone you trust, do check out the credentials of any consultant you approach. The Irish Financial Services Regulatory Authority (IFSRA) regulates financial services firms in the interests of consumer information and protection. Contact IFSRA at PO Box 9138, College Green, Dublin 2; Tel: 01-4104000; Consumer Helpline 1890-777777; Website: www.ifsra.ie.

Investing in Property

For over a decade, investing in property in Ireland must have seemed like a licence to print money, and many individuals have gained returns from property deals which far outstripped inflation. These include those who took advantage of favourable tax incentives to buy new property for rental, those who bought second-hand and also rented, taking advantage of high rental costs in cities like Dublin and Galway, and those who bought, held on to their property for a period, and then sold on in a continuously rising market.

This sounds like heady stuff and people would be forgiven for thinking that property investment is a sure-fire bet, because in many ways it has so proved to be. There are, however, some caveats when considering buying and/or developing a property.

When buying to rent, you need to consider if you want to be a hands-on landlord, or place the day-to-day concerns in the hands of a property management company, who will obviously charge a fee for their services. (Some new landlords who have taken a hands-on approach have had their fingers burnt with difficult, antisocial or intransigent tenants.)

Secondly, with any property you buy, you need a surveyor's report to ensure that the property is structurally and electrically sound. This is money very well spent. A detailed surveyor's report can either confirm that you have indeed a good buy, or alert you in time to future problems. You may also need to find out in advance how the local area will develop, as some developments could detract from the value of your property. Consulting development plans will help, as will a visit to your local authority offices.

Instructing a solicitor to act for you will sort out any legal issues involved in the purchase, ensuring, for example, that there are no "liens" (monies owed) on the property that you should know about, or any rights of way that emerge only after you have paid your money.

If you are thinking of buying a property to develop, you need a realistic budget which takes into account original purchase price, all fees, cost of refurbishment (including paying any subcontractors), time it will take, and VAT/capital gains tax implications. How much could your upgraded property realise? You will get some idea by checking out current prices for attractive and similar properties in the town/district.

STATE SOCIAL INSURANCE

When calculating income in retirement, find out if you are entitled to an income from the state social insurance plan and if so, how much? It can take time to get this information, so apply well in advance of retirement date. Have you any entitlements to state benefits from another country? This is particularly relevant if you have worked in the UK, as many Irish people have during their working lifetime. The most universal kind of pension scheme in Ireland is that provided for by the Social Welfare

Acts, which cover the provision of retirement and old age pensions to the employed and the self-employed and spouses' pensions to their surviving marriage partners.

Are you retiring before age 65? If so, you need to make sure that your contributions to the state scheme are maintained or your pensions could suffer. Your local Department of Social and Family Affairs office will tell you what you should do.

OTHER ENTITLEMENTS FROM THE STATE

Apart from a free travel pass for which everyone over 66 qualifies, there are very few universal benefits for you as an older person. There are, on the other hand, a very large number of payments, grants, types of pensions and benefits available from many sources — including social welfare, social insurance and health boards — for which you may be eligible. Conditions attach to each, which can be quite complex, and vary considerably from payment to entitlement. So don't automatically assume you are, or are not, entitled to a particular benefit.

If in doubt, apply. It is a surprising fact that many people do not get what they are entitled to simply because they do not know that they *are* entitled to them. The best advice if you think you may qualify for something is to apply for it. Generally speaking, nobody is going to come along and offer you services. Wives and husbands should each apply for benefits, as in many cases you may be individually entitled.

So what kind of packages are out there? Very briefly, you should be entitled to some kind of pension based on either your PRSI contributions, or a means-tested payment if your income is below a certain level.

There are other payments such as a Living Alone Allowance, rent or mortgage assistance, disability benefits or allowances, widows or widowers pensions. You may be entitled to treatment benefits such as dental, optical or hearing aids. In addition, if you are 66 and over, and receive a social welfare or health board payment, there is another package of benefits to which you may be entitled. These include an electricity, gas and fuel allowance, free colour television licence and free telephone rental. You may also be entitled to a medical card (see Chapter 6, pages 180–1). Again, the golden rule is, if in doubt, apply.

Where to? The Department of Social and Family Affairs manages the delivery of social welfare services. For information on Retirement/Old Age Contributory Pensions or Old Age Non Contributory Pensions, contact their LoCall service on 1890-500000, or write to the Department at College Road, Sligo. For information on the various free schemes such as fuel allowance, also telephone LoCall 1890-500000. For information on treatment benefits, LoCall 1890-400400, extension 4480 (dental and optical), extension 4524 (hearing aids).

The most comprehensive one-stop-shop guide is *Entitlements for the Over-Sixties*, an excellent booklet that is updated every year after the Budget. It is available free of charge from Comhairle, Hume House, Ballsbridge, Dublin 4; Tel: 01-6059000; E-mail: info@comhairle.ie; and is also available on their website, www.comhairle.ie.

WORK OPPORTUNITIES

For a number of reasons, you may wish to continue to work. You may find having done your sums that there is a shortfall and that you may need to remain in the same job (if you can) or look for another job, either full- or part-time. Or you may still want to work to keep your morale intact. You may want to try something different or you may actually enjoy "the thrill of the hunt". Analyse your skills and think outside the box, i.e. think creatively. For example, are you a keen gardener? Would you like to design and/or keep gardens? Are you any good at home repairs, painting, tiling? Have you thoughts of converting these skills and talents into generating money? A notice in your local garden centre or supermarket plus word of mouth and notifying neighbourhood groups are all ways of spreading the word. After age 66, continuing to work will affect neither occupational nor state pension.

With an increasingly contract-based workplace, opportunities do exist, and here are some pointers on how to find them:

1. Be clear as to what you want to do. Do you want to work five days a week or less? Do you want to travel in rush hour? Do you want to be self-employed? Do you want to be in the same career? How much do you want to be paid?

2. Identify your skills. Take a total view. What do you like to do and what gave you greatest satisfaction during your working lifetime? This will focus you on your real talents and then see how these could be applied in the job market. What retraining, if any, do you need? Where can you readily get it?

3. Research the marketplace. Contact a number of recruitment agencies. Look for those that deal specifically in the area you have selected. Meet them and emphasise your flexibility. For example, you can promote your ability to fit in without upsetting the career paths of those already there. You don't need fringe benefits or, to put it another way, you won't get them, so making you price-competitive!

4. Personally target small organisations. They are more adaptable and usually need experience and, again, the virtue is flexibility. In addition, it is usually easier to get a decision quickly since you will probably be dealing with an owner-manager.

STARTING YOUR OWN BUSINESS

This is becoming increasingly popular as individuals leave corporate employment earlier, and frequently with small pensions.

But if approached carelessly, this can be a real disaster at the time of your life when you don't need one. Be careful of two things — borrowings and partners. The first can dilute your current assets and commit your future pension income whilst the second can destroy relationships at the time you should be creating them. Up to 80 per cent of new businesses fail in the first year and only five per cent are still going after five years. One approach that combines control with opportunities is reinventing yourself as a self-employed consultant. What your subject is does not matter. As mentioned elsewhere, it could be garden design/maintenance, household repairs, financial advice, grinds, teaching adults or whatever. Visit your local FÁS office for ideas about employment in all its aspects and use its valuable website, www.fas.ie.

IF YOUR INCOME FALLS SHORT AFTER YOU RETIRE

Money Advice and Budgeting Service (MABS)

The Money Advice and Budgeting Service (MABS) is free at local level to members of the public. The service is delivered by money advisers who can assist you in drawing up a budget to pay routine bills and so gain more understanding and control over finances. MABS also helps clients work out a practical and feasible plan to address any debts or arrears. The type of debt regularly dealt with includes arrears in mortgage, rent, electricity, gas, phone, debts to moneylenders, catalogue sales, hire purchase, car finance, as well as debts to financial institutions including banks, building society, credit unions, and difficulties with credit cards and taxation.

The MABS service concentrates on cases of family or personal debt and is not geared towards debts in business. However, often help can be given in the case of a small business where the adviser works in co-operation with the person's accountant.

In resolving a debt problem, clients are offered a systematic process. The extent of the service will depend on individual needs, in that while a once-off visit may be suitable for one person, months of ongoing support may be necessary for another. MABS advisers work in a positive, non-judgemental way, with confidentiality guaranteed.

The money adviser can also negotiate with creditors and act as an "honest broker" between client and creditor, explain any legal processes, and help the client understand the legal consequences of non-payment of debts.

MABS also offers a Special Account Scheme operated in conjunction with the Credit Union Movement. Under this scheme, a client pays an agreed amount to their local credit union each week. This sum is administered by MABS, used to pay current bills and to make an agreed level of payments towards arrears. Many people have found that having such a structure in place to help them manage their weekly budget is a major advantage. They may also be encouraged to save a small amount every week in order to establish a credit rating. An added bonus is that there is no administrative charge for this service.

Another popular scheme, the "Household Budget Scheme" is operated by An Post in association with the Department of Social and Family Affairs. People in receipt of certain Social Welfare payments can have deductions made at source for routine bills such as electricity, local authority rents, telephone and gas. Again, there is no extra charge.

For information on local MABS round the country, contact your local community advice service, or contact The Support Unit, Comhairle, Hume House, Ballsbridge, Dublin 4; Tel: 01-6059024; Website: www.mabs.ie.

Financial Information Service Centres (FISC)

Financial Information Service Centres (FISC) is a voluntary service run by the Institute of Chartered Accountants in Ireland. Each centre provides free and confidential financial advice to people or organisations unable to afford the professional services of accountants. Centres are open to the public usually in conjunction with Citizens Information Centres and written queries can also be responded to.

For more information, contact your local community information centre, or Financial Information Service Centre, 87 Pembroke Road, Dublin 4, Tel: 01-6377361; E-mail: info@lsca.ie; Website: www.lsca.ie.

In Focus: The Federation of Active Retirement Associations

In 1978 a group of retired people in Dun Laoghaire, County Dublin, met in a local community room for afternoon tea and cards. Soon the group grew into the country's first active retirement association (ARA) and the card games had been joined by dozens more activities from language classes to gardening, DIY to shared holidays.

Too good an idea to keep down, the active retirement philosophy burst out of the confines of Dun Laoghaire, and associations began to form in other localities. Run for retired people by retired people, each group had its own ethos and its own range of interests. Local groups continued to come into being, and in 1985 the Federation of Active Retirement Associations (FARA) was established with a view to co-ordinating and encouraging the growth of ARAs as a national movement. FARA can be contacted at 1–2 Eustace Street, Dublin 2; Telephone: 01-6792142; E-mail: fara@eircom.net.

Today there are over 305 active retirement associations countrywide, with a total of 19,000 members. "We're heading for the 20,000," says FARA public relations officer, Jim Collier. Associations range in size from about 30 to 60 members, with a minority of very large associations with upwards of 250 members. Annual subscription is typically a modest €6, with members paying for outings and special activities. Originally an urban movement, rural membership has burgeoned, with associations now in almost every Irish county. The objectives of the movement are to:

- *Provide a focal point for active people, women and men, aged 55 and over, to meet and engage in educational, cultural, sporting and social activities;*

- *Promote a spirit of self-help and independence;*

- *Inspire members to use their energy, talents, skills, knowledge and experience to benefit each other and the community;*

- *Encourage a positive attitude to ageing and retirement.*

Some associations meet every day, others on one or two days a week, usually in daylight hours, in a location convenient to members. Activities remain eclectic and a random list could include some of the following:

- *Educational and hobbies: language classes, discussions, lectures, quizzes, woodwork, DIY;*

- *Cultural: flower arranging, music, singing, art, crafts, gardening, dancing, writing;*

- *Leisure: bridge, cards, indoor games, socials, holidays, tours, outings;*

- *Sport: snooker, swimming, table tennis, bowls, golf, tennis, keep fit, yoga, walking;*

- *Volunteering and community work.*

What do members get out of it? Here are some of their comments:

"It gives me an opportunity to meet people with similar interests."

"Life is now worth living."

"I was lonely, as my family are all married."

"The friendliness of members towards each other has enhanced our lives."

"It helps me keep active; I live for the bowling sessions."

"It makes me want to dress up and go out."

"I am no longer lonely. My life is full of surprises."

"I find it easier to relax and I am no longer depressed."

"I have made new friends and I have travelled to interesting places."

"I have something to do every day. Previously I only went out to shop."

"I always wanted to be artist and at last I'm getting my chance."

"I feel a new tolerance. It's great to feel needed."

"I'm in better physical condition than I was five years ago."

"I know I'm getting on, but I'm getting on with life."

"Once again my life has purpose."

Collectively, these statements reveal a lot about the issues facing many older people. For example, a possible lack of purpose in retirement illustrates what work/career can give in terms of routine, structure, goals. A number of people talk about loneliness — when children grow up and leave, when colleagues lose touch, when a partner dies. The member who has "always wanted to be an artist" speaks for the thousands who never got a chance when younger to pursue a gift or a talent. Finally, the person who remarks that because they now feel needed they have founded a greater tolerance in themselves exemplifies the fact that if any section of society is marginalised, then all of society is poorer in some way.

So the active retirement movement seems to be offering a lot — friendship, enjoyment, goals, physical activity, an opportunity to develop latent talents, a sense of belonging, emotional health, travel, and the chance to give to each other and to the local community. ARAs benefit the community by raising the status of retired people and older people in general by providing positive role models and helping to change negative stereotyping.

The concept of self-help has endured. Members draw first on the skills and talents within the association when looking for instructors, tutors and organisers, and so contribute further to member self-development As has been said, many associations work voluntarily in their neighbourhood, and FARA has spearheaded a new concept of retirement and ageing in Ireland.

The Federation is funded by the Department of Health, a recognition, says Jim Collier, of the contribution ARAs make to the physical, emotional and mental health of members. With its offices open each day Monday to Friday, the Federation operates a free information service for active retired and older people. Information is available in relation to relevant national and local organisations, social, cultural and sporting activities, travel and holidays, rights and entitlements for the over-sixties. "While our core business is active retirement, we are moving increasingly into the information and advocacy area and being seen in that light," says Jim Collier. "We are examining issues regarding older people such as travel, health care, grants and entitlements, and highlighting inequalities in these areas."

To find out if there is a retirement association in your area, ask around, or contact FARA. If there is none and you are interested in setting one up, they will help you. FARA provide an information pack, including a comprehensive handbook giving detailed guidance on how to set up an active retirement association. This covers the initial meeting, forming a committee, finding premises, planning an activities programme, funding, communications and duties of officers. FARA now have eight development officers — experienced active retirement members — to provide the assistance in setting up and continuing to support ARAs round the country.

One experienced member gives some informal do's and don'ts. "Get a few people together and elect a committee. Find premises available during the day or part of the day. Start small. You can choke yourself with too many ideas at the beginning. See what skills and interests there are in the group. You may have someone who can teach a language, another who does DIY; these could be your first classes."

TIME/ROUTINE

One simple approach to the new lifestyle which starts the first day after leaving your employment is to replicate what you enjoyed at work and avoid what you disliked. Of course, to do this you must first identify what these likes and dislikes, and again drawing up a list can be a good idea. For some people, though not all, high on the list of likes is socialising with others. Usually the pet dislike is travel to and from work! Draw up a list of potential activities; e.g. gardening, reading, visiting family, spending time with grandchildren, travel, studying, writing, learning a new skill, cinema, TV, etc. Prioritise them and have your spouse/partner do likewise. Compare the results. Discuss them with friends. Make plans.

RELATIONSHIPS

Of all the changes that come with retirement, changes in our long-term, close relationships can be the most traumatic. This is to be expected, since we are social creatures and living in relationship with partner, family, friends and colleagues is a vital aspect of our lives. A "rejection by the pack" was one retiree's description of the negative feelings created by an early retirement somewhat against his wishes.

Which brings us to a fundamental driver of how we react to retirement. Were you pushed or did you jump? In other words. did you choose the time and place of leaving or was it forced upon you? If the latter, there can be very negative reactions which will colour relationships both with former colleagues and with those nearest to us.

Married Couples

There are two extreme views of the effect of retirement on a lengthy marriage. One position can be caricatured as "the space invader syndrome", where couples struggle with too much togetherness. The opposite view is that of "the mature honeymoon", where the new, expanded time together is welcomed and managed well. Both points of view arise from the traditional relationship which had the husband working outside and the wife working inside the home.

The good news is that where there is reasonable preparation by both parties through discussion — and ideally a pre-retirement course — the result is a short-term period of mutual adjustment followed by a new life of greater companionship. One area that must be addressed very clearly and in detail is the financial one so that both are fully aware of the changes in lifestyle that may need to be made.

In the ideal world there will be more time spent together whilst still allowing for individual interests to be pursued. A degree of "cross-skilling", whereby household chores are shared, is recommended if desired by both.

Singles

An increasing number of single people, widows and widowers face into retirement in a society which is couple-centred. It is important, therefore, to become involved in community activities of all kinds — and possibly even taking up educational opportunities (see Chapter 3). Tell your friends very early in the transition of the forthcoming change in your life. Be open to their helping you.

Grown-up Children

An increasing trend, not really experienced by previous generations, is of grown-up children who leave the "family home" and return on a regular basis — or in some cases they may not leave at all! A certain degree of tension can exist when retirement occurs and suddenly there are a number of people experiencing life-changing events at the same time. A renegotiation of house rules may be needed at this juncture.

SOCIAL LIFE

Married or single, the need for friends and for the replacement of those faces one saw and related to during the working day is one of the challenges which the modern lifestyle has created. For example, it is not unusual for workers to be unacquainted with neighbours, local organisations, clubs and shops. With the fall off in church involvement, another part of the social fabric is missing.

As a result, it is important that in the years preceding retirement you prepare by establishing contacts which will lead to a fulfilled life after retirement. This does not mean there will be no further dialogue with ex-colleagues with whom you may have spent most of your working life but rather it will help you to "bloom where you are planted".

One of the best ways of meeting people is through volunteering in a charity or community group. The number of people engaged and the number of hours spent in voluntary activities has significantly declined in recent years. These were the findings of a recent survey completed by the National College of Ireland. It confirmed the trend in the US so brilliantly exposed in Dr Robert Putnam's *Bowling Alone: The Collapse and Revival of American Communities*. It gives the warning that the lack of involvement in our community by those living in it will seriously damage us all. (See also Chapter 2, "People Helping People".)

It has been found that social ties will help you live longer and more enjoyably — a concept that has become known as "social capital". At its simplest, the following questions illustrate what is at its heart. Are there people in your life whom you feel you can trust? How many clubs, societies or social groups have you joined? What really are the social contacts in your life?

A SPIRITUAL LIFE GIVES MEANING TO A PHYSICAL LIFE

At midlife and beyond we may ask questions that have faced all the great minds. Of what value is my life? Why I am here and where am I going? The basic belief that a spiritual life gives meaning to a physical life leads us to address the ultimate relationship: that of the individual and God.

The transition from work to the third age provides the space in which this aspect of one's life can also be examined, leading to a more serene approach to the years ahead. (See Chapter 10, "The Spiritual Dimension".)

SUMMARY

Let me finish by emphasising one thing that my 38 years of experience in this arena has taught me — all that matters is quality of life. The framework for this in the third age is accepted as:

- Adequate income

- Good relationships — family, friends, neighbours

- Involvement in social activities plus personal interests

- Health

- Appropriate accommodation

- A sense of purpose and control.

How to achieve these six main principles? The starting point is to prepare early for the unique adventure of the third age.

Chapter 2

PEOPLE HELPING PEOPLE

Clare McGuinness

"How does one keep from 'growing old inside'? Surely only in community. The only way to make friends with time is to stay friends with people. . . Taking community seriously not only gives us the companionship we need, it also relieves us of the notion that we are indispensable."
— Robert McAfee Brown

WHAT IS VOLUNTEERING?

The official Irish definition of volunteering is:

". . . the commitment of time and energy, for the benefit of society, local communities, individuals outside the immediate family, the environment or other causes. Voluntary activities are undertaken of a person's own free will, without payment, except for the reimbursement of out-of-pocket expenses." — White Paper on Supporting Voluntary Activity, Department of Social, Community and Family Affairs, 2000: 83

Volunteering is any type of unpaid work or activity which is freely undertaken by a person for the benefit of other people or a specific cause.

Voluntary activity has a long tradition in Irish society. One-third of the Irish population regularly volunteers in organisations. In fact, most of us have volunteered at some stage of our lives — whether we know it or not. It may have been formal volunteering through an organisation such as St Vincent de Paul, meals on wheels, or more recently the Special Olympics. More people again volunteer on an informal basis, e.g. with friends and family (Ruddle and Mulvihill, 1999) — whether by simply minding a neighbour's children, lending a hand at the local school or community centre, or helping out at a sports club. The total amount of time given to voluntary work per year is equivalent to some 96,454 full-time workers (ibid.). In 1995, the contribution of voluntary activity to the economy in Ireland was worth nearly €600 million (Donoghue, 1999).

In the past we have made a difference in our communities by giving some of our time to other people. So why stop now?

The results of voluntary effort — people helping people — continue to touch the lives of virtually every citizen in Ireland, through areas such as education, arts, sports, health or environment. Indeed, many people overseas also benefit from the voluntary efforts of people in Ireland, through fundraising campaigns, writing letters to governments and other activities.

Volunteering, in essence, is something that makes a difference. Volunteering boosts self-esteem, self-confidence and increases overall life satisfaction. Helping is a vital part of being human. Those who work in the sphere of helping others report the sense of joy, usefulness, power and self-worth that comes from the act of helping.

WHO CAN VOLUNTEER?

Quite simply: everyone, including you. All people have the right to volunteer. Volunteering provides equal opportunity, regardless of age, sex, sexual orientation, marital status, mental or physical health, race, colour, nationality, ethnicity, political or religious belief, or economic status.

WHY VOLUNTEER?

People volunteer for all sorts of reasons: to make a difference; to help others; to try out something completely different; to gain or improve skills; because they have some free time; to donate professional skills; to feel good; or because there is simply no-one else to do it. For many, volunteering is one way that people — old or young — can do their bit or give something back. Here's how some older volunteers describe their involvement in a Dublin get-together for older people:

> "We have played at the Wednesday Club every week for the past ten or twelve years. Why? Because we enjoy it. We do it for the satisfaction of being able to play in front of people who enjoy music and dancing, and sometimes we even get them up for a song. These days people give money — they don't give time. We think time is more precious." — Wednesday Club Senior Volunteer Band: Willie Shanks (spoons), Sean McGuinness (saxophone and clarinet), Jo Walsh (drummer)

While the motivations behind volunteering are endless, the positive contribution to society is also invaluable. And of course, the added bonus: according to the International Federation on Ageing (1999), volunteers live longer!

Ultimately, volunteering helps both the giver and the receiver. No matter how small you think your contribution is, remember — you can still make a difference.

Why Do People Volunteer? A Few Good Reasons

- To feel needed

- To be with people who are different

- To keep busy

- To get a better balance in life

- To make new friends

- As therapy

- To have something to get up for

- For fun

- To give something back

- As an excuse to do something they love

- To donate their professional skills

- Because there is no one else to do it

- To feel good

- To have an impact

- Because they can't do paid work

- To be part of a team

- To get out of the house

- To be challenged

- As an alternative to giving money

- Because they are asked

- To stand and be counted.

(Adapted from "Why people volunteer . . . a few possible motivations", *Volunteering Ireland Fact Sheet*, 2003)

TOO OLD FOR VOLUNTEERING? NEVER TOO OLD!

Older people in Ireland today are more healthy and active than ever. This is due to a combination of factors, such as early retirement, improved healthcare and changing lifestyles. Some people find they have extra time on their hands as they get older and wish to contribute to society in a meaningful and fulfilling way as active citizens. The beauty of volunteering is that you don't necessarily need to be young, or fit, or highly skilled in order to contribute — you just need to want to.

Organisations involve volunteers for a multitude of reasons. They benefit from the motivation and dedication of volunteers who want to help, to make a difference, to offer skills, expertise, experience and time. Many small and under-resourced organisations working for specific causes rely on the valuable contributions of those who give freely of their time and effort, without whom they simply could not function. Older people in particular represent a vital volunteer resource in society today and will continue to do so in the future. So what can you offer?

Maturity and Skills

Older people possess a wealth of knowledge, skills and experiences acquired over the years. Life experiences (e.g. employment, unemployment, marriage, child-rearing, bereavement) can put you in a position to be able to help others. Volunteering can be a very satisfying way of sharing this expertise, providing you with an opportunity to share your wealth of skills, knowledge and enthusiasm within the community.

Availability and Numbers

You may have extra time on your hands, due to retirement or redundancy from paid employment, or due to decreased family responsibilities. Volunteer-involving organisations consider older volunteers as a vital resource, as they often have more free time. The average retired man in Ireland has 91 hours of leisure each week; the average retired woman has 72 hours (Age & Opportunity, 1999). The Irish population is ageing, resulting in a larger pool of people who have the time to impart their knowledge and experience where it is needed most.

> "We are always looking for volunteers — especially retired people who have access to a car. People with poor mobility from outlying areas are often excluded from our services. I hate when people miss events like day trips, merely because they can't get a lift into town. All we need is someone who can spare a few hours a week and drive one of our service users to our centre. We look after them from there." — Volunteer Co-ordinator, Friends of the Elderly, Dublin

Commitment

Studies show that older people volunteer longer hours with organisations than any other age group, and are more likely to commit for a longer period of time than volunteers in any other age group.

Is Volunteering Right for You?

Before you start volunteering, think for a while about what you really want to give and what you want to get out of your volunteering experience.

What Do You Enjoy Doing?

What type of voluntary activity would you like to do? You may have a particular skill or qualification you want to use, or you may be interested in a hobby or a sport. On the other hand, you may wish to do something completely different and new. As well as being one way to share your knowledge and contribute to society, volunteering is also a great way to learn new skills, meet new people and share new experiences.

Think about whether you prefer team work or would rather work on your own; or perhaps you would like to work on a one-to-one basis with someone? Do you want to deal with the public or are you someone who prefers more practical work?

What Do You Care About?

Volunteering your time, energy and expertise is an ideal way to contribute to an area you are interested in and care about, for example: animals, arts, campaigning, children, community, culture, disability, education, environment, fundraising, health, housing, justice, media, people, poverty, retail, sports, welfare . . .

What Could You Do?

What skills do you have that you could use? Here are just a few examples of skills matched with voluntary roles:

- **Patience, kindness, empathy**. Helpline volunteer, victim support, mentor to young person, visiting people who are lonely.

- **Leadership, management qualities**. Management committee volunteer, youth leader.

- **Teaching**. Helping new immigrants to learn English, music teacher.

- **Practical skills**. Gardener, driver, painter, shop assistant, kitchen assistant, hairdresser.

- **Reading and writing**. Helping children with additional needs in homework clubs or teaching adults with literacy problems.

The range of volunteering opportunities are endless. From protecting children from begging on the streets, to planting seedlings in a forestry programme, to assisting at motor sports rallies, to visiting an isolated person in their own home . . . there's a lot of scope.

How Much Time Will You Give?

Consider how much time you want to give to volunteering. Make sure you don't commit too much of your time — remember to look after yourself and leave some time for yourself and your other commitments. Fortunately, there are many volunteering opportunities — short and long term — to avail of. Here are just a few:

- With one hour, you could give blood.

- With two hours, you could visit somebody in their home or write a letter to governments on human rights issues.

- With half a day, you could provide administrative support in a busy office or welcome visitors and tourists to popular sites of interest.

- With one day you could create a window display in a charity shop or plant some spring bulbs.

- With two days you could be part of a team renovating an apartment.

- With a week you could conduct research for an overseas children's charity.

- With three months you could be the quizmaster in a residential home.

Some volunteering opportunities may require only one day or one hour a week, but may need an ongoing commitment as they involve building up relationships, be it with older people in a nursing home or younger people in a youth group. Check the length of commitment required with the organisation before you decide on a volunteering position. If you only want to volunteer once in a while, contact Volunteering Ireland (details on page 70) for details of their Time Limited Commitment© service

(TLC©) where volunteers can do a few hours every so often if they so wish.

What Qualifications Do You Need?

The best qualification for being a volunteer is a genuine interest in the organisation's activities or in the person(s) requiring help.

Although specific skills are required for some voluntary activities, a willingness to learn and be involved is all that is required for others.

Nelly and Mary have volunteered in the Ritzy Rags Charity Shop, Dublin, for over ten years. Nelly found out through her church bulletin that people were needed, while Mary's sister told her about the opportunity in the shop. Both women love their voluntary work — they enjoy the company, love meeting new people and say their customers are nice. Both are keen to stress that the most important thing when volunteering is to be interested in the activity, and interested in other people.

Will It Suit You?

It is important to get a feel for the place and the task before you take on more. If you aren't suited to the organisation or activity, you can leave and keep looking for something you are happy with. That's the advantage of being a volunteer. If you are not happy with the position in the organisation, you may be able to change roles. In addition, some organisations offer training to volunteers — this may be an ideal opportunity to expand your skills and develop yourself further.

TOP TIPS FOR OLDER VOLUNTEERS

Do:

- Look for a volunteering position that you will enjoy, be able to do and that will fit in with your available time and activities.

- Choose a voluntary activity that you are interested in.

- Be willing to meet the organisation for an informal chat or interview — consider this a "getting to know you" exercise for both yourself and the organisation.

- Ask the organisation for a clear role description so that you know what tasks and activities you will undertake as a volunteer.

- Check if you need specific skills for the activity. If you can't fill the position, you may be able to find something else in the same organisation.

- Ask what supports you will receive as a volunteer, and from whom, e.g. the volunteer co-ordinator.

- Ask if there will be training opportunities to further supplement knowledge and skills, if you are interested.

- Ask if the organisation reimburses volunteers' out-of-pocket lunch and travel expenses. Mainly large (but also some small) organisations arrange this.

- Be aware that you may be asked by the organisation for Garda clearance if you want to work in direct contact with vulnerable groups, such as people with learning disabilities or children.

- Enjoy the experience!

Don't:

- Accept or remain in a voluntary position you are not comfortable with or are unable to commit to.

- Feel obliged to take on more that you can handle.

- Feel isolated; if you need support or advice, talk to your supervisor or your fellow volunteers. Remember, you are a valuable resource and your contribution makes all the difference!

In Focus: Become a Samaritan?

Could you be a Good Samaritan in 2004 and beyond? In Ireland every Samaritan branch is recruiting volunteers, with the Dublin branch in addition looking for people aged 50 plus. Older volunteers may be available during the day, able to make a solid commitment, bring particular life experiences and help to balance the age profile of the organisation. But whether you are aged 18 or 38 or 58 (and all age groups are welcome), what would you be taking on if you went forward?

According to the Samaritans' website their mission is to be available 24 hours a day to provide confidential emotional support for people who are experiencing feelings of distress or despair, including those which may lead to suicide (www.samaritans.org). Their vision is to create a society in which fewer people die by suicide, where people are able to explore their feelings and acknowledge and respect the feelings of others. Samaritans' values are based on these beliefs:

- *The importance of having the opportunity to explore difficult feelings*

- *That being listened to, in confidence and accepted without prejudice, can alleviate despair and suicidal feelings*

- *That everyone has the right to make fundamental decisions about their own life, including the decision to die by suicide.*

Between them Kevin Cronin, 62, and Judy Taylor, 70, have almost 40 years of Samaritan experience under their belt. Kevin joined 25 years ago in the midst of a busy working and family life. "I saw an ad for volunteers and felt I had a little time to spare. Without knowing too much about it then, the type of work struck me as being very valuable," he says. Judy was 56 with her family reared when she applied to train as a volunteer. "I was never very good at the bring and buy, coffee morning, fundraising circle and I wanted to do something, give something back, as you say. I am quite good at not telling people what to do, I knew Samaritans didn't give advice and felt this approach was something I could do."

After an initial interview, both were accepted for training, and Kevin looks back on his. "The most important thing I learnt was about listening, how it's so hard to listen. Through the training, role-play, reflection, I began to learn to listen. There is a sense before you get into it that maybe you're not doing anything. As Judy says, you're not giving advice, so I had to learn how effective listening can be."

Judy agrees. "In normal conversation we listen with both ears and sometimes we're not listening at all. One of the last lecturers we had talked about listening with the third ear, listening to the nuances, listening to what has not been said."

Volunteers are eased into the work with plenty of support and guidance. "Most of your cases are to do with human relationships, and the concerns that can arise from these. Sometimes they come right out with it, a row, a happening. Our aim is to help people try to express how they feel about whatever is going on. This is valuable because often you don't have time, don't have space to know how you feel. You might feel anger, but underneath there may be hurt of some sort. Saying how you feel can be a release and a relief," says Judy.

"You don't always know what the call is really about," says Kevin. "I would think some of the work is about people who don't fit in, who are lonely, depressed, isolated, who have trouble with relationships. People can be defined by their life experiences. Listening can be hard because we don't do the cheer up bit, though we can help people validate their feelings. Unless you express your feelings, you may not really understand them. Telling someone helps you know them yourself and hopefully will be a step towards coping."

The Samaritan message is to call if you feel suicidal, but you don't have to be suicidal to call, and volunteers are quite upfront in mentioning the S-word. Judy explains her approach. "If it seems right, I would bring in something about living and life itself. Outsiders often say that will put the idea of suicide into someone's head, but it's not like that. Sometimes a caller will say 'No, I never thought about suicide, it's nothing as serious as that', but there is often the response, 'Well, I do think about it, or I have thought about it'. Suicide is such a taboo subject that mentioning it gives people permission to talk about it if they need to."

Why does listening help so much? "Real listening is rare these days," says Kevin. "You are listening without judgement, without baggage, without criticism, trying to help them talk about it, open yourself to them. Sometimes there may be solutions that people can't see so you try to encourage them to look at their options and to find their own responses."

"People are bombarded with advice from all quarters — friends, family, media — we give time, space, and pace, there can be silence in a lot of conversations, and we just stay with the caller, we're still there," says Judy.

In an age with the expectation that every problem has a solution, the toughest calls to deal with, says Kevin, are from people in severe, ongoing difficulty. "People in terrible situations, very sick, terminally ill, in poverty, with little support and as far as you can see, there is very little they can do. I can feel very sad after such calls." "As Kevin says," adds Judy, "there are people in ghastly situations, though often at the end they say 'thank you very much for listening to me', and we still see a value in being there." Volunteers may suggest calling someone back if particularly concerned and some callers welcome this, while understanding that they will speak to a volunteer on duty rather than being able to access someone by name.

Samaritans offer a letter, e-mail, face-to-face and phone service. As well as initial preparation, volunteers receive regular refresher courses and, says Judy, constant support. "We get great support. After a very difficult call when you might be feeling inadequate, you can go to your team leader and talk through your feelings so that you don't take problems home with you. So we are Samaritans to one another." "There is enormous support in a broader sense too," continues Kevin. "Samaritans has a very good structure. We have a three-year rule, everyone changes their role after three years, so as well as being on the phones, which is the one constant, you get an opportunity over time at leading, training, being treasurer, director, all the jobs in running an organisation. It gives you a very broad base." The time commitment is from three hours a week and an overnight every two months.

Both Kevin and Judy see a value in having volunteers across the age range. "I think if you live long enough you have a sense of how arbitrary life can be," says Kevin. "I feel fortunate at how my life has gone, if it had gone another way, I could be a caller. This gives you a humility when listening to people who have been through so much." "We aim for a uniform response and believe that the age doesn't matter in terms of the service we give. In personal terms, as an older person, over the years, you learn when to talk and when not to talk, you learn patience, and, dare I say it, a bit of maturity," says Judy.

Finally, both volunteers say their involvement with Samaritans has helped them grow and develop themselves. "We are afforded the privilege to help people discover their inner feelings and to keep them company for a little while at a particular time in their lives," says Judy. "It is such a privilege to be allowed to be close to people at a time of crisis," agrees Kevin. "I've got far more out of it than I've put into it, and the kind of person we are looking for is not someone who feels they have all the answers, but who may be a bit diffident and wonder if they could do it. If they have the commitment, with training and support, they can."

If you would like more information call the Samaritans at 1850 609090 or e-mail jo@samaritans.org

WHERE CAN YOU FIND OUT MORE?

There are literally thousands of organisations around Ireland that depend on volunteers and desperately need your contribution. Social networks are the most common way of finding out about volunteering — friends, family, word of mouth. However, remember to look at other options that may display volunteering opportunities:

- Local volunteer bureaux

- Credit unions and libraries

- Social welfare offices

- Your local Citizen's Information Centre

- Community and Enterprise Director in your County Council

- FÁS offices

- Church bulletins

- Adult education centres

- Shop windows, newsagents, supermarkets

- Telephone directories

- Notice boards, newsletters, websites, promotional literature of small community and voluntary organisations.

Useful National Contacts

The following is a list of some national organisations that involve volunteers. While not comprehensive, it will begin pointing you in directions and serve as a starting point if you are interested in finding out more. Most of the organisations listed are based in Dublin, but have regional bases around the country, and will give you this local information on request. If in doubt, contact Volunteering Ireland.

- **Age Action Ireland Ltd.** Age Action Ireland uses volunteers in their library, as information officers, in their shops, in research and in administration. *Age Action Ireland Ltd., 30/31 Lower Camden Street, Dublin 2; Tel: 01-4756989; E-mail: info@ageaction.ie; Website: www.ageaction.ie*

- **Amnesty International (Irish section).** As a campaigning organisation, volunteers are vitally important to Amnesty International's work in a range of tasks, including administration and letter-writing activity. Increased involvement from older volunteers would be particularly welcome. *Amnesty International (Irish section), Seán MacBride House, 48 Fleet Street, Dublin 2; Tel: 01-6776361; E-mail: info@amnesty.ie; Website: www.amnesty.ie*

- **Barnardos.** Volunteers work in the charity shops and raise funds. They support professional staff in service provision for children and families. The members of Barnardos Board, which governs Barnardos, work on a voluntary basis. *Barnardos, Christchurch Square, Dublin 8; Tel: 01-4530355; E-mail: info@barnardos.ie; Web: www.barnardos.ie*

- **Citizens Information Centres.** If you enjoy working alongside other people and think you would like to volunteer with your local CIC, contact the head office to find out details of the CIC in your local area. *Comhairle, Hume House, Ballsbridge, Dublin 4; Tel: 01-6059000; E-mail: info@comhairle.ie; Web: www.comhairle.ie*

- **Conservation Volunteers Ireland** undertakes a variety of practical conservation work, such as collecting seeds, tree planting, forest tidying and litter clean-up. Volunteering Ireland's publication *Opportunity Knocks: Opening Doors for Volunteers with Additional Support Needs*, a comprehensive toolkit on inclusive volunteering, is available from them, price €10. *Conservation Volunteers Ireland Ltd., Steward's*

House, Rathfarnham Castle, Grange Road, Dublin 14; Tel: 01-4952878; E-mail: info@cvi.ie; Web: www.cvi.ie

- **National Adult Literacy Agency (NALA).** NALA involves over 5,000 literacy tutors, of whom over 4,000 are volunteers. The tutors provide an estimated 14,000 hours of tuition per week to people with low levels of literacy. The scheme extends to over 126 local Vocational Educational Committee (VEC) literacy programmes around the country. For details on your local literacy scheme, contact the head office in Dublin. *NALA, 76 Lower Gardiner Street, Dublin 1; Tel: 01-8554332; E-mail: literacy@nala.ie; Website: www.nala.ie*

- **Oxfam Ireland.** Volunteers are involved in a range of activities around the country, including the Oxfam shops. *Oxfam Ireland, 9 Burgh Quay, Dublin 2; Tel: 01-6777662; E-mail: oxireland@oxfam.ie; Website: www.oxfamireland.org*

- **Social Mentor Project.** The Social Mentor Project is a service provided by Comhairle and operates through a panel of volunteer mentors who share their expertise with organisations in the community and voluntary sector. The Project actively looks for retired or semi-retired volunteers with skills in strategic planning, management, project development, human resources, public relations, or other skills which may be helpful for the development of community and voluntary organisations. *Social Mentor Programme, Comhairle, Hainault House, The Square, Tallaght, Dublin 24; Tel: 01-4620444; E-mail: cora.pollard@comhairle.ie; Website: www.comhairle.ie*

- **Society of St Vincent de Paul.** Volunteers are involved at all levels, home and hospital visitation, running shops, serving in a voluntary capacity in administrative boards, and providing summer holidays for children and adults and more. *Society of St Vincent de Paul, 8 New Cabra Road, Dublin 7; Tel: 01-8384164; E-mail: info@svp.ie; Website: www.svp.ie*

- **The Senior Helpline.** Operated by over 300 volunteers from 11 centres nationwide, the service is available seven days a week from 10.00 am to 1.00 pm and from 7.00 pm to 10.00 pm. *Third Age Centre, Summerhill, County Meath; Tel: 046-9557756; Helpline: 1850-440444; E-mail: info@thirdage-ireland.com; Website: www.thirdage-ireland.com*

- **Volunteer Bureaux — Northern Ireland.** There is a comprehensive and well-established network of volunteer centres in Northern Ireland. The Volunteer Development Agency will have details of local centres throughout the province. *Volunteer Development Agency, Fourth Floor, 58 Howard Street, Belfast, BT1 6PG, Northern Ireland; Tel: 048-90236100; E-mail: info@volunteering-ni.org; Website: www.volunteer-ing-ni.org*

- **Volunteer Bureaux — Ireland.** Volunteering Ireland is the national resource for volunteering in the Republic of Ireland, supporting, facilitating and promoting volunteering right across the board. The placement service of Volunteering Ireland matches volunteers and organisations in the Dublin City Council area, and provides helpful and friendly advice, support and service on all volunteer issues. *Volunteering Ireland, Coleraine House, Coleraine Street, Dublin 7; Tel: 01-8722622; E-mail: info@volunteeringireland.com; Website: www.volunteeringireland.com*

- Volunteering Ireland organise an annual event each autumn **Volunteer Organisers Linking Together** (VOLT), bringing volunteer co-ordinators in different organisations to learn and share experiences. (See contact details above.)

Residential Volunteering Opportunities in Ireland

Listed below are the contact details of a few organisations that offer residential volunteering opportunities in Ireland, as well as non-residential volunteering options. For a more comprehensive listing, contact Volunteering Ireland and ask for a copy of their free fact sheet on this topic.

- **L'Arche Communities Ireland.** L'Arche is a worldwide federation of faith communities where people with and without learning disabilities live together. People who are searching for a deeper meaning in their lives often come to L'Arche. Community living attracts them to a life where spirituality is central. The communities welcome people of all denominations and those with no religious affiliation. Contact the Dublin office for details of your local L'Arche community. *L'Arche Dublin, "Seolta", Warrenhouse Road, Baldoyle, Dublin 13; Tel: 01-8394356; E-mail: dublin@larche.ie; Website: www.larche.ie.*

- **Camphill Communities of Ireland.** The Camphill Communities offer those in need of special care a sheltered environment in which their educational, therapeutic and social needs can be met. The nine communities in the Republic of Ireland were all founded through the initiative of parents of children with various disabilities and special needs. Each community has its own distinctive purpose and character. Volunteers who wish to get fully involved in the life of the community on a long-term basis (usually six months to a year or more) are encouraged to apply. *Website: www.camphill.ie*

- **Friends of the Elderly.** Friends of the Elderly provides full-time internships of between six months and one year to work with, and on behalf of, older people. *Friends of the Elderly, 25 Bolton Street, Dublin 1; Tel: 01-8731855; E-mail: info@friendsoftheelderly.ie; Web: www.friendsoftheelderly.ie*

- **Glencree Centre for Reconciliation.** This autonomous organisation seeks to work together with those trying to build peace. Volunteers usually come to Glencree for a year, starting in September, and undertake both practical work in kitchen and garden as well as programme work on peace issues and with community groups. Shorter placements, including weekends, can be arranged. *Glencree Centre for Reconciliation, Glencree, near Enniskerry, County Wicklow; Tel: 01-2829711; E-mail: info@glencree-cfr.ie; Website: www.glencree-cfr.ie*

Volunteering Holidays

The past decade has seen a huge number of charities who fundraise by offering a challenge and an opportunity to the general public. Third world agencies such as Trocaire, child disability supports such as Debra Ireland and cancer support services such as ARC are among a growing number of organisations who now use volunteers who are sponsored for walks, pilgrimages, treks in some of the world's most exotic beauty spots. During the trip, people tend to bond as a group, friendships are formed, experiences are shared, sights are seen and competencies challenged. Many who take part in such holidays are very positive about them.

If interested in this idea, look out for advertising of such trips on radio, television, newspapers and on charity organisations websites, and/or contact a number of charities to find out where such treks are being organised.

Volunteering Opportunities Overseas

The following contacts should provide a useful starting point if you are looking for international volunteering opportunities — and may also offer Ireland-based volunteering opportunities, e.g. fundraising or campaigning. Contact Volunteering Ireland for a more comprehensive listing of organisations that send volunteers abroad.

* **EIL Intercultural Learning.** EIL Intercultural Learning is a non-profit organisation which aims to promote global un-

derstanding. It runs a Volunteer Abroad programme providing opportunities for Irish people to work on community-based projects in several developing countries. This programme is open to people who are motivated and have a desire to learn. *EIL Intercultural Learning, 1 Empress Place, Summerhill North, Cork; Tel: 021-4551535; E-mail: info@volunteerabroad.ie; Website: www.volunteerabroad.ie*

- **GOAL.** GOAL recruits qualified volunteer doctors, nurses, midwives, accountants, administrators, engineers and mechanics to work in Africa, Asia and Eastern Europe. Applicants must have two years' work experience. The minimum commitment is usually one year. *GOAL, PO Box 19, Dun Laoghaire, County Dublin; Tel: 01-2809779; E-mail: info@goal.ie; Website: www.goal.ie*

- **Viatores Christi.** Viatores Christi sends lay missionaries overseas after a part-time training course, lasting about six months. Experience, professional skills and a Christian commitment are required. *Viatores Christi, Travellers for Christ, 38–39 Upper Gardiner Street, Dublin 1; Tel: 01-8749346; E-mail: viatoreschristi@eircom.net; Website: www.viatoreschristi.com*

- **Voluntary Service International.** VSI co-ordinates short-term international work camps, an Asia/Africa/Latin America exchange programme and various medium- to long-term volunteering projects. VSI publishes its guide to International Voluntary Work Projects each spring. This also lists work camps of between ten days and four weeks held each summer throughout Ireland. Most work is practical, environmental or with children. A small cost covers all food and accommodation. *Voluntary Service International, 30 Mountjoy Square, Dublin 1; Tel: 01-8551011; E-mail: vsi@iol.ie; Website: www.vsi.ie*

- **Wwoof (Willing Workers on Organic Farms)** is an international organisation giving travellers the opportunity to receive free accommodation and food on organic farms in Ireland, Europe and worldwide, in return for their labour. The help you give your host will be wide and variable, including sowing, making compost, gardening, planting, cutting wood, weeding, making mud-bricks, harvesting, fencing, building, typing, packing, milking, feeding. The help you give is an arrangement made between you and your host. You should negotiate beforehand with your host so that you know what they expect from you and the sort of volunteering you are happy to do. For more information, log on to www.wwoof.org

There are also a number of local volunteer centres around Ireland, some of which are still in the process of development. To find out more, contact Volunteering Ireland, who will be happy to direct you to your nearest volunteer centre.

References

Age & Opportunity (1999), *Volunteering*, Ireland.

Department of Social, Community and Family Affairs (2000), *White Paper on Supporting Voluntary Activity*, Dublin.

Donoghue, F. (1999), *Uncovering the nonprofit Sector in Ireland: Its Economic Value and Significance*, National College of Ireland.

International Federation on Ageing (1999), *INTERCOM*, USA, October/ November.

Mulvihill, R and Ruddle, H. (1995), *Reaching Out: Charitable Giving and Volunteering in the Republic of Ireland — The 1994 Survey*, National College of Ireland.

Mulvihill, R. and Ruddle, H. (1999), *Reaching Out: Charitable Giving and Volunteering in the Republic of Ireland — The 1997/98 Survey*, National College of Ireland.

Volunteering Ireland (2004), *Opportunity Knocks — Opening Doors for Volunteers with Additional Support Needs*, Holywell Press, Ireland.

Chapter 3

NEVER TOO OLD TO LEARN

Berni Brady

*"Old people are always young enough to learn,
with profit."* — Aeschylus

It is inspiring to listen to the learning journeys made by older people. Take Phyllis, for example. She left school years ago with a Primary Certificate, which gave her a good grounding in the three Rs. In 2002, she received her BA Degree at the age of 70+. Her description of her first day at a UCD lecture with over 300 young students made me laugh out loud recently. She was part of a focus group of adult learners who were telling their stories to Síle de Valera, Minister of State at the Department of Education and Science, and members of the Educational Disadvantage Committee in that Department. When I walk through UCD on my way to the monthly Governing Authority Meetings and see the crowds of fresh-faced students, I can just imagine how Phyllis must have felt.

Recently Phyllis gave a stunning stage performance at a conference on women learning organised by AONTAS, the National Association for Adult Education, as part of a drama highlighting the importance of support for women's education. She is still working as a volunteer with a women's group, as she has done for many years and is currently studying Greek and Roman civilisation. What would that equip one for, you might ask, especially in the context of creating competitiveness in the economy? A real love of learning is one answer; learning just for the sheer joy of it.

Phyllis wasn't the only adult learner who told her story. Others, men and women, gave testimony to the power of learning and how it changed their lives. Their stories also drew attention to the barriers they experienced in accessing learning opportunities. Phyllis provided an important role model for the younger adults there and indeed for anyone wishing to return to education, but nervous about taking the plunge. Of course, 50 years ago going to university was out of the question for people like Phyllis. Only rich people could do that. Unfortunately, 50 years on it is still only people who are reasonably well off who can afford to study part-time, or by distance learning, which is often the only way adult learners can fit their learning into busy lives.

CHANGING ATTITUDES

One of life's certainties is that all of us grow old, but how old is old? Inside all of us there is a young energetic person dying to get out, no matter what age we reach. The key to keeping that energy alive is to be constantly open to new experiences. "Never to old to learn" is a slogan often used by AONTAS in its quest to raise awareness of the importance of learning throughout life. It was also the title of a small research report published by AONTAS in 1988 looking at education for older people in Ireland. In its introduction, AONTAS set out to dispel the myth that older people do not want to do much; that they prefer to sit around listening to the radio or watching television and waiting for visits from friends and relatives. The report stated:

"A myth has been created, which unfortunately many older people themselves believe, that the last thing older people want to do is to learn something new."

The *Never Too Old to Learn* Report was one of the most requested publications ever produced by AONTAS. Perhaps the title said it all.

Nearly 20 years on, Ireland is a very different place, and attitudes to ageing are slowly beginning to change. This is partly due to the fact that people are living longer, healthier and enjoying more active lives. Brains, like bodies, need to be kept fit, and the best way to do that is to exercise them regularly. More than half of the 3,000 callers each year to the AONTAS Information Referral Service are older adults wishing to return to education now that they have the time, and very often the money, now that the kids have flown the nest. A recent article on ageing in the twenty-first century looked at the increasingly active population of older people in the UK. It examined the many activities now undertaken by older adults, especially those who had retired early from full-time work, but perhaps the one that tickled me most was called SKIing — no, not on the slopes, but Spending the Kids' Inheritance — on oneself! What an interesting idea. Well, why not, and why not spend it doing a PhD, or learning another language, or doing a TEFL (Teaching English as a Foreign Language) course or any kind of course for that matter?

However, despite the fact that attitudes are slowly beginning to change, there is still a culture of thinking about education as something you do when you're young in preparation for getting out into the big bad world of work, and certainly not something you can do when you are a granny or granddad. The notion of investing resources to ensure an active healthy life in older years is still seen as something of a waste, especially when we still have proportionally one of the largest young populations in Europe. Governments seem reluctant to provide education and training opportunities for anyone who is not going directly into the workforce at the end of their course. I was recently fascinated by a "quote of the week" in one of the Sunday newspapers from a South Korean election candidate suggesting that old people should not vote: "They do not need to decide the future because they will disappear in the future." While I am not suggesting that our politicians are quite as bad as the Korean candidate, inclusion of the welfare of older people on the social and political agenda sometimes feels quite low on the list of priorities here also.

Apart from the fact that during a long working life we all pay for the services we need when we age, such an attitude ignores the rich capacity of older people to contribute their abilities and experiences to the growth and development of a decent society for us all. AONTAS's work is based on the premise that learning is a right and we are, therefore, committed to the belief that it makes good sense to ensure that people have the right to learn throughout life, regardless of age. The most frequent question asked by adults seeking information about returning to education is, "Will I be able for it at my age? Or do you think the brain has gone too rusty for it?" After working in adult education for most of my career, I have seen at first hand what good and well-motivated learners adults make, given the right conditions. There is also plenty of evidence to suggest that mature students are very likely to complete their courses of learning once they get started.

ADULT LITERACY

The OECD *International Adult Literacy Survey*, published in 1997, showed that one in four Irish adults had insufficient literacy skills to enable them to undertake everyday tasks. Furthermore the survey drew attention to the substantially lower levels of literacy in older age groups. Following this study and prior to the general election in 1997, the first Minister of State with responsibility for Adult Education was appointed after a strong lobbying campaign by AONTAS and its sister organisation, the National Adult Literacy Agency (NALA). Both organisations campaigned for a political commitment to adult education and for investments to be made for the development of an educational sector that has been starved of resources. Since then, an increased investment has been made in the field of adult literacy and a number of innovative developments have been implemented in an attempt to tackle the literacy problem. The budget for adult literacy has risen to approximately €18.2 million in 2003 from €1 million in 1997 and a National Adult Literacy Strategy has been developed for the first time. The number of learners availing of literacy services has increased from 5,000 in 1997 to more than 30,000 in 2003. The number of adults aged 55 and over availing of provision currently stands at just over 10 per cent (NALA, 2004).

PROMOTING LIFELONG LEARNING

In August 2000, the government published the first ever White Paper on Adult Education entitled *Learning for Life*. The paper was warmly welcomed by everyone involved in adult and community education, as it provided, for the first time, a framework for the development of the Adult Education Service, and contained many exciting recommendations including specific investments for its development. The White Paper showed that 31 per cent of those currently aged between 55 and 64 had completed second level education as opposed to 67 per cent in the 25–34 age bracket. This pattern is common throughout the OECD countries, reflecting the very significantly increased investment and participation in second-level education since the 1960s throughout the industrialised world. The White Paper states:

> "These figures draw attention to one of the most persistent and pervasive inequalities throughout the in-

dustrialised world — that of age-based differentials in educational attainment."

While no one would dispute the importance of education for our young people, nonetheless the educational needs and desires of older adults must also be taken into consideration if lifelong learning is to become a reality. The White Paper devoted a short section to the educational needs of older people, stating that:

> "Strategies for active ageing stress the critical impor-
> tance of access to learning as a key tool in coping with
> change, and the importance of physical, social and men-
> tal activity to general well-being. In that respect, adult
> education can play an important role in contributing to
> active ageing, promoting social integration, reducing
> health costs, enhancing the quality of life, and providing
> training in new technology for those whose mobility and
> access to information might otherwise be restricted. . . .
> The consultation process highlighted the barriers for this
> group in accessing education and training through the
> use of criteria which are labour market focused, and
> highlighted in particular the importance of information
> technology training as an aid to mobility and communica-
> tion particularly in the remote rural areas."

Little progress has been made, however, in increasing specific learning opportunities for older people since the publication of this White Paper.

Also in the year 2000, the European Commission, following the European Council in Lisbon, produced a *Memorandum on Lifelong Learning* with the aim of developing a coherent overall strategy for education and lifelong learning in Europe. In its introductory statement, the Memorandum reads:

> "The scale of current economic and social change in
> Europe, the rapid evolution of the knowledge society,
> and the demographic pressures resulting from an ageing

population demand a fundamentally new approach to education and training."

Currently in Europe there are 35 people of pensionable age for every 100 of working age. By the year 2050, this figure will have increased to 75. It makes sense, therefore, to invest in the welfare of the population by providing learning opportunities throughout life and to regard this demographic trend as a rich source of opportunity rather than just a burden on the working population. The Memorandum defined lifelong learning as the common umbrella under which all kinds of teaching and learning should be united. It sees all learning as a seamless continuum extending from the early years through adult life, from cradle to grave. It also recognises various forms of learning including nonformal and informal, which are so often undervalued. Ireland has had a long tradition of non-formal learning, which is defined as learning that is done outside of the formal system and not necessarily recognised by certificates or qualifications.

NONFORMAL LEARNING AND COMMUNITY EDUCATION

Brian Friel's wonderful play *Translations* depicts the value and power of learning even in circumstances which could not be described as conducive to it. Yet people in the Ireland he writes about overcame many obstacles in their pursuit of education, seeing it as the key to escaping a life of poverty and marginalisation. The old headmaster in the play was the fount of all knowledge and experience. Each time I see this play, I am reminded of my grandmother, who died in 1963 — and whose own grandfather ran a hedge school — reading the local paper to a gathering of neighbours in her stone-floored cottage every Friday. It was only much later in life, when I began to work in the area of adult literacy, that I realised that most of those neighbours could neither read nor write, so my grandmother's skills in both areas were much sought after. I remember her reading out a report of a spacecraft orbiting the earth and her mispronunciation of a word new to the English language. The word was astronaut and the year was 1961. I was ten years old and was already being exposed to the power of words by a woman who had much less formal education than I had, even at that age, but who had a wealth of experience and an ability to engage people without making them feel uncomfortable.

In modern times in Ireland there is still a great wealth of nonformal learning taking place every day of the week. The 1980s saw the emergence of community-based women's education groups led by women who set about organising their own learning opportunities at a time when they were faced with unemployment and poverty and were often isolated in their own homes.

The women's groups spearheaded the development of what is now known as Community Education, which was centred on the needs of the learner and provided particular supports for women wishing to return to learning or to take up learning options that had been denied to them first time round. They organised courses and classes in any place they could find, from their own homes to church halls to leaky old prefabs left over from some other activity. The success of such classes lay in their accessibility and the acceptance of people and their individual experiences. Their work was recognised in the White Paper as crucial, not only to individual women but also to the communities to which they belonged. Since then thousands of groups providing learning opportunities have sprung up all over the place, providing hundreds of courses in everything from flower arranging to forensic psychology. The women's groups provided a model which is being replicated by other groups targeting men, disabled people, travellers and so on. More recently, they have welcomed people from other countries and cultures.

OVERCOMING THE BARRIERS

Currently AONTAS estimates that more than 300,000 adults in Ireland participate in some kind of education and training every year. Although there is no official breakdown of statistics by age, we know that many of these are older adults. Usually, however, they also tend to be adults who already have quite a good level of education and who can afford to pay for courses. Paying for courses is still a major barrier for adults returning to education and AONTAS has been campaigning for many years for the fees waiver to apply to part-time distance and modular courses at third level. Other barriers include low levels of confidence and initial education, while lack of transport and isolation are major issues for older people living in rural areas.

For older adults who wish to enter the workforce, similar barriers exist. Recently the Equality Authority published a report entitled *Ageing and Labour Market Participation*. One finding was that the increase in the 1990s in the proportion of people between 50 and 69 in employment was mostly due to women entering jobs from home duties. This return to work has been encouraged by the government as it seeks to fill skills shortages. But the report also found that the likelihood of employment for older people is highest among those with third-level education. Yet because few older people have third-level education, they are losing out. There are fewer choices about the type of work people have access to. Most of these people will go into service or sales jobs or other low-paid, low-skill jobs.

And while we're on the subject of work . . . we are hearing rumbles from our own and other governments about their plans to increase the age at which we can retire. For myself I think this might be rather a mixed blessing, as I am looking forward to giving up full-time work after about 40 years and really concentrating on the oil painting, the gardening and writing that novel! And then there's the TEFL course; I reckon this will be a good one to choose now that the EU has opened up its gates to all those new countries. And teaching English is one of those things I could do in my own time in between the gardening and painting and writing the novel! Now that I've got the hang of using the computer, courtesy of the class in the local community school and some workplace training, the bestseller might well just become a reality, not to mention the e-mail conversations I can have with my mother in Northern Ireland — and she is only 88. Never too old to learn indeed!

CHOICES, CHOICES

So now that we've looked at some of the issues, let's turn to what's available out there for you if you want to return to learning. The first step is to realise that anyone can learn at any time and at any age. Okay, sometimes we might have to adopt different methods for remembering things, or go a little bit slower than we did when we were younger, or organise ourselves a little bit differently, but by far the biggest thing is getting over the fear of trying out something new. The old adage that you can't teach an old dog new tricks simply does not apply and only adds to the myth we are trying to dispel.

The first thing you need to do is to sit down and have a think about what you might like to study and why. Would you like to gain a certificate in something that you did not have an opportunity to achieve before? Like Phyllis whom I remembered earlier, you might want to take advantage of the fact that you no longer have direct family or work responsibilities. Do you want to study something which will equip you for work to supplement your income? Or is there something that you are very good at and would like to formalise with a qualification? Perhaps you want to travel more and would like to learn another language, or learn how to use a computer and the internet. After all, online shopping and banking facilities could come in very handy and now you can pay your car tax online, you could save yourself all that queuing. Perhaps you have family and friends living abroad and would like to keep in touch with them by using e-mail. Having even basic IT skills opens up all sorts of possibilities. You might want to learn a craft or become involved in a drama or reading group. Your motivation might be social, as getting involved in learning circles opens up the possibility of making new friends. What about a wine-tasting course combined with a nice trip to a wine-making region? Or maybe you didn't have the opportunity to complete your early schooling and you might like to brush up on your reading, writing and maths.

Once you have had a think about what you might like to learn, the next question is how much time and money you have, how far you are prepared to travel or whether you can learn at home with the support of a computer programme or tutor. If you have friends or family who have done something themselves, talk to them. Ask them how it felt to go back, how they coped with homework or studying. Once you have done your groundwork you can look around at what is available. The best starting point is in your local area. Each county has a Vocational Education Committee (VEC) and in some of the larger urban areas there is more than one.

Overall there are 33 VECs providing a wide range of courses through their school and college networks. All of the VECs have Adult Education Organisers who are the first point of contact. The Adult Education Organiser will be able to provide information about courses and programmes in their own catchment area, including literacy and second-chance education courses, which are free of charge or charge a nominal sum only. The VECs generally have locally advertised enrolment dates and brochures which are often hand-delivered in local areas or are advertised in community newspapers, so look out for these, especially in early September and January.

There are thousands of courses to choose from and, as has been said, they are generally within the financial range of most people. The Adult Education Organiser may refer you to the local Community Education Facilitator or the Adult Literacy Organiser or other members of the VEC team. Some VECs have Guidance and Information services which can help you to make decisions about your own learning. All of these people are used to dealing with adult learners so don't be afraid to ask questions or discuss issues with them.

Keep an eye out around your area. Have a look at the shopping centre or community notice boards. There may be a local community group which provides daytime courses at times and places that suit you best. If you are interested in having a go at a third-level course, there are a number of Foundation, Access and Return to Learning courses run by universities and third-level colleges. The best way to find out about them is to call the college and ask for the access officer. Third-level colleges also offer a range of courses which cater for a wide variety of interests. AONTAS provides an information referral service for adults and has compiled an Information Pack which contains a number of fact sheets dealing with general information, distance education, repeating the Leaving Certificate as well as lists of contact numbers for adult education organisers, third-level colleges and other useful information.

You might also be interested in the University of the Third Age (U3A). Any group of older people can participate in learning through the U3A, whether they are living independently or in residential care. Age Action Ireland promotes the concept in Ireland and can put those interested in starting a U3A group in contact with others who have already done so. (See *In Focus* below.)

Your public library is also a good source of information and you could purchase a copy of the *Wolfhound Guide to Evening Classes* or, if you live in Dublin, *Dublin's Evening Classes* by Oisin Publications. These are widely available at local bookstores/

newsagents and are also available at your local library. If you've already mastered the internet, you could have a browse through www.nightcourses.com. Many third-level institutions and other adult learning providers also have their own websites. Access to some of these is available through the AONTAS website, www.aontas.ie.

_____

In Focus: The University of the Third Age (U3A)*

The University of the Third Age, or "U3A", is a worldwide movement encouraging older people in the "third age" of life to take up or continue educational and other interests in friendly and informal settings.

No qualifications are required to join — and no qualifications or degrees awarded. Members are encouraged to see the value and take pleasure in learning for its own sake.

U3A defines "third age" as coming after the "first age" of youthful growth and education and the "second age" of maturity, career and/or home-making responsibility. It comes after full-time employment, usually with retirement and senior citizen status, but U3A does not specify any minimum age for membership.

The movement was founded in France in 1972, where it was closely linked to universities. When it came to Britain it became more of a self-help organisation. Most of the teaching and tuition comes from the ranks of its own members. It is a unique educational self-help co-operative.

The movement has spread to many other countries, though the name is not always the same. It is not a univer-

_____

* Reprinted and adapted from the central website of the University of the Third Age in the UK, www.u3a.org.uk; and from Age Action Ireland's website, www.ageaction.ie.

sity except in the medieval sense that participants teach each other in an informal setting that involves co-operative learning. In Britain, the word is used in its ancient meaning of "a community of scholars".

The precise pattern varies from place to place, but a typical U3A will offer a range of interest groups from language classes to archaeological and philosophical studies and from art and craft groups to music appreciation and creative writing.

As leadership comes from the members themselves, a U3A member may be a student in one group one day and the leader or tutor the next. It is not always necessary to have an expert as a leader. In some subjects, members learn from each other and the role of the leader is to encourage everyone to take part.

Interest groups are often quite small with meetings or classes taking place in members' homes. Not only does this save on accommodation costs, it makes for friendly contact among members.

Costs are kept as low as possible so that members can take part in as many groups as they wish. Quite often members join to try out a subject that they always fancied. Others join because they are looking to make new friends in their retirement.

Basic Principles

Since its inception, the University of the Third Age movement has operated on a number of fundamental principles which determine its unique character and style. The original "Objects and Principles" were largely determined by the late Peter Laslett, the distinguished educationalist and one of the founding fathers of U3A.

However, in 2004 in the light of changing circumstances over the past 21 years, the National Executive Committee of the Third Age Trust has produced a new set of "Aims and Guiding Principles".

They have been drawn up following an extensive consultation throughout the organisation over the past two years. *The new document retains the spirit of the original but sets out the philosophy of the movement in language and style more appropriate to the new century.*

The first aim is "to encourage and enable older people to help each to share their knowledge, skills and experience". Another is "to celebrate the capabilities and potential of older people and their value to society" while a third is to encourage the establishment of U3As in every part of the country.

Among the guiding principles on styles and methods of learning is the recognition that "the pleasure of learning" is a driving force in U3As and that U3A members see themselves as both learners and teachers.

In summary, the University of the Third Age is:

- *A self-help model of lifelong learning organised by older people.*

- *An international movement of learning organised by older people for older people in a spirit of co-operation in which "everyone teaches and everyone learns".*

- *A model of learning that can be adapted to include both older people living independently and those living in long-term residential care.*

The University of the Third Age in Ireland

The University of the Third Age is administered in Ireland by Age Action. Mary Colclough, Age Action's Education Officer (U3A), is responsible for the support of existing University of the Third Age (U3A) programmes and expansion of the network countrywide. She can help to generate a learning programme that gives older people what they want, as well as harnessing community support to set up a centre for lifelong learning.

It is recognised that older people are happy to learn from their peers. Any group of older people can participate in this style of learning, whether it be a new group, or an existing group wishing to expand the horizons of its activities, for example, active retirement groups.

It is the job of Age Action, and the U3A branches with which Age Action has been involved, to get across the U3A message, inviting the general public to accept that education need not be competitive, or related economic goals, that it is a good in itself. So Age Action is now becoming involved also in the University of the Fourth Age — basically education for people in long-stay settings. Because a person is very old, it does not mean their education should stop.

Health professionals working in day centres or residential care can get involved in the U3A movement by developing learning centres in these facilities. You can collaborate with residents on learning projects that express their diverse interests and the wealth of their life experience. Health involves the whole person and the whole community — a sense of wellbeing that rests on participation, sharing and diversity.

I'm Not Finished Yet by educationalist Pamela Whittaker is a guide to self-help learning for older people which breaks out of the boundaries of traditional education and includes a guide to U3A branches in Ireland. Wisdom of the Ages by Pamela Whittaker looks at the Fourth Age and the needs/opportunities surrounding education in residential care settings. Both are Age Action publications.

Activities undertaken by Irish U3A groups to date include:

- *Computers*

- *Arts and crafts*

- *Storytelling*

- *Book clubs (talking books, large print books)*

- *Creative writing*

- *Poetry writing*

- *Reminiscence*

- *Local history*

- *Complementary health (massage, aromatherapy, reflexology)*

- *Current affairs or debating club*

- *Personal safety*

- *Woodwork*

- *Gardening*

- *Dinner outings*

- *Music clubs (sharing recorded music)*

- *Live music performances*

- *Sing-a-longs.*

Since the beginning of 2004, three new U3A groups have been formed in Dublin, one in each of Ballymun, Darndale and Terenure. In addition the U3A or Lifelong Learning group in Dundalk has been revitalised. These new ventures were made possible by the support of organisations such as Terenure and Ballymun Libraries, Darndale/ Belcamp Resource Centre and Dundalk County Museum. Community links like these are essential for the success of new groups. Existing U3A groups, Dublin City U3A (formerly known as Chester Beatty U3A), Lucan U3A, Blackrock U3A, Waterford U3A and Errigal U3A continue to operate well.

There are also nine U3A groups in Northern Ireland and, over time, it is hoped that cross-border links can be enhanced.

Other groups that adhere to the U3A ethos include the Cork Retired People's Network, Ballincollig Senior Citizens Club (Westgate Foundation), The Golden Circle Club, Rathdangan and Daonscoil (Dublin Folk School).

Contact information for any of these groups can be obtained by getting in touch with Mary Colclough at Age Action on 01-4756989.

TAKE THE PLUNGE

So now you know where to go and what you want to do, how about getting started? It's time to take the plunge. Returning to learning can be very nerve-wracking, especially if you left school many moons ago, or maybe school wasn't a very happy place for you. When I worked with the Dublin Literacy Scheme, every day I listened to people who had walked round the block many times before plucking up the courage to get themselves in the door. Their most persistent fear was of being thought stupid. After lots of tea, and sometimes far too many cigarettes, adult learners would begin to relax and work up the confidence to have a go. There was always a great feeling of relief at being taken seriously and not being regarded as odd for "wanting to come back to school". Mind you, I blame this aspect of my work then for the development of a smoking habit, as I came out in sympathy with the nervous adults in front of me! Luckily I've since given up.

I suppose what struck me most strongly during those literacy scheme years was the fact that many adults dismissed their time in the University of Life as unimportant. Later when they gained in confidence and self-esteem, they began to realise how significant and valuable was their own experience of life in general. Our oldest learner at that time was a sprightly 88-year-old just like my mother, and she began to publish her poems in a booklet published as part of the scheme and read them out at our evenings to encourage less confident participants. While many adults feel rusty and inadequate when they start, don't forget: adults make very good learners. They are highly motivated and almost always succeed. I can only assure people that once you get hooked on learning, like the old cigarettes, it's totally addictive. If you don't believe me, the following quote from an older learner who became involved with her local community education group says so much:

"Being involved in a group like this has made me feel like a person again — an important part of society. This group has brought out so many qualities that had been dormant in me. I just want to keep on learning."

References

Department of Education and Science (2000), *Learning for Life, The White Paper on Adult Education.*

The Economist, "Europe's Population Implosion", 23 April 2004.

European Commission (2000), *Memorandum on Lifelong Learning.*

McCarthy, Mary (1988), *Never Too Old to Learn, A Study of Education for Older People in Ireland*, AONTAS.

Russell, H. and Fahey, T. (2004), *Ageing and Labour Market Participation*, The Equality Authority.

WERRC, AONTAS (2003), *At the Forefront: The Role of Women's Community Education in Combating Poverty and Disadvantage in the Republic of Ireland.*

Chapter 4

ARTS AND LEISURE

Ann Leahy

*"Creativity is a mysterious thing. It's an attribute of every
human being, not just the great and the gifted, not just
the young. Age can bring an enriched sense of self and,
often people are more creative in their later years."*
— C. Golman, "Late Bloomers", quoted by Fi Frances
in *The Arts and Older People*, 1999

GROWING MORE CREATIVE

Why older people and the arts? If someone hasn't taken up
painting, theatre or dance, or hasn't produced a book by the
time they reach retirement, why expect them to do so then?
Well, many people believe that we are all creative — you see it
in the way someone lays a table, tying roses with gold string
around the napkins, or in the way another has a knack for making stories out of ordinary events — keeping a whole roomful
spellbound telling about what happened at the butchers. One
woman I know (who happens to be in her 90s) enjoys hanging
the washing on the line — she chooses what colours and shapes
to put side by side and makes it an expression of herself.

Not everyone who picks up a pen is going to write as well as
Yeats, but, if they find a way to write that is authentic for them, it

may not only be a source of tremendous satisfaction, but it may also give them a unique way to explore aspects of their life story and, indeed, of what it is to be human. Because in today's world there is such a fuss made about young artists — with prizes and bursaries aimed at discovering the next big talent— it can sometimes be forgotten that the creative faculty is not confined to youth. Take Yeats, since he has been mentioned already — he wrote his most impressive poetry during the last two decades of his life. Countless artists — writers such as PD James and William Trevor; painters such as Louis le Brocquy and Pauline Bewick; actors, Jeanne Moreau and Brian Dennehy — are living testament to the human capacity for creative challenge and growth, no matter what our age.

People who become active participants in the arts in the course of their lives will very likely continue as such no matter what their age. And involvement in the arts is not confined to the gifted: through active involvement in the arts — be it through painting, singing, writing, photography, dance or attending films or theatre — we can all enrich our lives. This is about "keeping the windows open" as we age, to use a phrase coined by the late Peter Ustinov. Interviewed in his seventies, Peter Ustinov said, "I'm learning something you can't learn when younger — that the spirit doesn't age."

A well-structured arts programme can allow people of any age to express thoughts and feelings about what it is to be human; it can afford the chance to reflect on the challenges that life throws at us. But there are many older people who had little or no access to the arts when they were younger. Visual art was a low priority; creative writing as a discipline, film and theatre studies — all of these had hardly been thought of. When such people come to engage with a thoughtful, well-planned arts programme — one which engages them in a learning process — tremendous energy and enthusiasm can be unleashed. Professional artists facilitating programmes with older people have often commented on this and on the great leaps of personal growth and empowerment that they witness.

MORE ART, BETTER HEALTH

"Our results show that people attending cultural events seem to live longer than those who attend rarely. . . . The importance of stimulating activities is obvious, and there is hardly any need for medical arguments for attending a theatre, cinema or sports event, for reading books and periodicals or for making music." — Professor Lars Bygren, *British Medical Journal*, Volume 313

Most people would agree that being active and engaged after we retire is good for us, and increasingly studies are establishing a proven link between involvement in arts programmes and better mental health and well-being, and even with better physical health. This message is again confirmed by a US study of 300 people completed in 2004, assessing the impact of ongoing involvement in high-quality arts and cultural programmes.

Take, for example, the Senior Singers Chorale at a school of music in Washington DC who participated in the four-year study. Dr Gene Cohen of George Washington University is evaluating this chorus and participants in similar ongoing programmes for independent people aged over 65 in New York and San Francisco. His theory is that the challenge of learning from professionals improves health. The singers' average age is 80; the youngest is 65 and the oldest 96, and a preliminary report suggests that participants get more than enjoyment and emotional support from their involvement. Compared with others of a similar age, they suffer less depression, make fewer doctor visits a year, take fewer medicines, report themselves as having higher morale and as being less lonely.

People who have retired from work or childrearing represent a potentially great resource to the arts sector. After all, the vast majority of over-65s live independently in the community — they have the time to take an interest in the arts, and, more important, the experience. It has been said that the imaginative and interpretative process relies on the accumulation of sensations, knowledge and so forth garnered through the passage of life. And life experience is something that older people have — in spades.

Over the past decade, arts organisations have a much greater awareness of older people as part of their constituency. Increasing numbers of arts organisations participating in Bealtaine — the national festival celebrating creativity in older age — is one indication of this. In May 2004, Bealtaine included nearly 700 events in 26 counties and is now the biggest arts festival in the country.

There are additional reasons why arts organisations are increasingly committed to facilitating the engagement of older people. One of these is that when people are exploring their creativity — learning a new skill or taking their learning further in a particular artform — they themselves embody a challenge to prejudices that often go unquestioned in society. I have in mind the sort of unquestioned assumptions that are abroad about older age — that it is always a time of rigidity, of resistance to new challenges, a time of stagnation and sedentariness. Any such notions would be exploded for anyone who knows the St Michael's Parish Active Retirement Group.

This Active Retirement Group are long-time participants in the older people's art programme at the Irish Museum of Modern Art. They have had their own work exhibited at the Museum and elsewhere, and they have curated exhibitions of the Museum's permanent collection. Their experience of this programme — making art, having discussions with artists, exploring the Museum's collections has, they will tell you, added immeasurably to their lives.

ARTS IN CARE SETTINGS

The potential for creativity does not end with frailty or with the onset of disability. Many people living in residential care are capable of remaining engaged in life in ways that are meaningful to them — not just in "activity" for its own sake. Arts programmes can play an important part in helping older people who have had to leave their own homes to live in nursing homes and hospitals to express their reactions to the losses and the joys that have been, and that continue to be, part of their lives.

Anyone who hears visual artist Deirdre Walsh talk about her work with the residents of the Sacred Heart Hospital, Castlebar will realise how arts continue to contribute in care settings. Artist-in-Residence with Mayo County Council Arts Office, Deirdre is passionate about the value of this kind of work: "I would love to see all care centres having a dedicated space for arts workshops. It may seem obvious but it is often forgotten, that only good artist-quality materials should be used." She also says that for her it is essential to trust in the creativity of the people with whom she is working. Striking exhibitions of the work produced by older people in her workshops have been well received in arts centres in Castlebar and in Sligo.

There are other examples of arts programmes in care settings. A unique training course accredited by FETAC (the Further Education and Training Awards Council) is offered to staff of the Midland Health Board. It allows nurses and other care workers to learn how to work in the arts with the older people in their care. Outcomes from these courses continue to go far beyond the making of art — in some care settings, there is now much more awareness of how much residents enjoy contact with the local community — so there are trips out and there is an effort to bring the outside in — plants, pets, children. After one excursion, a resident was profoundly moved by everyday aspects of nature — she said that she'd forgotten how green the grass was.

According to Elly McCrea, arts educationalist and facilitator of the Age & Opportunity/Midland Health Board Arts in Care Course: "I have seen the benefits for the care-workers as well as for their clients. Communication between staff and residents engaged in the creative process is different. It operates at a different level; it is two-way. Nobody knows the answers but there will be different rules. Rules that enhance self-expression."

It is important that health authorities and government learn from programmes like these in care settings, and from studies such as the American one described above which was conducted with people living in the community. High-quality arts/cultural programmes could improve the health and well-being of a generation. Perhaps a modest amount spent on arts programmes could yield savings in health spending. An added bonus would be the harnessing of the energies of older people and the promotion of understanding between the generations through the active involvement of all ages alongside each other in their local communities.

ALL ABOUT BEALTAINE

Maybe you have been wondering if you could revive an old arts interest or start a new one. How do you do it? Well, why not go along to an arts event during next May's Bealtaine? It would be ideal for dipping a toe in the water — attending a workshop or two to see if it's for you. For many people the Bealtaine festival has operated as a springboard for more sustained involvement.

> "Up to [Bealtaine 2003] it had been nearly 30 years since I'd been in a theatre . . . all of this has added a new and exciting dimension to my life — new interests, new friends. Getting older is fun now, an adventure full of possibilities and opportunities." — Gabriel McGovern, participant in "Affairs of the Arts", Bealtaine 2003

In Dublin during Bealtaine 2004, you could have signed up for a four-week workshop exploring modern art, or attended a two-day introduction to theatre, film and contemporary art (called "Affairs of the Arts"). In Kerry you could have taken Irish language masterclasses with writer Louis de Paor. In Cork you could have gone along to your local library and learned lace-making or portraiture, participated in a storytelling session or tried your hand at "weaving a landscape". In Donegal there was a joint exhibition by older people and schoolchildren, looking at similarities and differences in their lives. There was also a film tour to 27 venues countrywide. Most of these events were free, or came at a nominal cost — intended to attract people who don't ordinarily participate in the arts. You can get a Bealtaine programme in April each year by contacting Age & Opportunity; contact details are in Appendix 2.

Increasingly, the organisations involved in Bealtaine arrange ongoing programmes aimed at retired people throughout the year — not just once-off events for May. Find out if there are opportunities near you for involvement throughout the year:

Local Authority Arts Officers represent a local resource to groups interested in the arts as participants and audience. Most have specific programmes for Bealtaine. But they are there year-round, operating as a local information and access point on everything to do with the arts. Many also make grants available.

Regional and local arts centres aim to bring the arts to the public. Some offer concessionary rates to older people and groups on performance admissions. Others offer courses and some have outreach programmes (see list of organisations on the next page).

Don't forget that many public libraries organise arts events, run reading groups that you can join and also offer computer and other learning programmes from time to time. Many put on extensive programmes of workshops, readings and exhibitions during Bealtaine. Year round they will also be able to give you information on local arts opportunities. During Bealtaine 2004, nearly 20 library authorities were involved in providing a huge range of arts events in branch libraries from Bantry to Foynes and from Dundalk to Longford.

Among the events organised by Cork City Library were gramophone recitals and readings by authors. In Cork County there were dance performances, storytelling, art exhibitions and readings as well as craft workshops in textiles, lace-making, weaving and more. Dublin City libraries offered work-shops such as glass painting and silk painting. In Fingal librar-ies there was drawing, painting, storytelling and poetry. Dun Laoghaire-Rathdown libraries offered readings, jewellery-making and an introduction to watercolours.

This gives just a flavour of the range available to retired people at libraries during May — with most events free of charge. (See also library section later in this chapter.)

ARTS ORGANISATIONS AND OLDER PEOPLE

Some organisations/venues have ongoing programmes specifi-cally targeted at older people. Here are just some of the arts organisations that offer such programmes:

- Abbey Theatre, Middle Abbey Street, Dublin 2; Tel: 01-8872223; E-mail: outreach@abbeytheatre.ie. The Theatre Matinee Club involves people meeting up once a month from February to December to visit the Abbey or Peacock Theatre on a Saturday afternoon for the matinee perform-ance. Afterwards the group meets with an artistic and/or technical theatre practitioner involved in the production. Membership of the Theatre Matinee Club is €80 for the full year or €40 for a half year, including theatre tickets at a dis-counted rate. The Script Club has a smaller membership intended to offer a more in-depth experience. Participants meet writers and explore a chosen text.

- Draíocht Arts Centre, Blanchardstown, Dublin 15; Tel: 01-8852610. Draíocht's art group for older people, the Dabblers, meet twice a month. They have recently spent six months on painting and six months on clay work, working with facilitators to ensure a high-quality experience. Director of Draíocht, Emer McGowan, says: "It's important to involve the people in decision-making about what they would like to do and explore. It is about giving skills and allowing them to be creative." Open to new members in autumn.

- Irish Film Institute, 6 Eustace Street, Temple Bar, Dublin 2; Tel: 01-6795744; E-mail: wildstrawberries@irishfilm.ie. The IFI has an ongoing film club called Wild Strawberries specifically for older people. This club has a membership of 250, with around 120 attending on a regular basis. They view a varied range of films from Hollywood classics to foreign language films and frequently have question-and-answer sessions with people involved in making particular films. Admission is free to older people and anyone can attend, but you need to put your name on their mailing list and telephone in advance of each film to confirm your attendance. The IFI's Outreach service also works with groups of older people teaching film-making skills and facilitating the making of short films.

- Irish Museum of Modern Art, Royal Hospital Kilmainham, Dublin 8; Tel: 01-6129912; E-mail: lisa.moran@imma.ie. Older People's Programme, the general programme for older people, includes free guided tours of exhibitions, talks and lectures, and visits to the artists' studios. Charcoal and Chocolate is a new programme to introduce older people to contemporary art through drawing. Facilitated by professional artists, this programme involves a combination of gallery visits and workshop sessions looking at, and making, drawings. No previous experience of either drawing or contemporary art is necessary.

- Mayo County Council Arts Office, The Mall, Castlebar, County Mayo; Tel: 094-9024444; E-mail: artsstaf@mayococo.ie. Artist in residence, Deirdre Walsh, who works in two care centres, facilitating workshops for older residents, is now engaged in a mentoring scheme which supports other artists working in residential care centres for older people throughout Mayo. As well as organising a large Bealtaine programme of events each May, there is an older people's programme in Achill throughout the year, and ongoing funding of programmes with active retirement groups throughout Mayo, usually in visual arts, creative writing and dance.

- Sligo County Council Arts Office, Market Yard, Sligo, County Sligo; Tel: 071-9140985; E-mail: arts@sligococo.ie. Sligo Arts Office is involved in many innovative projects, a number of which involve bringing older people and school children together and engaging them jointly in an ongoing arts programme. Projects include:

  o The Maugherow Project — Students and older people from the Maugherow area work together in the local primary school with professional artists, using a variety of art forms.

  o Abbeyquarter Arts — Another intergenerational programme involving older people and students, this time from the eastward area of Sligo town. The programme takes in drama, dance, creative writing and visual art elements such as printmaking, painting, drawing, bookmaking, collage and feltwork.

  o Arts/Health Programme for Older People, St Anne's, a community centre in Sligo town — This is an arts programme for older people who attend day care in a community setting. Workshops take place in St Anne's Youth and Community Centre. The programme includes visual arts, painting, printing, feltwork and storytelling.

- West Cork Arts Centre, North Street, Skibbereen, County Cork; Tel: 028-22090; E-mail: westcorkarts@eircom.net. Current programme includes a series of workshops designed for over-55s who wish to explore the arts, the arts centre and develop their creative skills. Each week a two-hour session is offered where participants are invited to take part in a creative challenge in a relaxed sociable atmosphere. Once a month, there is a guided tour of the current exhibition to inspire and inform the creative process. Justine Foster from the centre says: "It is important to create a safe and appropriate space for creative development and above all social enjoyment to encourage participation." Beginners and newcomers are very welcome to the sessions.

- Westmeath County Council Arts Office, County Library HQ, Dublin Road, Mullingar, County Westmeath; Tel: 044-40781; E-mail: ckelly@westmeathcoco.ie. For the Children of Lir Project, artist Lorraine Mimnagh worked with pupils from St Cremin's National School, Multyfarnham and clients from St Mary's Care Centre, Mullingar. The intergenerational arts programme involved painting and printing and the project continues to be developed as a collaboration between the clients of St Mary's and Music Network.

One of the main aims of Age & Opportunity is to promote greater participation by older people in all aspects of society, including in the arts. Age & Opportunity believe that the chance to engage with an artform is the right of everyone who so chooses no matter what their age; it may also change their lives. Involving people of all ages in the arts makes sense — not just for individuals but also for arts bodies and for society as a whole — especially when older people are making up an increasing proportion of the general population. As has been described, each May Age & Opportunity co-ordinates Bealtaine.

SOME SURPRISES AT YOUR LOCAL LIBRARY

Art workshops, membership clubs, author readings, reading groups, free (or reasonably priced) internet access, foreign language conversation classes, music tapes, exhibitions of art work, gramophone circles — all of these are offered by public libraries and many are available in your local library. If it's a while since you popped down there, you may be surprised. Oh, and, of course, there are books — books on everything from DIY to self-help psychology, from "chick lit" to contemporary poetry. And books come in different formats — on tape and in large print — as well as in the usual format.

There are over 330 public libraries in Ireland as well as a number of mobile and hospital libraries. They attract 12 million visits and issue some 12 million books every year. Libraries are one of the few public places that are open to everyone and their services are generally free or come at nominal cost. A nationwide survey published recently by the Library Council suggests that 94 per cent of library visitors considered their visit successful.

What retired people generally have is leisure time. There is an obvious match between the desire of libraries to serve their local community and the wish on the part of retired people for a meaningful outlet for their time and energy. And being an active participant in your local community can even affect your health. Studies show that social connectedness — links with friends and community — is good for health and well-being.

Reading Groups

Increasingly, retired people are becoming active members of a movement that has become widespread in public libraries: reading groups, also called "book clubs" or "reading circles". Part of the inspiration for this development has been the LV Book Club at Cork City Library — a reading group that has been meeting since 1989 and aimed at people aged 55 and over. The LV was the original, but there are now some five other senior reading groups meeting in libraries across Cork city.

A recent informal survey carried out amongst public libraries by Age & Opportunity shows that there are reading groups meeting and open for new members in libraries the length and breadth of the country. While library reading groups tend to be open to all members of the public, many attract a membership of more mature people, especially those that meet during the day. You'll find them from Kiltimagh, County Mayo, to Laytown, County Meath, from Bantry in Cork, to Carndonagh in Donegal, and from Blackrock in Dublin to Blanchardstown via Clondalkin. Most meet monthly and most read novels; some also read non-fiction, biographies and nineteenth-century fiction, and a few occasionally include poetry. According to Pat Egan of LV Book Club, Cork, "Belonging to a book club or reading circle socialises reading." A comprehensive list of reading groups meeting in public libraries is available on Age & Opportunity's website, www.olderinireland.ie.

So what does it mean to belong to a reading group? Well, sharing a book brings it to life. As well as providing the chance to share thoughts and opinions on books, it allows for reflection on the stories read and the wider issues raised — on life itself — allowing members to contribute at a level at which they feel comfortable.

In case this all sounds a bit too academic or too literary, it is worthwhile remembering that the approach to reading taken in most reading groups is "reader-centred", putting the experience of each reader first. In other words, you start from the subjective reading experience of each member, not from any notions about what constitutes literature. It accepts that there is no correct response to a book: each reader is an expert on their experience. This tends to create an atmosphere that is non-threatening and inclusive. Remember too that many reading groups also have a social side, particularly long-standing ones, where companionship and friendships grow between members.

Library-based Groups around the Country

Some libraries foster other types of groups. Wexford town library is a case in point; their Thursday Club members came together first to attend a computer learning course offered by the library to retired people. Now a core group of about 20 meets each Thursday morning with a flexible agenda. Usually they meet as a reading group one day per month, have a guest speaker on another day, and have two less structured sessions per month. The group members derive education and enjoyment from their involvement with the library, but the benefits flow the other way also. Thursday Club members are loyal supporters of other general library initiatives — such as "Reading Down the Ages", where people selected favourite poems and short passages to share and discuss. According to Wexford librarian, Susan Kelly, "If I was organising a trip to Mars, a Thursday Club member would pop next door for a new toothbrush and be ready at the bus stop in five minutes."

Other unusual groups fostered by libraries include gramophone circles, which are a particular feature of Cork libraries, where people meet to listen to music in the library's music room. Often members take turns sharing their favourites from the library collection, introducing others to music they may not have listened to before.

Libraries can be the starting point for a research project looking at local history. Indeed, reading groups can even be organised around history and heritage. For example, Louth libraries facilitated a reading group for people from two care centres in Ardee and Dundalk, looking at townland maps, early workplace memorabilia, and early motor tax lists. In Wexford, the Thursday Club are participating in a structured learning course, "Our Literary Heritage", a reading programme focusing on Wexford writers of the nineteenth and twentieth centuries.

*In Focus: Getting into History**

It is not the great battles and statesmen that "make" history; they are its symptoms. We the people are the makers of history, and we are the reservoirs of its detail, of much vital information and ideas derived from our lived experience. We have lived the endless cycle of change and renewal that is history. That is why through a new involvement, we can now be both contributor and beneficiary.

There are many facets of history — and it might be interesting to consider which particular facet takes your fancy: political, military, social, personal. You may want to know more of the history of designs and inventions in areas like transport, power generation, or the history of achievement in leisure subjects, or sports, cinema, reading, gambling; or more individualistic and personal areas such as fashion in clothes, shoes, furnishings, food, toys; or perhaps in aspects of the history of education, of religions, of work and careers. The scope is as broad and as exciting and intriguing as are people themselves.

Third age citizens are — often unknown to themselves — a valuable history/heritage resource for their local community. The mythic Irish poet Amergin asked the ques-

---

* Written by Seamus Cashman, Consultant to Age & Opportunity.

tion: "Who but I knows the secret of the unhewn dolmen?" People whose lives span 60 or more years carry many "secrets" with them unknowingly. These include the detail of childhood lives and times, of earlier now lost lifestyles, a knowledge of the process of change through the decades. We all have experienced how a small question can trigger a stream of knowledge. For instance, you live near a weed-infested stream or river, now without fish. So what fish were here? Your answer — that once, in living memory, it provided a harvest of trout or pinkeens or dase or mullet — may lead to more interesting queries — why, when, what now? Perhaps this could be the beginnings of a localised environmental history, where your contribution and participation will undoubtedly energise you as you are in turn energising the community. Or in a city, that interesting building you've always known and is now being demolished — what is its story? Can you find out and tell it? Little steps can lead to an enjoyable and beneficial walk. We can all find our story and tell it.

But what to do, where to go, how to begin? Opportunities in history and in heritage abound no matter where you live, no matter what your age, sex or financial resources. Are you interested in sports — then, what is the history of your sport in your area and/or in your province or country? — or motorbikes, or shop signs, or clothes, or historic sites such as graveyards, churches, castles, forts and ancient places — all have a history, and all have a local history.

It may be that you want to test the waters first, rather than get involved in a longer-term search process. Heritage sites, networked throughout the country, provide a wonderful and most satisfying opportunity, and at very little or sometimes no cost. These are the ideal first steps if you are retired and keen to go, and the information you need on possibilities abounds. Apart from national organisations such as Dúchas and tourist offices, every public library is a vast and friendly resource — the notice board, the librarian, and of course the books; most towns have an information centre. Remember, many of us have never been tourists in our own country! It is time to begin.

In my twenties, in then very distant Africa, I met travellers who always asked "What is Killarney like?" But I couldn't tell because, though living next-door in County Cork, I had never been there. Where have you never been — to Craggaunowen, Scattery Island, Dublin Civic Museum, the Fry Model Railway Museum, Garnish Island, Carrickfergus Castle, Lough Key Forest Park, the Irish Famine Museum, the Blasket Centre, the National Museum? There are hundreds of places to begin. I myself like the Hill of Tara — it is free, magical and at the core of all our histories. And if you are over 60, discounts and special rates will apply at heritage centres.

Such first steps may lead to the subject of local history. A sense of place has been a powerful force in Irish literature and folklore and within our culture generally. To become involved in a local history activity is to participate in that relationship between people and their place of living. Local history projects allow us to find and tell the stories of both.

In childhood, we looked to grandparents and old people to tell us the stories of their lives, and we were frequently amazed and disbelieving at how different their way of life seemed. The pace of change has been vastly greater since the 1960s, so we should perhaps realise that our stories will amaze and entertain too. I remember in the 1970s waiting for 18 months to get a phone installed for my business! The story is in the detail: local history is the detail of national history; and people carry the detail of local history, be it of place names, field names (so many lost), folklore, architecture and buildings, business styles, farming methods, crafts, trades — the blacksmith, carpenter and wheelwright, weaver, stonebreaker, lace-maker, dressmaker and tailor, and so much more.

With Transition Year in secondary schools today, opportunities exist for involvement in intergenerational history projects — such projects already exist in other areas

*and the scope for imaginative sharing and contributing in
history and especially local history is undoubtedly great.*

*Two interesting local history projects I have some
knowledge of are a community project in the village of
Conna in rural east Cork, and a youth project in the sub-
urban village of Portmarnock in north County Dublin. Both
had many characteristics in common — the search for
new information about local place names, ancient sites,
community institutions and businesses, some family histories, local political and economic histories. Each was initiated for very different reasons. In Conna, it was a desire
among some long-time residents to add to the already
substantial knowledge of the parish history that existed
but was unstructured, untested, and vitally, not available
for presentation to future generations. Their work began in
libraries and books, progressing to lore and legend, and to
interviewing local people in search of the detail or memory
that often escapes recording.*

*The Portmarnock experience was very different. Here,
the project was initiated to give work experience to young,
unemployed people. They knew nothing of the local history when they began; their task was to discover all they
could about their home place by meeting with and interviewing the older generation who had known Portmarnock
as a country village decades earlier, collecting documents,
letters, photographs and stories wherever possible. With
guidance from an adult director, they worked on different
aspects of the area, meeting regularly to record and co-
ordinate their discoveries into a coherent account of their
home place.*

*A key lesson learned from both ventures was the im-
portance of not losing the knowledge and lore of the older
people in the area: these people were reservoirs of vast
amounts of valuable information — sometimes inaccurate,
sometimes previously unknown, always valuable as an
expression of local and personal histories. The projects de-
pended on the Third Age to succeed; and in so doing gave
to those who contributed enormous satisfaction and involvement. And to transmit their stories to future genera-*

tions, both projects ended up in book publication: Conna: In History and Tradition; *and* Portmarnock: A Closer Look. *These ventures were independent parts of the growth in local history projects that has been evident through Ireland in the past decade.*

But not all local history projects need to aim at expensive book publication. Completed work can be lodged in public libraries where they are available and preserved for the next generations, or kept as part of a personal library that will pass on down the family. A useful book to read as an initial guide is Doing Local History: Pursuit and Practice *by Hill and Gillespie. It should be in your local public library, where your project could fruitfully begin. The process, activity and sharing of information and ideas which the work involves can be in itself the achievement and purpose of a project.*

A core aspect of both the projects described above was the automatic crossover of involvement and activities between the generations. Both projects involved young and old in order to succeed. History and heritage live in us all and getting involved with local history projects, or indeed initiating them, can provide ready-made opportunities for intergenerational understanding and exchanges — the sharing of the ideas and activities that bind us.

E-Libraries

Some people go to the library regularly but rarely take out a book. Their interest is in computers and access to the internet. All public libraries have computers that provide internet access to the public. This is often provided free of charge, but some libraries charge for use — trying to keep their charges modest in order to keep the service accessible for as many people as possible. You can research anything on the internet — from angiogram to Zionism — you can send e-mails to friends and fam-

ily abroad. You can also type a report, a flyer, a story, an essay.
. . . anything!

There is no doubt that many retired people take to using information technology enthusiastically when given the chance. The stereotype of older people being intimidated by computer technology doesn't stand up to scrutiny — in an Age Concern/ Microsoft study of over-50s, 81 per cent found it easy to use a computer, with just 19 per cent saying they experienced some difficulty at first. Close to home, in Ennis Information Age Town, many retired people have been active participants in computer learning. One Ennis group of seniors publishes its own on-line magazine, *Sunset*.

> "Over-60s have taken on board technology and adapted more to it than the 35–40 age group." — Triona McInerney, Ennis Information Age Town Project, Age & Opportunity *Challenging Attitudes Newsletter*, Autumn/Winter 1999

However, a bank of screens can be off-putting, especially if you have never learned how to use a computer. Many libraries recognise that retired people have generally had fewer opportunities for access to information technology, and are, therefore, disadvantaged when it comes to using this service. Some organise computer learning targeted specifically at retired members of the community. Wexford town library ran a computer course for over-50s using a trainer provided by the local VEC. Other libraries, like Clonmel, have also targeted computer training at retired people. Such computer training is also widely available at local level.

Finglas Library in Dublin came up with the idea of organising a peer learning programme — where older computer users volunteered to impart their skills to other older library users. Librarian Anne Marie Kelly sees tremendous potential for this idea, especially where it is possible to harness the skills of retired people with a technical background. Like other branch libraries, Finglas Library gets lots of enquiries from older library users for computer learning and especially for internet training. Occasional courses are offered to the general public, and retired people are well represented among participants.

Other Library Activities

There are many other things that you may not know about your local library. For instance, you can pick up application forms for motor tax and passports. You can get information about other resources in your area, like whether there is an active retirement group, an arts centre or a computer class. Many libraries are also glad to hear from active retirement groups who want space in which to exhibit artwork and some have rooms available to groups for meetings. Even if you find it hard to get out of the house, the library may still be of service, as many public libraries deliver books to the homes of people who are housebound as well as to residential care units.

So, if all of this has spurred some interest, why not visit your library and find out if they have a reading group, a course or workshop to suit you? Maybe they will be involved in an arts programme for next year's Bealtaine or they may be prepared to organise a computer learning course aimed at mature learners. While you're down there, you might also borrow a music tape, a video or, for that matter, even a book!

Age & Opportunity collaborates with public libraries around the country in a number of ways. They organised workshops in collaboration with the Library Council aimed at librarians and intended to give them the skills to establish reading groups. Age & Opportunity has published a guide to running reading groups: *Sharing a Personal Pleasure: All You Need to Know about Senior Reading Groups* written by Anne Dempsey. It covers ground rules, do's and don'ts, suggestions for getting started, choosing books, and a comprehensive list of resources for book clubs. The guide is available in public libraries or to download from the Age & Opportunity website, www.olderinireland.ie. Age & Opportunity also keeps a list of public libraries that run reading groups.

Chapter 5

FIT FOR LIFE

Anne Dempsey[*]

*"Of all the causes which conspire to render the life
of a man short and miserable, none have greater
influence than the want of proper exercise"*
— Doctor William Buchan, 1762

LAZYBONES

When asked what he did when he felt the urge to take exercise,
Winston Churchill is said to have replied, "I lie down until the
feeling passes." Many Irish adults seem to follow his example,
as successive surveys indicate we are becoming more static
with each decade, with people aged 55 and over the least active of all.

So what's going on? Back in 1996, a National Survey of Involvement in Sport and Physical Activity found that four in
every ten adults described themselves as sedentary, that is,
they had taken no sustained activity lasting 20 minutes or over
in the previous month. The number of older people so describing was greater than the average.

---

[*] The author would like to thank Mary Harkin of the Go for Life programme at Age & Opportunity for her assistance with this chapter.

A year later, a 1997 pan-European survey confirmed this age-related decline in activity, while providing interesting insights into what active older people actually choose to do. It showed that 56 per cent of the over-55s participated in walking, 37 per cent in gardening, 12 per cent in cycling, 6 per cent in keeping fit, 5 per cent in swimming, 5 per cent in golf, 5 per cent in dancing and 1 per cent in football. Comparing these levels with participation rates of the general population, older people held their own when it came to walking, gardening and keep fit, but after that the gap widened.

A few years later the 1997–1999 Irish Universities Nutrition Alliance (IUNA) Study confirmed that levels of physical activity were relatively low among Irish adults and also decline significantly with age. Over half of the women in the 51–64 age group reported no vigorous activity.

In 2001 a study similar to its 1997 pan-European predecessor showed that participation levels in all the earlier activities — except swimming — had declined among all age groups and that the number of people who said they took no activity had risen from 13 per cent in 1997 to 23 per cent in 2001.

Finally, the second Slán Survey 2003 into health and lifestyle commissioned by the Department of Health and Children found that over one third of Irish people over the age of 55 do not exercise at all. So the verdict is that all age groups are taking progressively less exercise, with older people as a group taking least of all. Does this matter? It does, for many reasons. First, if children, young and middle-aged adults become less active, they will arrive at old age even less fit and able to face it. And older people who settle into a passive, less mobile lifestyle are depriving themselves of the many physical and emotional benefits of exercise, and in some cases, will be shortening their lives.

In the fitness stakes, the organisation "Go for Life" divides the population into four categories: couch potatoes, modest movers, healthy hustlers or regular revvers. Which are you?

- **"I'm a couch potato** — I have very little physical activity in my life, I'm too tired at the end of the day, I sit around a lot, I'm an armchair sports person, and I would tend to drive everywhere rather than walk."

- **"I'm a modest mover** — I do my share of household jobs, have an occasional walk, we have a small garden and I take care of it."

- **"I'm a healthy hustler** — I'm quite active every day. Running the house — vacuuming, cleaning, bedmaking, shopping keeps me moving, and I choose to walk with friends during my free time."

- **"I'm a regular revver** — I'm on my feet for most of the day, my life keeps me very busy, and I've energy left over for the bowling club and for a game of tennis".

Who can exercise? Just about anyone, at any age, can do some type of activity to improve their health. Even if you have a chronic condition (such as cardiovascular disease or diabetes), you can still exercise. In fact, physical activity may help your condition, but only if it is done during times when your condition is under control. During flare-ups, exercise could be harmful. You should talk to your doctor for guidance.

In Focus: Managing Change and Getting Fit

The problem with the promises we make ourselves — to do better, to grow fitter or to take more exercise — is that we often don't bridge the gap between articulating the hope and planning for its reality. Making a major life change is not an event, it is a process. Now new research suggests that people go through six stages on the way to successful behaviour change. These are pre-contemplation, contemplation, preparation, action, maintenance and relapse.

This "stages of change model" was originally used in America in motivational interviews between doctors and patients when patients were trying to change their behaviour. Now the stages are being applied successfully and widely in a wide range of settings — such as, for example, helping people to stop smoking, or helping individuals in a group to look at their lifestyle and what changes they would like to make.

Managing the stages of change is also something you can do on your own, or with a friend or partner. The stages of change are often represented diagrammatically as follows:

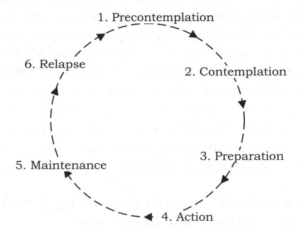

1. Pre-contemplation — when you have no intention of changing behaviour

> *"I often make unhealthy choices, but I don't really feel I can change."*

You are unhappy with your current lifestyle but don't quite know what's wrong. List some of the changes that would make life better now. For example, you may know that you're putting on weight and feeling more tired, and it's not a feeling you like or enjoy. But change seems too much of an effort. Or it might be a long time since you have taken any exercise, and doubt your ability to get into shape again. In order to move from this stage, you must have some idea that you could change. Begin thinking about the benefits of the new lifestyle. Even a little exercise will help you sleep, give you more energy and keep weight under control. Give yourself other reasons why it could be good to change.

2. Contemplation — when changing behaviour is being considered

> *"I do make unhealthy choices,*
> *but I'm hoping I could change."*

You are now actively considering change, but you may still lack a belief that you can. Will you be able for it? Will it be too much hassle? What supports can you muster now to encourage you? Talk to trusted friends. Find out what professional advice is available. Visit your GP for a check-up and make sure that a programme of exercise, such as a regular walk, joining a fitness club or learning to swim, is within your capability and carries no risk factors for you. Continue to strengthen your resolve by drawing up a list of the benefits you would gain from your change.

3. Preparation — when preparing for change already involves new behaviours

> *"I want to change and am making*
> *some preparations to help me."*

You're at the starting blocks getting ready for the whistle. Get practical. If you want to lose weight, for example, as well as gain more energy, look for healthy eating guidelines from your GP. It may not be necessary to go on a diet. Eating differently may be enough. Stick to three meals a day and give snacks the thumbs down. Cut down on fats, sweets, confectionery and alcohol. Don't go on a diet, just eat differently, majoring on fruit, vegetables, breads, potatoes, rice, cereals, pastas.

If planning to begin a regular walk, build in some support by asking a friend to come with you. Invest in a good *pair of sports or walking shoes to absorb impact. Plan your route. Look at any remaining obstacles which could prevent you from keeping your resolve. Be honest and don't fool yourself. Do you really want to make changes? What will stop you? How can you help yourself?*

4. Action — when preparations are over and core behaviour is changed

"I feel I've turned over a new leaf."

Take action. Join the gym. Get walking. Join the exercise class. Get out the bicycle. Take one day at a time, and remember that many major changes can take months to achieve. Build in realistic goals. For example, if you have been inactive for years, deciding to walk quickly for an hour a day is unrealistic. Study the Go for Life walking programme in this chapter; it could be a better model for you, particularly the warm-up and cool-down exercises. So one big step may need a number of smaller steps on the way to achievement. Start small and build up.

5. Maintenance — when changed behaviour is sustained, built upon and obstacles overcome

"The changes I made are now part of my life."

Acknowledge yourself for your new status. You are a walker, a gym club member, an exercise class participant. This will take effort after the honeymoon of the first few weeks. As days become cooler, as a favourite television programme beckons, you may not want to go out to fulfil your exercise regime. Persevere. Push through the obstacles which are part of managing change. If you are exercising on your own, again consider enlisting a friend or family members, joining a self-help group, walking group or gym to help stiffen your newfound resolve.

6. Relapse — when the newer behaviour is discontinued

"For some reason I've slipped back,
I'm disappointed and a bit perplexed."

Relapse is now built in as part of change, acknowledging that trial and error can be part of permanent change. If you falter, pick yourself up and start over. You won't be back to square one. You can by-pass pre-contemplation and contemplation, and move immediately to action or maintenance.

If, in hindsight, you feel you didn't prepare properly, move to preparation. Maybe you need to rethink your motivation? Maybe you need more support?

It would be important to identify reasons for your relapse. The best laid plans can be scuppered for a million reasons — from overwork to the weather. Examine what you liked about your changed behavior. (For example, feeling healthier, saving money by giving up cigarettes, losing weight and fitting into a smaller size, feeling good about yourself for doing something you find difficult, and so on.)

What was the downside? See what you can put in place to make it easier or more manageable next time. Don't beat yourself up for failure. Try again. Next time you've a greater chance of success. And remember, even if takes a couple of attempts to achieve sustained change, always reward yourself for effort.

WHY EXERCISE?

Many of us believe that as we grow older the need for physical activity decreases. Recent scientific evidence, however, proves that keeping moving is one of the most important things we can do to maintain our physical and psychological health and quality of life as we move through the decades. For most older people a key aim is to remain independent, to continue to be able to do what we want when we want. And those who have been the most inactive have the most to gain, so it's never too late to start.

The benefits of active living are social, psychological and physical.

Social Benefits

Many activities mean getting out and about, meeting people, working co-operatively or in competition with others, and often having fun.

Psychological Benefits

Setting and meeting goals such as taking a regular walk, participating in a game of bowls or kicking a ball about with your grandchildren will help you to feel better about yourself. Fulfilled people are more relaxed, have less stress, and may sleep better. Also, more vigorous exercise releases feel-good endorphins which underline that feeling of well-being.

Physical Benefits

Regular moderate to vigorous exercise strengthens muscles and bones, improves heart and lung fitness, increases joint flexibility and balance, raises energy levels and helps people to maintain a healthy weight. Eating healthily also has a part to play in being well and maintaining a correct weight for your size (see Chapter 6, pages 146–150).

So if regular, moderate physical activity is helpful at any age, it confers particular benefits as we grow older. Improved flexibility, balance and muscle tone can help prevent falls, which are a major cause of disability, dependency and distress among older people. Keeping active is good for co-ordination, endurance, motor control and even cognitive function — in other words, keeping us more mentally alert. Getting out and about provides the opportunity for social interaction, reduces feelings of loneliness and social exclusion, can improve self-confidence, self-sufficiency and mental well-being.

OLDER PEOPLE AND EXERCISE BARRIERS

So given the benefits of exercise, why is it that older people seem to turn off keeping fit? A survey carried out in 1999 among older people in Ballymun, north Dublin, identified the key local barriers to being more active as:

- Lack of facilities, difficulties with access

- Lack of programmes to meet their specific needs

- Lack of transport

- Concerns about health/fitness/age.

Somewhat similar points were made in facilitated discussions with older people conducted as part of a Quality of Life survey by the Limerick County Development Board in 2001. Respondents said they would welcome more opportunities to be active. But some suggested that lack of money restricted their choice. Others complained that community halls were often unavailable because of licensing and insurance problems. There was interest in countryside activities, but concern about the quality of paths and walkways. There was strong criticism also of the lack of information relating to activities, events and courses.

Some of these barriers involve perception rather than fact. For example, it is possible to become more active without having to invest large amounts of time or money. It is not necessary to have lots of free time, to be sporty or to be a member of a gym or fitness club to keep physically fit. What came through from the discussions is that the social element of physical activity was extremely important for older people, so herein perhaps lies the key to facilitating people to remain mobile. Activities for older people have a better chance of success if they are sociable, enjoyable and accessible and don't need too much in the way of equipment, transport or expense.

It is also true that exercise involves effort. You've got to make a start, extend yourself, get yourself going. Nobody else can do it for you. You may be helped to get started if you begin to think about the exercise you currently take and build on that. For example, anything that gets you moving is good. All forms of physical activity, whether it's housework, gardening, chasing round after grandchildren, walking to church each Sunday, dancing at home to the radio . . . all are of value. Your body doesn't know the difference between the jobs you have to do and those you want to do; the important thing is that you move it regularly.

So plan on making a bit of exercise a part of your everyday life. Do things you enjoy. Go for brisk walks, ride a bike, dance. And don't stop doing the routine maintenance work you've always done around the house — even if takes you longer and you build in a few breathers. Trim your hedge with a shears rather than a power tool. Climb stairs. Rake leaves.

SAFETY FIRST

Check with your doctor first if you are a man over 40 or a woman over 50 and you plan to do any vigorous activity or if you've been very unit for a number of years and want to turn over a new leaf. If you have any of the following problems, it is important to check with your doctor before increasing your physical activity:

- A chronic disease, or a high risk of getting one — for example, if you smoke, if you are obese, or if there is a family history of chronic disease.

- Chest pain

- Shortness of breath

- The feeling that your heart is skipping, racing, or fluttering

- Blood clots

- Infections or fever

- Undiagnosed weight loss

- Foot or ankle sores that won't heal

- Joint swelling

- Pain or an irregular walk after you've fallen

- A bleeding or detached retina, eye surgery or laser treatment

- A hernia

- Hip surgery.

Four Golden Rules for Exercising Safely

1. Start slowly. Build up activities and your level of effort gradually. Doing too much, too soon, can hurt you, especially if you have been inactive.

2. Avoid holding your breath while exercising; breathe through the effort — particularly if you have high blood pressure. The rule is to exhale during muscle exertion; inhale during relaxation, so if lifting a leg or arm, say, breathe out on the lift; breathe in on the release.

3. Use safety equipment to prevent injuries. For example, wear a helmet for cycling or protective equipment for activities like skiing and skating. Wear knee and elbow pads and eye protection as appropriate. If you walk or jog, wear stable shoes made for that purpose.

4. Unless your doctor has asked you to limit fluids, be sure to drink plenty when doing endurance activities that make you

sweat. Many older people tend to be low on fluid much of the time, even when not exercising.

Warming Up

Warming up before any exercise may help reduce the risk of accidents and help you get more out of your activity. The aim of the warm-up is to prepare your heart, lungs, joints and muscles for the activity. A good warm-up will move all parts of your body — arms, legs, trunk, hips, neck and shoulders — raise your heart and breathing rate and your body temperature. As the name implies, you are literally warming up your body, rather like running the car engine before driving off. The mobilising exercises will help to loosen and lubricate your joints, stretch your muscles and enhance your ability to exercise well and safely.

A simple on-the-spot warm up devised by Go for Life, the National Programme for Sport and Physical Activity for Older People (see later in this chapter) offers exercises to mobilise the body and raise pulse, breathing and temperature.

Mobilisers

- Move gently and fluidly; don't jerk or bounce

- Repeat each activity at least five times before moving on

- Repeat movements for one side of the body on the other side

- Don't work through pain or discomfort.

Fingers and Wrists

- Clench and stretch fingers

- Slowly circle hands in each direction

- Shake out gently.

Elbows and Shoulders

- Slowly raise hands to shoulders and lower

- Copy swimming strokes (breast, backstroke, crawl)

- Shrug and circle shoulders forwards, then backwards.

Hips and Knees

- Using a support, stand on one leg while gently swinging the other forward and back

- Still using support, raise your heel behind to your rear, then lower.

Ankles and Toes

- Using the support, point your toes, then pull them to you

- Circle your ankles right, then left

- Clench, stretch, then wiggle your toes.

Pulse/Breathing/Temperature Raisers

- Toe tap — tap the toes of your right foot in front, repeat with left

- Toe to heel — keeping your toes in one spot, raise each heel off the ground

- On-the-spot walk — raise each foot slightly off the ground and walk on the spot

- Body walk — gradually involve arms, shoulders and body into the on-the-spot walk

- March — exaggerate knee lifts and arm action until you are marching lightly; don't pound

- Heel to rear — raise each heel behind to your rear, simultaneously lifting bent arms to the side with each step

- Stand-up swim — copy breaststroke arm and leg action

- Side step — Step to the right with right foot, bring your left alongside; repeat step to left.

Keeping Warm, Cool and Hydrated

As we get older, our body may become less likely to trigger the urge to drink, so we may need water but not feel thirsty. Protect against dehydration by drinking liquids when involved in activity that causes fluid loss through sweat. The rule of thumb is that, by the time you notice you are thirsty, you are already somewhat dehydrated (low on fluid). This guideline is especially important in hot weather, when dehydration is more likely. Conversely if your doctor has asked you to limit fluids, be sure to check before increasing the amount you drink while exercising. Congestive heart failure and kidney disease are examples of chronic diseases that may call for fluid restriction.

Also, older adults can be particularly affected by heat and cold. In extreme cases, exposure to too much heat can cause heat stroke, and to very cold temperatures can lead to hypothermia caused by a dangerous drop in body temperature. If exercising outdoors, dress in layers so you can add or remove clothes as needed.

T'AI CHI

T'ai Chi is a Chinese system of slow, meditative, physical exercise designed for relaxation, balance and health. The word "chi" means energy and the potential of t'ai chi is to work on every internal organ in the body, creating a free flow of energy and so helping physical, emotional, mental and spiritual health. As both an exercise and an emotional health programme, it is suitable for people of all ages. In China, the groups you see going through their slow, rhythmic movements in the public parks and squares before going to work are doing t'ai chi, and you will see many older people within the ranks.

A t'ai chi health board research project set up to investigate ways to improve the physical health of older people in 2003 led to classes in south Dublin and Wicklow. The study found that participants enjoyed improved balance and flexibility and the incidence of falls decreased by almost 50 per cent following the classes. The East Coast Area Health Board study was carried out by the Centre for Sports Science and Health at Dublin City University. For more information contact the health board, DCU, or the Federation of Active Retirement Associations (FARA), as a number of active retirement groups were involved in the project.

T'ai chi classes are sometimes advertised locally in health centres, libraries and community halls. Martial arts organisations may also have information on such groups/classes.

WHAT KIND OF EXERCISE?

It is helpful to know that different kinds of exercise confer different benefits in terms of (1) endurance/stamina, (2) muscle strength/balance and (3) flexibility.

1. **Endurance or stamina** is staying power, the ability to work harder for longer, to keep going without gasping for breath. Endurance exercise improves the circulation in the heart and lungs because oxygen has to be pumped in sufficient quantities to the working muscles. The more vigorous the exercise, the greater the demand for oxygen in the blood, and the better the exercise for heart and lungs.

2. **Strength** is the extra muscle power needed for pushing, lifting or carrying. Strength is improved by regularly increasing the amount of effort required of your muscle. Many exercises to help strengthen the lower body also help with balance.

3. **Flexibility or suppleness** is the ability to bend, stretch, twist and turn as you wish. The more supple you are, the less likely you are to suffer from aches and pains caused by stiffness or to have accidents due to slow reaction.

Endurance Exercises

So having more endurance helps keep you healthier and improves your stamina for the tasks you need to do to live and manage with independence — climbing stairs and grocery shopping, for example. Endurance exercises may delay or prevent many diseases associated with ageing, such as diabetes, colon cancer, stroke, and others, and reduce overall death and hospitalisation rates.

Improving Your Endurance

Endurance exercises are any activity that increases your heart rate and breathing for an extended period of time. Examples of moderate endurance exercise includes swimming, cycling, cycling on an exercise bike, gardening (mowing, raking), walking briskly on a level surface, mopping or scrubbing floors, golf (without a cart!), tennis (doubles), volleyball, rowing, dancing.

How Much, How Often?

When you are ready to progress, build up the amount of *time* you spend doing endurance activities first, then build in more *effort*. For example, first gradually increase your time from five to 30 minutes over days, weeks or months by walking longer distances, then start walking up steeper hills or walking more briskly. Examples of vigorous endurance exercise include climbing stairs or hills, brisk cycling, digging in the garden, tennis (singles), swimming laps, cross-country skiing, downhill skiing, hiking, jogging.

Your goal is to work your way up from a moderate to a vigorous level that increases your breathing and heart rate. Even a moderate level of sustained activity is beneficial. Once you reach your goal, you can divide your exercise into ten-minute sessions (less than that won't give you the desired cardiovascular and respiratory system benefits, except when you're starting out and small amounts are helpful). Aim for a minimum of 30 minutes of endurance exercise on most or all days of the week. More often is better, and every day is best.

Keep Safe

Endurance activities should not make you breathe so hard that you can't talk. They should not cause dizziness or chest pain. One doctor describes it this way: "If you can talk without any trouble at all, your activity is probably too easy. If you can't talk at all, it's too hard." So find your level.

Warm up with a little light activity first like walking on the spot. Cool down afterwards with some stretching activities while the muscles are still warm.

Muscle Strengthening and Balance Exercises

Strength exercises build your muscles, increase your metabolism, helping to keep your weight and blood sugar in check. That's important because obesity and diabetes are major health problems for older adults. Studies suggest that strength exercises may also help prevent osteoporosis. Keeping your muscles in shape can help prevent the falls that cause broken hips or other disabilities because when the leg and hip muscles that support you are strong, you're less likely to fall. And using your muscles may make your bones stronger, too. Even very small changes in muscle size can make a big difference in strength, especially in people who already have lost a lot of muscle. An increase in muscle that is not even visible to the eye can be all it takes to improve your ability to climb the stairs at home.

So it is important to keep using your muscles. People lose 20 to 40 per cent of their muscle — and, therefore, their strength — as they age. But some of this is down to lifestyle. Older people who still use their abdominal muscles to get out of a chair, who carry moderate amounts of shopping, who walk regularly — in other words, who continue to do what they've always done within reason — will retain proportionally more strength and muscle power. It is lack of use, rather than age, that lets muscles waste away. In other words, you either use it or lose it.

Balance exercises can also help prevent falls. There is overlap between strength and balance exercises; often, one exercise serves both purposes.

Improving Your Muscle Strength and Balance

Don't stop day-to-day activities involving lifting, carrying and moving, which strengthen arm, leg and back and stomach muscles. Regular walking helps to strengthen leg muscles, and many sports build up muscle tone and strength also. Properly organised keep-fit classes and exercise programmes will have a progressively paced series of exercises to strengthen the main muscle groups.

Muscle-building gym equipment involves lifting or pushing weights and gradually increasing the amount of weight used. DIY equipment such as hand and ankle weights are sold in sporting-goods stores; or you can make your own weights with socks filled with dried beans and tied at the ends; or buy a resistance band, which looks like a giant rubber band — stretching it helps build muscle.

Some of the warm-up exercises described above help with balance. A simple balance exercise is to stand on one foot, then the other. You may need to begin by holding on to something for support, but may gradually be able to hold your balance without support. Focusing on an object in the room will help as you balance. When doing this exercise, check your posture and relax your body.

Help your balance by standing up from sitting in a chair without using your hands or arms. Every now and then, walk heel-to-toe (the toes of the foot at the back should almost touch the heel of the foot), an easy exercise.

How Much, How Often?

- Do strength exercises for all of your major muscle groups at least twice a week. Don't do strength exercises of the same muscle group on any two days in a row.

- Depending on your condition, start out using as little as one or two pounds of weight.

- Gradually add weight to progressively but gently challenge your muscles.

- When doing a strength exercise, do eight to fifteen repetitions in a row. Wait a minute, then do another set of eight to fifteen repetitions in a row of the same exercise. (While waiting, gently stretch the muscle you've just worked on.)

- Build up your balance through practice. Many balance exercises take just a few moments and can be done many times a day.

Keep Safe

Don't rush at the everyday jobs. Don't lift weights or move large objects that may cause strain or injury, get help if necessary. Learn the correct way to lift, which allows your lower body, rather than your back, to take weight.

- Don't hold your breath during strength exercises. Breathe normally. Holding your breath while straining can cause changes in blood pressure. This is especially true for people with heart disease.

- If you have had a hip repair or replacement, check with your surgeon before doing lower-body exercises.

- Avoid jerking or thrusting weights into position. This can cause injuries. Use smooth, steady movements.

- Don't lock arm or leg joints too tightly; stand more loosely.

- Breathe out as you lift or push, and breathe in as you relax. For example, if doing leg lifts, breathe out as you lift your leg, and breathe in as you lower it. This won't feel natural at first, and will take practice.

- Muscle soreness lasting up to a few days and slight fatigue are normal after muscle-building exercises, but exhaustion, sore joints, and unpleasant muscle pulling aren't and mean you're overdoing it.

- None of the exercises should cause pain. The range within which you move your arms and legs should not hurt. If you can't lift or push a weight without a huge amount of effort, it's too heavy for you.

- Stretch after strength exercises, when your muscles are warmed up. If you stretch before strength exercises, be sure to warm up your muscles first (through light walking and arm pumping, for example.

Flexibility Exercises

Flexibility exercises help keep your body supple by stretching the muscles and the tissues that hold your body's structures in place. Physiotherapists often recommend certain stretching exercises to help patients recover from injuries and to prevent injuries from happening in the first place. Flexibility also may play a part in preventing falls. Stretching exercises give you more freedom of movement to do the things you need to do and the things you like to do. Flexible exercises which bring the arms, legs and trunk through a range of movements are also beneficial. Swimming slowly and deliberately for maximum joint flexibility is also beneficial.

Improving Your Flexibility

Get into the habit of stretching already-warmed muscles after a bout of activity such as a brisk walk.

Many keep-fit programmes include stretching exercises to improve suppleness. These show safe and effective ways to stretch your back, legs, upper and lower arms; stretch your neck and upper shoulders also to ease out any tensions there. Many of these exercises require no equipment and can be done at home.

How Much, How Often?

- Get into the habit of including some stretching exercises into your every day.

- Do each exercise three to five times each session.

- Slowly stretch into the desired position, as far as possible without pain, and hold the stretch for 10 to 30 seconds. Relax, then repeat, trying to stretch farther.

Keep Safe

- If you have had a hip replacement, check with your surgeon before doing lower body exercises.

- Always warm up before stretching exercises. Stretching your muscles before they are warmed up may result in injury.

- Don't bounce or jerk into a stretch; this could cause tightness and possible injury. Make slow, steady movements instead.

- Avoid locking your joints into place when you straighten them during stretches. Your arms and legs should be straight when you stretch them, but not hard or rigid.

GET WALKING

Walking is one of the best exercises around and fulfils the criteria that many older people ask for — it costs little or nothing, it is socially enjoyable and extremely accessible. Walking is good for us. A huge body of well-researched evidence now clearly proves that regular walking:

- Helps increase bone density, so helping to prevent osteoporosis (brittle bone disease);

- Improves overall physical and emotional health;

- Helps to preserve independent living;

- Reduces the risk of developing coronary heart disease;

- Helps in the control of stress, becoming overweight and diabetes.

Some practical tips when walking:

- Wear proper walking shoes.

- Wear bright clothes and reflective armbands if walking at dusk or at night.

- Wear layers of light loose clothing that can be removed as you warm up.

- Use wind/waterproof gear to protect you against the elements.

- Walk the talk — walk with a friend or family member as well as enjoying a walk alone.

If suffering from health problems or worried about any aspect of your health, ask your doctor's advice before you start a walking programme.

A Health Promoting Walking Session

A healthy walking session should last at least 20 minutes, but if you haven't walked for a while or if you're very unfit, start by taking shorter sessions (five to ten minutes). Also, don't ignore the benefits of a short walk. Walking to the shop to get the paper in the morning is always better than taking the car, even if (or especially if) the shop is five minutes away from home. For longer walks, bring a bottle of water to keep yourself hydrated.

Begin by walking slowly for five minutes; this gently loosens out joints (ankles, knees, hips, elbows, shoulders), acts as a wake-up call for heart and lungs, muscles and joints and prepares them for an increased walking pace.

Gradually increase your pace to a point where your heart is beating a little faster (but not thumping), your are breathing a little deeper and faster (but not breathless), and you are perspiring slightly, but not sweating profusely.

This means that the pace is challenging you a little, making it one from which you'll gain most benefits. Stick to this. This section of the walk should last five to 15 minutes depending on your level of fitness.

As you near the end of your walk, ease your speed for five minutes until you are walking quite slowly again. Allow your body to relax mentally and physically. At the finish, gently shake and loosen your joints and take three all-over stretches, like a full body yawn. Hold for ten seconds, breathing normally as you do so.

GO FOR LIFE PROGRAMME

Go for Life is the Irish National Programme for Sport and Physical Activity for Older People. Its aim is to involve more older adults in all aspects of sport and physical activity more often. The thrust of the programme is to empower and enable older people by reaching out to active retirement associations, senior citizens groups, day care and community centres around the country, to ensure that more older people are more active, more often.

Go for Life is an Age & Opportunity initiative funded by the Irish Sports Council. The Go for Life team at Age & Opportunity administers the Programme in partnership with the Health Boards and the Local Sports Partnerships (LSPs). There are many different elements to the Go for Life programme, including Activity and Walking Challenges for individuals and groups, leadership training programmes, group presentations explaining the benefits of activity to older people, and the national grant scheme to help increase older participation in sport and physical recreation.

The Get Active Challenge

This involves doing three activities each week for five weeks. You can pick one activity or a mixture, choosing easily accessible activities like gardening or walking, or out-and-about exercise such as dancing, bowling, swimming or pitch-and-putt. You can mix them any way you wish during the five consecutive weeks.

You are more likely to succeed if you choose something you enjoy, enlist your partner, a friend or a family member to do the challenge with you, or do the challenge with a group you belong to, or form a group for the purpose.

You will gain from the opportunity to experience the range of physical, mental and social benefits associated with physical activity. And you'll be presented with a personalised Get Active Challenge Certificate if you complete the Challenge. Find out more, but remember too to get your doctor's advice if you know you should before starting on an activity programme.

The Get Walking Challenge

This involves walking for at least 100 minutes each week for five weeks, which can break down into 15 minutes a day, or 20 minutes for five days, or whatever combination you decide. This could include a ten-minute stroll in the morning and a 15-minute ramble later in the same day. A personalised Get Walking Challenge Certificate is awarded to successful Challengers.

Learning about Being Active

Go for Life has trained tutors to deliver presentations to groups of older people about the benefits of physical activity. These presentations are Get Active, Going Strong and Better Balance. To find out more, contact your local health board and speak to the Go for Life co-ordinator.

Leadership Training

Go for Life runs a series of day workshops offering information, ideas and skills to older people who wish to train as Physical Activity Leaders (PALs). The workshops would be useful for activity organisers/managers in active retirement groups, day care centres or local groups. A PAL can lead people in short exercise routines, dances, fun games and recreational sports. Again the contact for more information is the Go for Life co-ordinator at your local health board.

National Grant Scheme

One of the main elements of the Go for Life Programme is the National Grant Scheme for Sport and Physical Activity for Older People which supports/funds physical activity programmes or helps to buy sports equipment for older people's organisations In 2003, 525 successful applicants nationwide, representing every county, shared in over €300,000. These applicants included active retirement associations, senior citizens clubs, ICA guilds, sports clubs, day centres and community centres. Details of the annual grant scheme are announced in September each year and available on the Go for Life website, www.gfl.ie

Publications

Go for Life has produced a range of fact sheets offering helpful information for older people, publishes an annual newsletter, and a quarterly newsletter to PALs. Go for Life, c/o Age & Opportunity, Marino Institute of Education, Griffith Avenue, Dublin 9; Tel: 01-8057733, E-mail: gfl@mie.ie. All publications can be found on www.olderinireland.ie if you click on the link to "physical activity".

Chapter 6

In Sickness and in Health

Janet Convery and Anne Dempsey

"If I'd known I was going to live this long, I'd have taken better care of myself." — Eubie (James Herbert) Blake

Most older people in Ireland are reasonably healthy, active participants in normal daily life. Some are still in paid employment or working for themselves. Others are involved in voluntary work, many pursue hobbies, sport and leisure interests and an increasing number share in the care of their grandchildren.

Although it is true that people over 75 are the heaviest users of our medical services, the number in full-time long-term residential or hospital care is small. This number has not increased in recent years, in spite of popular perceptions to the contrary. Furthermore, a number of recent research projects show that the vast majority of over-65s surveyed stated a clear preference to spend their final years in their own homes and not in institutional care. This chapter will discuss the factors that are critical to maintaining good health in old age and provide some information about available services and how they can be accessed. Also included is information about services that are useful once health deteriorates, including nursing and medical services.

PREVENTION IS BETTER THAN CURE

The present generation of over-75s grew up in hard times. Many spent their formative years in houses that were damp and unheated. Their nutrition was poor; they may not have received proper medical attention when they needed it as children and young adults; they smoked; and many left school at age 14. Ireland has a high percentage of over-75s who never married. These factors have undoubtedly contributed to our present place at the bottom of a 17-nation list compiled by the World Health Organisation on life expectancy at age 65.[1] When you factor in adjustment for time spent in poor health, Ireland comes last out of 23 countries on the "Healthy Life Expectancy" tables. Clearly we should be doing better.

The challenge for Irish third agers is to take better care of ourselves and do whatever we can to improve our chances of a long and healthy life. Clear links have been established between good health and lifestyle. People who take regular exercise, have a network of friends, participate in activities they enjoy and are able to understand and express feelings are going to have a more positive ageing experience than those who don't. Those who progress through this stage of their lives drinking alcohol in moderation only and without cigarettes will do even better. (See Chapter 5.)

It is noticeable that in the United States — though there may be dramatic differences between socioeconomic groups — people in general seem to pay more attention to their health than in Ireland. Regular check-ups with the GP are routine for many US citizens over 50, and even younger. There is public awareness of the danger signs for a range of conditions/diseases such as heart disease, cancer (including skin cancer), and respiratory illnesses, all of which are equally prevalent in Ireland. While the

---

[1] Eamon O'Shea (2003), *Report on Healthy Ageing*, National Council on Ageing and Older People.

US health system is gravely flawed in many respects, Americans are way ahead of us in taking responsibility for their own health. In Ireland we are much more fatalistic about our health, and many people seek advice and services only after symptoms present themselves; and even then, we may wait too long to do something about it.

This was brought home to me when my husband was diagnosed with melanoma, the most dangerous form of skin cancer, a few years ago at age 58. It seems that a minor wound on his ear had never really healed in the 18 months since he bumped his head on a low doorway when we were holidaying in Greece. By the time he got medical attention, the cancer had reached Stage 2 and required surgery, followed by a lot of anxiety during what seemed like a very long wait to hear that it had not spread further. It struck me that this particular scenario would not arise with my relatives in the US. Those who, like my husband, have sensitive skin and are thus more at risk of developing skin cancer, go regularly to the doctor for check-ups. Where suspicious growths are identified, they are immediately removed. While cynics here might suggest that this leads to unnecessary time, expense and even contributes to hypochondria, we've been sufficiently frightened to know better.

HEALTH PROMOTING SERVICES

Health promotion is not only about check-ups and going to the doctor earlier rather than later. It's also about lifestyle and the things we do to our bodies in the day to day. Chapter 5 has focused on the importance of physical activity and fitness, and opportunities to participate in physical activities as an individual and part of a group are on the increase. Below are other factors that influence our health and the quality of our life in later years.

Nutrition

"You are what you eat." Increasingly, we are waking up to the fact that what we eat is critical to good health. Although conflicting messages can be given regarding what foods to enjoy and what to avoid, awareness of the need for a balanced diet, of the dangers of overindulgence in certain types of foods (be they fats, sugars or carbohydrates), and of the health risks of being overweight are gradually permeating the public consciousness. So how do you eat sensibly? One way is to use the Food Pyramid to guide you to make healthy food choices. Below is a Food Pyramid designed specifically for older people.

Food Pyramid for Older Adults

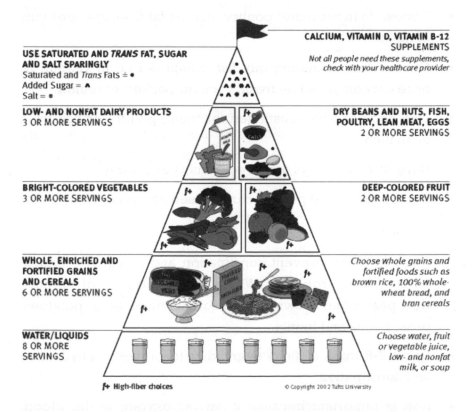

Source: Developed by Tufts Nutrition Centre, Tufts University. Reprinted with permission.

As you can see, it is better to eat more foods from the bottom of the Food Pyramid and less from the top. A brief word of explanation: saturated fats become hard at room temperature and are typically animal fats, found in meat, lard and so on. Trans fats are oils which also harden during food processing. Trans or saturated fats are less healthy than unsaturated or polyunsaturated fats which remain liquid at room temperature.

In summary:

- Enjoy a wide variety of foods.

- Eat at least six servings of bread, cereals or potatoes each day.

- Eat four or more servings of fruit and vegetables.

- Choose lean meat and poultry; cut the fat from cheaper cuts of meat.

- Choose fish, including oily fish which is rich in vitamin D, once a week. It can be fresh, vacuum-packed or tinned.

- Two eggs can be substituted for meat, poultry or fish for a main meal.

- Have three servings of dairy products every day.

- Herbs, spices and pepper can be used as alternatives to salt.

Remember:

- Fibre helps to prevent constipation and safeguard against other bowel problems. Whole grain varieties of cereals, rice, pastas and brown breads contain fibre, as do potatoes, peas, beans and lentils.

- Drink 6-8 cups of fluid every day to prevent dehydration and constipation.

- Iron is important because it carries oxygen in the blood. Meat, poultry, fish, offal (liver, heart and kidneys), green leafy vegetables, peas, beans, fortified breakfast cereals are rich in iron.

- Vitamin D helps your body to absorb calcium from foods and is needed for healthy bones. As people age, their skin is less able to produce vitamin D, so older people need to eat foods rich in vitamin D like oily fish, milk with added vitamin D, margarines, eggs and liver.

Food Tips for Older People

There is a wealth of information available from Health Promotion departments of the health boards and from nutritionists and dieticians working in hospitals and the community on how to eat well at every age. The booklet "Food Tips for Older People" recommends that you:

- Eat three main meals daily

- Eat a wide variety of foods.

- Try to drink one pint of milk each day.

- Choose more high fibre foods, including wholegrain cereals, wholemeal bread, fruit and vegetables.

- Drink 7–8 cups or 5–6 mugs of fluid daily. Try water, fruit juice, fruit squash, soups and milky drinks instead of tea and coffee.

- Have two or more portions of fruit daily; fresh, tinned or stewed.

- Eat two or more servings of vegetables daily — fresh, frozen or tinned.

Store Cupboard Cookery

Keep a food store cupboard with some of the following for days when you can't get out to shop: tinned/packed soup, tinned stew, tinned fish, skimmed milk powder, instant mash, baked beans, tinned vegetables, tinned rice pudding, powdered/ready-made custard, tinned/dried fruit, crackers or crispbread, breakfast cereal, Complan/recovery food or build-up.

Use dried foods regularly as they don't keep as long as tinned foods. Throw food out if it is past its "use-by" date.

See also the "Meals in Minutes" booklet, available from the Health Promotion Department of your local health board.

Certain Conditions and Food Awareness

How you eat, what foods you choose and what foods you avoid may be particularly relevant if you

- are obese

- have fluid retention

- suffer from constipation or diarrhoea

- have high blood pressure

- have diabetes

- suffer from heart disease

- suffer from anaemia

- suffer from osteoporosis

- suffer from coeliac disease

- have food allergies or food intolerance

- have difficulty gaining weight.

These are just some of the many conditions which may be affected by the way you eat, and if you suffer from any of them, your GP or consultant will already have talked to you about diet and possibly encouraged a particular regime. For extra advice, you may also contact the community dietician employed by each health board. Also, the organisation dealing with your particular complaint, such as, for example, the Irish Heart Foundation or the Coeliac Society of Ireland (Tel: 01-8721471) may also supply information and support.

How to Access

- The Department of Health and Children has in recent years significantly increased funding of Health Promotion services in the health boards. This has resulted in a wealth of sometimes very good literature on healthy diet, including leaflets and booklets specifically aimed at older people. Most health boards now have senior nutritionists for older people, and although their numbers are still small, they are a very important resource to health board staff and community groups.

Smoking

The recent high-profile introduction of legislation prohibiting smoking in any workplace, including pubs and restaurants, has done a lot to raise Irish public awareness of the dangers of smoking, and hopefully, this move will encourage many to give up the habit. It's never too late to stop! We now know that our lungs and general health actually improve when we stop smoking, regardless of how long we may have smoked or what age we are.

For those people who find that they cannot give up smoking on their own, there is help available in many forms. Your GP may have help and advice in the form of information and literature. One-to-one or group help may be available from your health board, which is funded to employ Smoking Cessation Officers who also give talks to community groups. The Irish Cancer Society also offers stop smoking support. Private practitioners are available offering a range of complementary therapies such as hypnotism and acupuncture, which claim to help people to stop smoking. There is also nicotine replacement therapy to help give up smoking in the form of gum, patches and inhalers.

How to Access

- Contact Smoking Cessation Officers at the Health Promotion Department in your local health board or through your local health centre, or the Irish Cancer Society Smoking Quitline 1850 200 700.

- Complementary therapists are listed in the Golden Pages. Find out if the person you choose belongs to a professional body; alternatively, contact the professional body, also listed, and ask for a list of professional members.

- Nicotine replacement therapy products are available at your local pharmacy. Again, ask for advice, as different products have been produced to suit different types of smokers.

HEALTH ISSUES AS WE GROW OLDER (1): PHYSICAL HEALTH

Although growing older is not and need not be about developing sickness and frailty, it is a fact that, as we age, our chances of developing certain illnesses or conditions do increase. However, there are things we can do to reduce our chances of becoming ill or disabled. Taking better care of ourselves at every age is one way. There is no excuse not to at least attempt to do what we can to keep ourselves healthy into old age. Eating healthily, giving up smoking, taking exercise and finding ways to reduce stress is one part of the equation. Regular check-ups is another way to ensure that we are doing everything we can to prevent physical deterioration that diminishes our ability to lead a full and happy life. Prevention has not routinely been a part of Irish health care up to now; but if we don't take responsibility for our health, no one else will.

Because my father died at age 62 of heart disease, I decided to go for a complete check-up in a private clinic as I approached 60. My own GP does not have the facilities to undertake such an assessment and it seemed a good idea to go someplace where I could have a whole battery of tests done at one time. Twice since then, GPs in other settings have questioned me about why I had done so, implying that it was an unnecessary, self-indulgent and even wasteful exercise. I find this attitude very curious in a country where life expectancy is relatively low and disease prevalence in old age so high. Fortunately, the check-up showed that I was healthy in most respects except for a high cholesterol count, and that is something that is easily sorted. Given my family history, with heart disease on both sides, I still question why I should have to defend my decision to go for a check-up to health professionals. Peace of mind regarding lack of evidence that anything else was wrong with me was almost as valuable as finding out that my cholesterol was unacceptably high. While we do not cover all major illnesses here, we do out-line some of the most common problems affecting older people.

Heart Disease

Risk of heart disease increases with age and is one area where early prevention and regular check-ups, depending upon fam-ily history and personal circumstances, can make a difference to healthy ageing. Large numbers of both women and men are affected by heart disease in Ireland, and the risks increase after menopause for women. High blood pressure and high choles-terol combined with smoking and poor diet are among the sig-nals of potential heart problems in later life. But family history may be an even more important factor. If either of your parents, aunts or uncles or grandparents suffered from heart disease, it is advisable to go for a medical assessment and follow the ad-vice of professionals should a problem be identified.

Strokes

Risk of strokes also increases with age. Again, chronic high blood pressure, smoking and poor diet may increase your risk of developing a stroke. Family history is also very important. Going for a medical assessment is the responsible thing to do, especially if any of the above are relevant (see also the section on physiotherapy below).

Osteoporosis

Osteoporosis — thinning, brittle bones — is a common condition as we age. Prevention can be helped by diet — for example, switching to milk enriched with Vitamin C and D — and its progress managed by medication. Early detection is important and testing via a bone density scan is becoming increasingly accepted as an effective way to control osteoporosis. All women are advised to get tested, as women are more susceptible than men to the disease.

Incontinence

Incontinence is a problem that causes embarrassment and, in extreme cases, may seriously limit ability to leave the home and carry out normal activities. Early intervention can be important to prevent the development of a serious, chronic problem. Where there are no other solutions, incontinence wear is available to manage the problem. If you have a problem with incontinence, don't accept that this is a normal part of old age. There is help available from the GP, public health nurse, physiotherapists and other health professionals for this very common problem.

Mobility Problems

> "Now here, you see, it takes all the running you can do, to keep in the same place. If you want to get somewhere else, you must run at least twice as fast as that!"
> — *Through the Looking Glass* by Lewis Carroll.

As we age, we may experience sensory or mobility problems that can get in the way of normal daily activities like dressing ourselves, taking a shower or bath, making a meal, shopping, or getting about. As the quotation above suggests, we may simply have to work harder in order to maintain our previous lifestyle as we age. Part of this phenomenon is a natural part of the ageing process, although not everyone ages the same and some people may experience few difficulties as described into advanced old age.

For others, mobility problems can arise gradually over time or following a limb fracture, a heart attack or stroke, hospitalisation for an acute illness episode or flare-up of a chronic condition. While such difficulties may not create total barriers to activity, they do impact on quality of life and so taking preventive action in time is worth exploring if there is any chance at all that improvement is possible. Sometimes the solution may be more about compensating for lost ability than about treatment.

Physiotherapy

Physiotherapists are the people to approach when you have problems with your muscles and joints, when it hurts to bend over and when you suffer aches and pains that inhibit you from walking, moving, lifting or bending to do ordinary things. Physiotherapists work to restore and maintain mobility and movement in order to improve independence and quality of life following an accident, an illness, stroke or in the case of progressive debilitating conditions. They are the people to approach for walking sticks, insoles or shoes if you have special footwear needs. The focus is on helping your body to function better through treatment, exercise and/or provision of aids. Physiotherapists work in hospitals as well as in the community.

How to Access

- **Hospital services:** referral from GP to hospital in- and outpatient physiotherapy department.

- **Community services:** referral from GP, public health nurse, hospital physiotherapists, medical social worker and others or directly from clients and their families to the physiotherapy department in your local health board.

- **Private physiotherapy services** may be accessed by contacting the Irish Society of Chartered Physiotherapists, (Royal College of Surgeons, St Stephen's Green, Dublin 2; Tel: 01-4022418), whose members are listed in the Golden Pages. Members of the Irish Association of Physical Therapists are also governed by the Society's regulations. Mobility equipment may be available from health appliance shops and private providers but it is advisable to get professional advice before buying. Health board physiotherapy services are free, and private health insurance may cover the cost of private physiotherapy services for those members.

Foot Problems

Foot care becomes more important as we grow older. This is especially so for people who have diabetes and other circulation problems, but also for those with ingrown toenails, bunions, or other minor abnormalities which cause pain and can prevent us from being able to walk or move around, even in our own homes. So taking care of our feet through good hygiene, wearing shoes that fit properly, including walking shoes to absorb impact, can be basic to maintaining independence in later life. If problems do occur, you should visit a chiropodist sooner rather than later.

My sister-in-law, aged 55, lives in San Francisco which, as she tells us regularly, has the best of everything imaginable. Except chiropody. On visits to Ireland, she routinely sets up appointments with a chiropodist because this service is not easily available in California at affordable prices. On the last visit, she even brought her 23-year old daughter along. She says that her visits to the chiropodist make her feet feel better and this improves her everyday quality of life.

How to Access

- Medical card holders are eligible for free visits to the chiropodist with the number of visits varying by health board. Chiropodists usually work as private practitioners but some are under contract to the health boards to take medical card holders as clients. There is a form to fill out, available at your local health centre.

- Private chiropody services are listed in the Golden Pages or may be located by contacting the Society of Chiropodists/ Podiatrists of Ireland, 68 Granville Road, Dun Laoghaire, County Dublin; Tel: 01-2024939. It is a good idea to ask about qualifications before making an appointment.

Hearing Problems

Three out of four adults who are hard of hearing are over 60, suffering developmental loss due to inner ear damage which can be caused by ageing. Not all such loss is serious. Hearing loss can be caused by wax which builds up in your ear. Soften the wax with a little warm olive oil for a number of nights before visiting your GP who can remove the softened wax by syringe.

Tinnitus refers to noises heard in the ears which do not come from an external source. Antibiotics can clear up tinnitus due to an infection of the middle ear; minor surgery may also help. The condition may also be managed by a tinnitus masker which emits a gentle sound diverting attention from tinnitus noise. Learning to relax through breathing or other techniques may also help.

If concerned about your hearing, contact your doctor who can refer you to a qualified audiologist to have your hearing tested. A hearing aid may be useful for anyone with a mild to moderate hearing loss and current models are small and discreet. Getting accustomed to a hearing aid may take a little time because you may have ceased to hear many background noises and need time to adjust to hearing them again.

For more profound and long-term problems, contact the National Association for Deaf People, 35 North Frederick Street, Dublin 1; Tel: 01-8723800; E-mail: nad@iol.ie; Website: www.nadi.ie. Another website, www.irishdeaf.com offers an annually updated Irish directory of resource organisations of interest to deaf people.

I Can See Clearly Now

Seven out of ten people over 40 wear glasses at some time, mostly for close work, with the numbers creeping up over the following decades. This is because the ciliary eye muscles which allow the lens to focus become less flexible with time. The most common corrective measure for bad eyesight is a pair of glasses or contact lenses.

Have a full eye examination and full consultation with a qualified optometrist before buying a pair of glasses. The optometrist can diagnose existing problems and may also spot potential difficulties. Low-cost glasses may not be best for you. Different types of eye problems may require special lenses or glasses with special coatings to protect against glare.

The Association of Optometrists Ireland have a register of members and offer some advice and information to the public. Contact them at 18 Greenmount House, Harold's Cross Road, Dublin 6W; Tel: 01-4538850; E-mail: info@optometrists.ie; Website: www.optometrists.ie.

Medical cardholders are entitled to free eye tests and certain types of lenses and frames. You may receive information on this at your GP surgery or local health clinic. Employees paying PRSI may also be entitled to some optical benefit. Contact the Optical Benefit Scheme, Department of Social and Family Affairs, Letterkenny, County Donegal; Tel: 01-8748444/074-25566.

The main eye diseases associated with ageing are cataracts, glaucoma, and macular degeneration. A cataract is a cloud on the central lens which blurs vision. Today the lens can be replaced in situ and people well into their eighties are being operated on successfully for cataract removal. With glaucoma, pressure builds up inside the eye, affecting side vision. It may be treated with surgery or medication.

People in the 70–80 age group are commonly affected by degeneration of the macula, a small spot at the back of the eye, which gives some of our finest vision. Proper use of low vision aids and an understanding of using light effectively can help.

The National Council for the Blind in Ireland (NCBI) has services for people suffering from a range of vision difficulties. These national/regional/local services include community resource officers, rehabilitation officers, plus personnel offering mobility and technical support. The organisation also offers peer and family counselling and has a low vision clinic for people recently diagnosed with vision impairment offering vision aids. Contact NCBI at PV Doyle House, Whitworth Road, Drumcondra, Dublin 9: Tel: 01-8307033; E-mail: info@ncbi.ie; Website: www.ncbi.ie.

Speech and Language Difficulties

Being able to communicate with others is such an important part of who we are and so basic to quality of life. For people who experience difficulties with speaking, speech and language therapists can provide services that can help overcome these difficulties. For stroke victims, it is important to get speech and language therapy as early as possible, as the chance of improvement may diminish over time. Speech and language therapists also work with people who have difficulty swallowing, and timely intervention can mean the difference between being able to continue to live at home and having to stay in hospital or long-term care.

How to Access

- **Hospital services:** referral from consultant physician or GP to in- or outpatient services

- **Community services:** referral from GPs, consultant physicians, psychologists and public health nurses, carers and other family members. Contact the Irish Association of Speech and Language Therapists, 29 Gardiner Place, Dublin 1; Tel: 01-8787959.

Other Common Ailments

Arthritis is a common nuisance for many and in some cases it may be serious enough to result in serious loss of independence. Hearing loss, sight problems, speech and swallowing difficulties, circulatory problems and other conditions may negatively impact on older people's quality of life, but the good news is that a proper medical assessment followed by prescribed treatment is available to help you to cope better with such problems (see Medical Services below). New assistive technologies, some relatively inexpensive, are being developed all the time to make life easier and increase our ability to continue to care for ourselves. Like everything else, access to these may be directly related to your income, but public services are very good when they can be accessed. Your GP, public health nurse, or local health centre should be able to help you find out what you need to know about local available services. In general, there is no charge for services directly provided by the health boards.

Male Health Issues

Men have a lower life expectancy than women and while different causes may be advanced for this, it is likely that attitude plays a part. Men, in general, do not look after their health as well as women do and may have a lack of interest or knowledge

in preventive and protective health measures. In repeated surveys, many men admit to leaving problems too long before going for medical advice.

Men and Heart Disease

While heart disease — its causes and treatment — is discussed
elsewhere in this chapter, we mention it again under men's
health, because men are more prone than women to heart disease. The classic heart disease candidate is typically a rushed,
work-driven male, and while this may be a stereotype, learning
to relax and broaden your range of interests and enjoyment will
undoubtedly benefit your general and heart health.

Male Cancers

Over 6,500 men are diagnosed with cancer each year, with skin
and lung cancers the main types. Almost 1,000 men die in Ireland from specific male cancers each year. Colorectal cancer
narrowly leads the field, with 1,011 new cases and 561 deaths in
1999, according to figures from the National Cancer Registry.
There were 1,378 new cases of prostate cancer the same year
with 499 deaths, and 105 new cases of testicular cancer and
nine deaths. When you add the 953 men who contracted lung
cancer in 1999 and the 915 who died from it, the figures climb
even higher.

In spite of the numbers of families affected, male cancers
have received relatively little publicity. In November 2003, Ireland's first Men's Cancer Action Week was launched by the
Irish Cancer Society. It aimed to raise awareness specifically
regarding prostate, colorectal, testicular, bowel, lung and skin
cancers. Men are encouraged first to make any lifestyle
changes necessary, such as quitting smoking, eating a low-fat,
high-fibre fruit and vegetable diet, taking regular amounts of
physical activity, keeping weight within a healthy range and
avoiding over-exposure to the sun. Knowing your family history

of cancer and taking your doctor's advice about reducing any risk will also benefit.

The causes of **skin cancer** are prolonged or repeated exposure to sunlight, or to certain chemicals. Warning signs are dry, scaly patches or skin sores that don't heal, warts or moles which change in size or appearance or unusual skin lumps.

Reduce your risk factors for skin cancer by avoiding excessive exposure to sun. Wear protective clothing and follow recommended procedures. If in doubt about work hazards, contact the Health and Safety Authority, 10 Hogan Place, Dublin 2; Tel: 01-6147000; Website: www.hsa.ie. An annual campaign from the Irish Cancer Society directed at men who work outdoors encourages them to wear a sun block with a high sun protection factor, and to cover up even on a cloudy day.

Cigarette smoking has been established as the main risk factor for **lung cancer**. Warning signs are persistent cough, difficulty in breathing, chest pain or coughing up blood. **Lip cancer** is also associated with smoking. Symptoms are sore or cracked lips which don't heal, though these can be due to other causes also. If worried about any such symptoms, visit your GP.

Prostate cancer is at last receiving public attention as something that may endanger older men's lives. Early detection is critical to treatment and cure, and the test for prostate cancer is simple and painless. There are now high-profile public health campaigns urging men over 50 to go for testing for prostate cancer and this issue is being confronted openly.

The prostate is a walnut-sized gland that sits just under the bladder, and men are advised to go to their GP if there is a noticeable persistent change in bladder habits for no good reason. Difficulty with urinating doesn't necessarily mean the presence of prostate cancer, but should not be ignored. Watch out for more frequent urination, getting up more at night, discomfort or burning sensation when urinating.

Ageing is a risk factor for contracting prostate cancer and the disease is rare in younger men. So the campaign strongly advises men aged 50 and over to consult their GP about the merits of screening, which involves a physical examination and blood test to measure Prostate Specific Antigen (PSA). While a raised PSA does not necessarily mean the presence of cancer, it is a valuable early warning system, as prostate cancer can be treated very successfully if identified early. Population-based screening is not currently available in Ireland, and the jury is still out internationally as to whether such catchall action increases chances of cure.

Knowing how your testicles usually feel and checking regularly for anything unusual such as a lump, thickening or swelling can be a protection against **testicular cancer**.

Cancer of the bowel (colon and rectum) affects both sexes but is more common in men, typically aged 50–70. This cancer is linked to diet and is highest in western countries where people eat over-refined foods. Warning signs are changes in bowel habits which may include constipation or diarrhoea or blood in the bowel, and unexplained weight loss. To guard against bowel cancer eat plenty of wholemeal bread and cereals, fruits and fibrous vegetable such as potatoes, parsnips and turnips.

For a copy of "Manual for Men on Cancer Prevention and Early Detection", contact the Irish Cancer Society Helpline Freefone 1800-200700; Website: www.cancer.ie.

Male Menopause

Many men suffer a range of physical and psychological symptoms in middle age which if untreated can drag on. Symptoms can include fatigue, depression, loss of libido, impotence, insomnia, dry skin and anxiety attacks. Some professionals believe this mid-life crisis is due to the pressures of everyday life, sadness around unfulfilled ambitions and the prospect ahead of ageing.

If some of the above symptoms sound familiar, take action. If you can, talk to your partner, family or a close friend about how you feel. See your GP and discuss any lifestyle changes you feel you could make. Try to take more exercise, have a look at your diet. If necessary, visit a counsellor to talk through your symptoms and possible causes.

Hernia

A hernia is a weakness in the abdominal wall, and the most common type of hernia occurs when part of the intestine bulges through this causing a swelling which may be visible. Such hernias are common in the groin area, they can be both painful and dangerous and need surgical repair. Hernias often develop gradually. Warning symptoms include weakness, pain, swelling in the groin area when you cough or strain, digestion problems or constipation. Any hernia can become strangulated, i.e. when the blood circulation to the protruding part of the bowel is cut off, producing acute pain. Emergency action is then needed.

Impotence

Penile erectile dysfunction is the inability to achieve or maintain an erection for intercourse. This can become more common in middle or older age. Such permanent problems may have a physical root including taking certain drugs (particularly drugs for hypertension), some medical conditions including heart disease and diabetes. Your GP can discuss physical causes, change your medication if appropriate or refer you to a urologist. Psychological problems which can lead to temporary impotence include stress, depression and alcohol abuse. Treatment options include hormone medication, making some changes in lifestyle. Psychosexual counselling and more general personal or couple counselling is also an option.

Female Health Issues

Women on average live longer than men. This may be partly because they look after their physical health needs better. It is also accepted that women approach emotional problems in a way that allows them receive more support from family and friends, so lowering stress levels. Health difficulties for many women may revolve around their childbearing years, so older women can often enjoy better health than in earlier years. However, the loss of the hormones oestrogen and progesterone can remove some protective function and many women find the menopause itself both stressful and difficult.

Women and Heart Disease

While most women dread a diagnosis of breast cancer, they are ten times more likely to die from heart disease, the single leading cause of death among Irish women today. In 2001, 5,774 women died from diseases of the heart and circulatory system. The rate of heart disease in women is similar to that of men, but onset in women is on average ten years later than in their male counterparts.

The image of heart disease as a male phenomenon has harmed women in a number of ways. First, the ECG and/or stress test to accurately diagnose the disease is more geared to pick up male symptoms and may not identify female heart disease, or conversely may show up in female patients as either false positives or false negatives. Often more tests become necessary creating more delay in women getting treatment.

Symptoms can be more difficult to diagnose in women whose symptoms may be vague and diffuse, and may include side and back pain, nausea and vomiting, rather than more classic symptoms. The advice from the Irish Heart Foundation is for women to look at their lifestyle, understand their own level of risk for heart attack and stroke and to recognise the signs and symptoms including chest pain. If you are beginning to suffer from unexplained pains in chest, arms, back, if you experience nausea or shortness of breath, do consult your GP. It is particularly important to have regular health checks if there is a history of heart disease in the family.

Female Cancers

Irish women suffer the second highest rate of cancer death in the EU and many of the guidelines given above to lower risk factors for men apply also to women. **Skin cancer** affects one in 12 Irishwomen by age 75. While most skin cancers are curable, women should take particular care in the sun. There have been a number of public warnings against unsafe use of sunbeds. Reputable salons should have guidelines on maximum time exposure to the UV rays of the sunbed. You may also need to space your visits. If in doubt, get advice from your GP, or the Irish Cancer Society.

About 80 per cent of **breast cancers** occur in women over 50 years of age, and while treatment options are much more hopeful than they used to be, breast cancer still poses a major threat to health to those women who develop it in later life. Stopping smoking, taking exercise, keeping within a healthy weight range for height, eating a diet containing a good amount of fruit, vegetables and fibre and keeping stress at a manageable level can contribute to reducing risk levels of contracting breast cancer. But family history does play a part, making regular breast monitoring important.

Mammograms at recommended intervals — every two to three years — are also helpful. BreastCheck, the National Breast Screening Programme, is a free health service which aims to reduce deaths from breast cancer by finding and treating the disease early.

The programme offers free screening (a breast x-ray) every two years to women aged 50–64 living in Leinster and the Midlands, with ongoing plans for a national programme. Screening can help to detect small changes in the breast before any other signs or symptoms are noticeable. And the sooner these changes are found, the better. Programmes similar to Breast-Check have significantly reduced deaths from breast cancer in other countries. For further information, Freephone 1800 454555.

As a woman's chances of developing breast cancer may increase after age 65, organisations such as Age Action are campaigning for inclusion of over-64s. Meanwhile, it is important to be aware of any changes and seek treatment early. The Irish Cancer Society promote a five-point breast awareness code as follows:

1. *Know what is normal for you.* If you know what is normal for you, then you will find it easier to spot any changes.

2. *Know what changes to look out for.* Get into the habit of looking at your breasts from time to time. Stand in front of the mirror and look from different angles for changes.

3. *Look and feel for any changes.* Get into the habit of looking at and feeling your breasts from time to time. An easy way is with a soapy hand in the bath or shower.

4. *Talk to your GP straight away if you find any changes.* Most changes you find in your breasts will be completely benign (non-cancerous), but this doesn't mean you shouldn't see your doctor straight away.

5. *Act by attending routine screening if you are aged 50–64 years.* Screening can help to detect small changes in your breast before any other signs and symptoms are noticeable.

More information is available from the Society's Action Breast Cancer helpline on 1800 309040.

Cancer of the cervix, or neck of the womb, can be detected at a pre-cancerous stage and is completely curable if caught in time through regular smear tests. Principally a disease of sexu-

ally active women, it is the second commonest female cancer in
women under 35. However, older women too can contract cervical cancer and a cervical smear test every few years has
proved to be an effective way of detecting this disease. Regardless of the results of your most recent smear test, see your GP if
you notice unusual vaginal bleeding. When caught early,
treatment involves laser therapy or cryosurgery (freezing) to
excise the abnormal cells.

Cancer of the womb and **ovarian cancer** occur mainly after menopause and are more likely to affect women who have
never had children. Warning signs include unusual vaginal
bleeding and — with ovarian cancer — unexplained weight
loss, stomach swelling, a bloated feeling in the pelvis, and
change in bowel or bladder habits. Ovarian cancer can run in
families. If you have a mother, sister or daughter who developed ovarian or breast cancer at a young age, ask your doctor
about a health screening which involves blood tests and ultra-
sound scans. Treatment for both cancers involves surgery.

Menopause

Menopause means the end of the menses or monthly period.
Women usually reach menopause around age 50 and menopause lasts on average two to five years. It occurs when the
ovaries stop functioning, which leads to a drop in the levels of
the hormones oestrogen and progesterone. Many women sail
through this time, glad to say farewell to their periods and the
need for contraception. However, the decrease in hormone
levels can lead to physical and psychological symptoms such as
hot flushes, night sweats, dry vagina (which can contribute to
lowered libido), insomnia, depression, anxiety, sadness and
loss of concentration.

Women can help themselves through the menopause by
taking regular exercise, eating healthily, receiving help from
spouse, family and friends and keeping their plans and dreams

alive. Hormone replacement therapy (HRT) treats the symptoms by replacing the declining hormones. HRT also protects against osteoporosis. There are different types of HRT and you should discuss with your doctor which combination will suit you — if any. HRT may not be suitable for women with a history of thrombosis, or severe liver or kidney disease. There is ongoing debate about the suitability of HRT for women who have a history of breast cancer or heart disease, and these days, many professionals offer the least possible dose to deal with the physical symptoms.

HRT can cause side effects in some women, such as breast tenderness, weight gain, nausea, headache, mood swings and fluid retention. If HRT is not suitable for you, or you are reluctant to use it, ask your doctor for alternative ways of dealing with symptoms. These may include Vitamin E for hot flushes, non-hormonal medication to treat other symptoms and complementary alternatives such as homeopathy. Complementary medicines which seem to help with menopause are Evening Primrose Oil, Royal Jelly and Vitamin B6.

Osteoporosis

Osteo means bone and *porosis* refers to the holes that occur in bone when the structure breaks down. As stated earlier, the greatest risk factor for osteoporosis is being a woman. The disease is up to six times more common in women than in men, because women develop less bone mass than do men and because after menopause women lose the ability to retain bone calcium. It is calcium that keeps bones strong, dense and rigid. Osteoporosis can cause pain and places sufferers at risk of fracture through falls.

Preventive measures include taking regular weight-bearing exercises such as brisk walking or aerobics and taking enough calcium. Walking in the open air has another benefit as calcium cannot be absorbed without the help of Vitamin D. Our bodies manufacture the vitamin when the sun shines on the skin, but this absorption ability slows down with age. Vitamin D-enriched milk, cod liver oil and oily fish are good sources of the vitamin. The foods that supply calcium include dairy products, green leafy vegetables, tinned fish and red meat. Repeated hospital studies among older women found that drinking milk fortified with Vitamin D over six months significantly increased vitamin and calcium levels.

The Irish Osteoporosis Society provides information to the public and health professionals on all aspects of the disease and offers support to people with osteoporosis and everyone at risk from the disease. Contact the Irish Osteoporosis Society at 33 Pearse Street, Dublin 2; Tel: 01-6774267; Website: www.irishosteoporosis.ie

HEALTH ISSUES AS WE GROW OLDER (2): MENTAL AND EMOTIONAL HEALTH

Loneliness and social isolation can be a problem for some people as they get older. Loss of a spouse or partner, the scattering of grown-up children, shrinking of social networks because friends have either died or moved away, the loss of physical mobility; all can cause loneliness and contribute to emotional problems that may make us more vulnerable to physical illness.

It is extremely important to maintain friendships where you can. It may also mean reaching out for help if that is the only way you can stay in touch with what is going on around you. Accepting help from others can be hard, particularly if you are someone who has prided yourself on being independent throughout your life. The widow who won't let her neighbours give her a lift to Mass or cut her grass or do messages for her, although she would obviously benefit from such assistance, is depriving herself and frustrating others who may sincerely wish to help. Sometimes we refuse because to accept may make us somewhat dependent on others. But it needn't be all one way. If you receive from others, you may also be in a position to give — your time, your attention, some quality or skill you may have that others could benefit from.

Group activities aren't for everyone, but many locations have an active retirement association. (See Chapter 1, pages 44–8.) Most communities have day centres, bridge clubs, bowling groups, arts groups or other local groups that welcome new members and provide a network for people who may be otherwise alone in the day to day. To find out what's available in your area, contact the Citizens' Information Centre, ask someone in your parish, or look at notices in local shops.

If loneliness or depression are causing major problems in your daily life, seek medical advice as detailed below.

Depression and Other Mental Health Problems

First, mental health problems are not a normal part of the ageing process, although they may be common in old age. If you are experiencing feelings of hopelessness, if you are having trouble sleeping, if your appetite is poor and you find it hard to get out of bed in the morning, you may be depressed, or you may have another problem that will respond to therapy or medical treatment. Don't accept it as something you have to live with. Get help. Your mental health is as important as your physical health.

So although development of mental health problems is not a part and parcel of the ageing process, research suggests that there is a high incidence of depression in people over 65 and that under-diagnosis is a problem in Ireland. There is still mystery around mental health problems that inhibits us from identifying a problem in the early stages and doing something about it. This reflects a lack of awareness on our part about the risk factors and indicators of poor mental health, a lack of training of health professionals, and ageist assumptions about ageing and older people — that is, the belief that depression or, worse, dementia, is just a normal part of old age. It's an assumption we can make about ourselves and create a self-fulfilling prophecy.

It is natural to expect that people may experience considerable losses as they grow older. They may lose partners, friends and other family, and in some cases loss of control over their lives through illness or disability. This can cause sadness and depression. While feelings of shock, anger and sadness may be a normal reaction to such losses, some people may become stuck and need help to move on to the stage of acceptance of the situation. In these cases, help from a bereavement group like the Bethany Group (contactable through your local Church) or other parish or community support groups may be very helpful. Professional private counselling may also be helpful. To find out about your local Bethany Group, enquire at your parish office, community centre or Citizens' Information Centre. The service is free and confidential.

The national organisation Aware, which supports people in defeating depression, has 60 support groups countrywide. Their national helpline is 1890-303302. For information about the organisation, telephone 01-6617211.

If you are experiencing periods of disorientation, memory loss, or bad dreams bordering on hallucinations, seek medical help to determine the cause of the problem. There are many physical explanations for these symptoms, and they can often be treated with medication. Most importantly, doctors can help to reduce anxiety about the possibility that you may be suffering from other mental health problems, which may or may not be age-related. (See also "In Focus: Don't Let the Blues Hang Around" below.)

How to Access

- Mental health problems should be reported first to the GP who will either treat or refer on to specialist services. These may include consultant physician, consultant geriatrician services/consultant Psychiatry of Old Age Services — which offer assessment, diagnosis and treatment.

- Other options are day hospital service offering assessment, therapy and treatment, community psychiatric teams of medical and nursing personnel with therapists who monitor health and refer to community services, or generic day centre, respite care or other community services that may accept people with mental health problems.

- As well as Aware, other organisations such as Schizophrenia Ireland, and the Mental Health Association of Ireland provide advice, information, carer support and sometimes directly provide services for the person with mental health problems.

- Psychology services for older people are almost non-existent in the public sector, but as mentioned counselling, including bereavement counselling, may be available from church or community groups in your area or from the growing number of people offering private counselling services. The Irish Association of Counselling and Psychotherapy maintains and regulates standards for professional practice; members are listed in the Golden Pages. IACP, 8 Cumberland Street, Dun Laoghaire, County Dublin; Tel: 01-2300061; E-mail: iacp@irish-counselling.ie; Website: www.irish-counselling.ie

In Focus: Don't Let the Blues Hang Around[*]

Everyone gets the blues now and then; it's part of life. But depression is different. Clinical depression has been described as feeling there is a glass wall between you and the rest of the world. This wall, which imprisons you be-

---

[*] Reprinted and adapted with permission from the National Institute of Aging (US) — www.nia.hig.gov.

hind it, separates you from other people, and from the joys, pleasures and ordinary problems of life.

Being clinically depressed over a period of time is not a normal part of growing old. But it is a common problem, and medical help may be needed. For most people, depression will get better with treatment. Counselling, medicine, or other treatment methods can ease the pain of depression. You do not need to suffer.

There are many reasons why depression in older people is often missed or untreated. Depression can be tricky to recognise. Some signs of depression are more likely to be seen as crankiness or grumpiness. Confusion or attention problems caused by depression can sometimes look like Alzheimer's disease or other brain disorders. Mood changes and signs of depression can be caused by medicines older people may take for arthritis, high blood pressure or heart disease. It can be hard for a doctor to diagnose depression, but the good news is that people who are depressed often feel better with the right treatment.

What Causes Depression?

There is no one cause of depression. For some, a single event can bring on the illness. Depression often strikes people who felt fine but who suddenly find they are struggling with a death in the family or a serious illness. For some people, differences in brain chemistry can affect mood and cause depression. Sometimes those under a lot of stress, like caregivers, can feel depressed. Others become depressed for no clear reason.

People with serious illnesses such as cancer, diabetes, heart disease, stroke or Parkinson's disease sometimes become depressed. They are worried about how their illness will change their lives. They might be tired and not able to deal with something that makes them sad. Treatment for depression helps them manage symptoms of the disease, thus improving their quality of life.

Genetics can play a role. Studies show that depression may run in families. If either parent suffered from depression, there may be a higher risk of depression.

What to Look For

How do you know when you need help? After all, as you age, you may have to face problems that could cause anyone to feel low and sad. Perhaps you are dealing with the death of a loved one or friend. Maybe you are having a tough time getting used to retirement. After a period of grieving or feeling troubled, most older people do get back to their daily lives. But, if you are suffering from clinical depression and don't get help, you might not feel better for weeks, months, or even years.

Here is a list of the most common signs of depression. If these last for more than two weeks, see a doctor.

- *An "empty" feeling, ongoing sadness, and anxiety;*
- *Tiredness, lack of energy;*
- *Loss of interest or pleasure in everyday activities, including sex;*
- *Sleep problems, including trouble getting to sleep, very early morning waking, and sleeping too much;*
- *Eating more or less than usual;*
- *Crying too often or too much;*
- *Aches and pains that don't go away when treated;*
- *Difficulty focusing, remembering or making decisions;*
- *Feeling guilty, helpless, worthless, or hopeless;*
- *Being irritable;*
- *Thoughts of death or suicide; a suicide attempt.*

If you are a family member, friend, or health care provider of an older person, watch for clues. Sometimes depression can hide behind a smiling face. A depressed person who lives alone may briefly feel better when someone stops by to say hello or during a visit to the doctor. The symptoms may seem to go away. But, when someone is very depressed, they come right back.

Don't ignore the warning signs. If left untreated, serious depression can lead to suicide. Listen carefully if someone of any age complains about being depressed or says people don't care. That person may really be asking for help.

Getting Help

The first step is to accept that you or your family member needs help. Perhaps you are uncomfortable with the subject of mental illness. Or, you might feel that asking for help is a sign of weakness. You might be like many older people, their relatives, or friends, who believe that a depressed person can quickly "snap out of it" or that some people are too old to be helped. They are wrong.

A health care provider can help you. Once you decide to get medical advice, start with your GP. The doctor should check to see if your depression could be caused by a health problem or a medicine you are taking. After a complete examination, your doctor may suggest you talk to a counsellor, psychologist, psychiatrist or social worker. The special nature of depression in older people has led to a different medical specialty — geriatric psychiatry.

Don't avoid getting help because you are afraid of how much treatment might cost. Often, only short-term psychotherapy (talk therapy) is needed. It may be covered by health insurance. Also, some health board counselling is free and there are volunteer counselling services, offering sessions at free or reduced costs.

Be aware that you might have to explain your symptoms as fully as possible so that your GP can understand. If your doctor is unable or unwilling to take seriously your concerns about depression, you may want to talk to another health care provider who can help.

Treating Depression

Different therapies seem to work in different people. For instance, support groups can provide new coping skills or social support if you are dealing with a major life change. Improving your general health, taking some exercise, eating sensibly, may also improve your mental/emotional health.

Several kinds of "talk" therapies are useful as well. One method might help give you a more positive outlook on life. Always thinking about the sad things in your life or what you have lost might have led to your depression. Another way works to improve your relationships with others to give you more hope about your future.

Counselling or psychotherapy can help people deal with depression with or without medical intervention, depending on the cause. General counselling may also help clients understand the reasons for their depression, including coming to terms with early childhood events which may have given rise to feelings buried, denied or misunderstood. It has been also found that group counselling benefits older people enabling them to be more clear-minded and more able to express anger. A recent study carried out by researchers in University College, Cork, and Stanford University in the US used gestalt therapy to assist a group of older people express their angry feelings, thereby dissipating them, and allowing a more healthy relationship with themselves and others. It is often found that underneath feelings of depression and sadness there can be feelings of strong anger.

For more information about finding an accredited counsellor/therapist, contact the Irish Association for Counselling and Psychotherapy (see page 172).

Don't forget to let family and friends help you. Getting better takes time, but with support from others and treatment you will get a little better each day.

Antidepressant drugs can also help. These medications can improve your mood, sleep, appetite and concentration. There are several types of antidepressants available. Some of these can take up to 12 weeks before you are aware of real progress. Your doctor may want you to continue medications for six months or more after your symptoms disappear.

Some antidepressants can cause unwanted side effects, although newer medicines have fewer side effects. Any antidepressant should be used with great care to avoid this problem. Remember:

- *The doctor needs to know about all prescribed and over-the-counter medications, vitamins, or herbal supplements you are taking;*

- *The doctor should also be aware of any other physical problems you have;*

- *Be sure to take antidepressants in the proper dose and on the right schedule.*

Help from Family and Friends

If you are a family member or friend of someone who seems depressed, try to get that person to a health care provider for diagnosis and treatment. Then help your relative or friend to stay with the treatment plan. If needed, make appointments for the person or go along to the doctor, mental health specialist, or support group.

Be patient and understanding. Get your relative or friend to go on outings with you or to go back to an activity that he or she once enjoyed. Encourage the person to be active and busy, but not to take on too much at one time.

Preventing Depression

What can be done to lower the risk of depression? How can people cope? There are a few practical steps you can take. Try to prepare for major changes in life, such as retirement or moving from your home of many years. One way to do this is to keep and maintain friendships over the years. Try to find someone you feel you can talk to. Friends can help ease the loneliness if you lose a spouse/partner.

You can also develop a hobby. Hobbies can help keep your mind and body active. Stay in touch with family. Let them help you when you feel weighed down or very sad. If you are faced with a lot to do, try to break it up into smaller jobs that are more easily finished.

Being physically fit and eating a balanced diet may help avoid illness that can bring on disability or depression. Follow the doctor's directions on using medicines to lower the risk of developing depression as a side effect.

Dementia

Dementia, including Alzheimer's disease, is receiving increasing attention in Ireland. As we grow older, our chances of developing dementia increase, although dementia is not a normal part of ageing. Even for people over 80, less than 20 per cent will experience dementia-related problems. As has been said, some symptoms which might suggest dementia are actually manifestations of physical illnesses. So don't jump to conclusions without having a complete medical assessment.

The GP is the first stop for people who suspect they may have dementia, or for their carers. Psychiatrists of Old Age services, accessed through the GP, now established in every health board, deal with behaviour problems like aggression and wandering. Consultant geriatricians also treat people with dementia. Home help services, personal care services, day care services and other home care and community care services (see Chapter 7, pages 209–224) can all be of great support to people with dementia and their carers.

How to Access

- Community and home support services can be accessed through the GP, public health nurse or directly.

- Specialist medical services require a referral from your GP.

- The Alzheimer Society of Ireland offer advice and information regarding dementia itself as well as about services available to people with dementia and their carers. They have carer support groups around Ireland, day care services in some areas as well as more limited residential and home respite services. The Alzheimer Society of Ireland, 47 Northumberland Avenue, Dun Laoghaire, County Dublin; Tel: 01-2846616; National Helpline 1800 341341; E-mail www.info@alzheimer.ie; Website: www.alzheimer.ie

ALTERNATIVE THERAPY

Homeopathy, Chinese medicine, acupuncture, and other alternative therapies are gaining popularity and credibility and may have something to offer older people looking for ways to feel better and improve the quality of their lives. While the medical profession often dismisses the benefits of such therapies and point to the lack of scientific evidence to back up practitioners' claims, individuals may experience relief or reduction of symptoms following treatment and popular demand for alternatives to conventional drug treatment is growing. The qualifications of practitioners vary widely, and it is advisable to check out the background and training of a therapist before signing up. Personal recommendation from someone you know who has been helped is sometimes a good guide.

Caveat emptor or "buyer beware" is a good principle when approaching an alternative therapy, and people suffering from life-threatening diseases may be particularly vulnerable. While most complementary practitioners are committed and professional, an unregulated profession can lead to difficulties. There has been a recent controversy in Ireland where patients suffering from cancer were offered so-called light treatment which does not appear to have been helpful in many cases.

Also, the herb St John's Wort, used to treat depression and to alleviate the symptoms of seasonal affective disorder (SAD) was removed as an over-the-counter drug in recent years and is now available on prescription only. This was due to concerns by the Irish Medicines Board about possible side-effects when the herb was combined with other medication.

Today, in the absence of regulation, many complementary practitioners are forming their own associations where members need to have undergone a standard of training to register, and to comply with a code of conduct after joining. Enquiring whether such a body exists and whether the practitioner you wish to consult is a member of such a body may offer some guarantees of good practice.

How to Access

- Your GP may be able to refer you to clinics offering alternative therapies.

- The Golden Pages lists many practitioners under "Alternative and Complementary Medicine". Ask questions about the qualifications of the person offering the therapy and try to get a recommendation from a health professional or from someone who has experienced the particular therapy/technique which interests you.

MEDICAL SERVICES

Medical Card Patients

A medical card is effectively a statement that you have "full eligibility" for health services; that is, you are entitled to a range of services free of charge. It is a plastic card, similar to a bank or credit card, which is issued by the Health Board to anyone who has established that they are eligible.

The medical card is available now to everyone over age 70, although you must apply in order to get one, and for people under 70, eligibility is according to income. The medical card entitles the holder to free GP visits, approved medications, and public hospital services, as well as a range of personal social services (including community nursing and chiropody). You may also be entitled to have travelling expenses to outpatient hospital services and/or to day hospitals refunded by the health board, although the situation here is not uniform. You will be entitled to some dental and optical treatment free of charge, and to some hearing aid appliances as well as medical and surgical aids and appliances.

While everyone has a choice of GP, GPs may choose not to take medical card patients in favour of private patients or their list of such medical card holders may be full. Those who qualify for a medical card also have the option to attend their doctor as a private patient and pay for services as they go.

Are you Entitled to a Medical Card?

For those under 70, in order to qualify for a medical card you need to satisfy a means test, with special medical needs and exceptional expenses taken into account. If in doubt apply, especially if your income has been reduced since you stopped working. Means thresholds are updated each January, and you can find out what your threshold is by applying to your local health centre or health board. Your GP surgery may also have this information.

So the golden rule regarding a medical card as with all entitlements is, if in doubt, apply. Consider applying particularly if your income is somewhat above the guideline figure and you have heavy or ongoing medical expenses.

Drug Refund Scheme

The Drug Refund Scheme was introduced to offset the cost of medication for certain ongoing conditions. If you qualify, you pay a current maximum of €78 per month, irrespective of the real cost of medication. For further details, contact your GP, health centre or enquire at your local pharmacy.

General Practitioner Services

As we age we may become more and more dependent upon our GP to help us maintain our health. While an increasing number of GPs are forming group practices, many single-handed practices remain, with one GP and a receptionist. Group practices may provide diagnostic services, counselling or other services under one roof, and the practice nurse may be able to deal with many problems that previously required the doctor's full attention. Single-handed practices offer the advantage of continuity and many of us like to know we will see the same doctor each time we visit. GPs offer many services including advice and information; assessment, diagnosis and treatment of illness, and referral to specialist medical services where appropriate. Your local surgery also provides 'flu vaccinations; you may be charged an "administration fee" but the vaccine is provided free by the health boards.

New GP Developments

In many parts of Ireland, GP out-of-hours services have been developed on a co-op basis, ranging from evening and weekend services to 24-hour services. In some areas, GPs may have direct access to x-ray, physiotherapy, endoscopy and other hospital-based services, although coverage is patchy.

Some GPs participate in national and regional initiatives including:

- The ***Diabetes Shared Care Programme*** where the patient sees the GP, specialist dietician and specialist nurse (both supplied by the health boards) in the local surgery on a regular basis.

- ***Heartwatch***, a national programme for the secondary prevention of cardiovascular disease. The service is free to patients who have suffered a heart attack or who have undergone a heart bypass or angioplasty and it involves four visits to the GP per year. Participating doctors and their practice nurses get specialist training, and patients have access to clinical dietetics services and smoking cessation services from the health boards.

- The **Cardiac Diagnostics Programme** allows GPs to refer patients directly for cardiac tests, including stress tests, ECG, echo cardiograms, 24-hour blood pressure and ECG monitoring.

- In each health board, there is now a **Primary Care Implementation Project** which brings together GPs, nurses, physiotherapists, occupational therapists, social workers, psychologists and home helps into a Primary Care Team aimed at providing integrated care to patients of participating GPs. Benefits to patients will include easier access to a comprehensive range of services through development of a "one stop shop" which is linked to the GPs' surgeries and better communication and co-ordination between services.

In Focus: Talking with Your Doctor *

For some older people, the local GP is a point of social contact, someone who they have known for years and in whom they feel they can confide. For others, even contemplating a trip to the doctor can be a terrifying experience.

A basic plan can help you communicate better with your doctor, whether you are starting with a new doctor or continuing with the doctor you've seen for years. The following tips can help you and your doctor build a partnership.

Getting Ready for Your Appointment

- ***Be prepared: make a list of your concerns***. *Before going to the doctor, make a list of what you want to discuss. For example, are you having a new symptom you want to tell the doctor about? Did you want to get a flu shot? If you have more than a few items to dis-*

---

* Reprinted and adapted with permission from the National Institute of Aging (US) — www.nia.hig.gov.

*cuss, put them in order so you are sure to ask about
the most important ones first. Take along any information the doctor or staff may need such as insurance
cards, names of your other doctors or your medical records. Some doctors suggest you put all your prescription and over-the-counter medicines in a bag and bring
them with you. Others recommend bringing a list of
medications you take.*

- ***Make sure you can see and hear as well as possible***. *Many older people use glasses or need aids for
  hearing. Remember to bring your glasses. If you have a
  hearing aid, make sure it is working well, and wear it.
  Let the doctor and staff know if you have a hard time
  seeing or hearing. For example, you may want to say, "I
  have hearing difficulties. Could you speak slowly?"*

- ***Consider bringing a family member or friend***.
  *Sometimes it is helpful to bring a family member or
  close friend with you. Let them know in advance what
  you want from your visit. They can remind you what
  you planned to discuss with the doctor if you forget,
  can help you remember what the doctor said, or can
  take notes for you to review later.*

- ***Plan to update the doctor***. *Let your doctor know
  what has happened in your life since your last visit. If
  you have been treated in an accident and emergency
  department in hospital, tell the doctor right away.
  Mention any changes you have noticed in your appetite, weight, sleep or energy level. Also tell the doctor
  about any recent changes in the medication you take
  or the effect it has had on you.*

*Your doctor may ask you how your life is going. This
isn't being impolite or nosy. Information about what's
happening in your life may be useful medically. Let the
doctor know about any major changes or stresses in
your life, such as marital difficulties or the death of a
loved one. You don't have to go into detail; you may
just want to say something like, "My sister died since*

my last visit with you" or "I had to sell my home and
move in with my daughter".

Sharing Information with Your Doctor

- **Be honest**. It is tempting to say what you think the
  doctor wants to hear; for example, that you smoke less
  or eat a more balanced diet than you really do. The
  typical Irish response is "I'm fine"! While this is natural, it's not in your best interest. Your doctor can give
  you the best treatment only if you say what is really
  going on.

- **Stick to the point**. Although your doctor might like to
  talk with you at length, each patient is given a limited
  amount of time. Give a brief description of your symptoms, when they started, how often they happen, and
  if it is getting worse or better.

- **Ask questions**. Asking questions is key to getting
  what you want from the visit. If you don't ask questions, your doctor may think that you understand why
  he or she is sending you for a test or that you don't
  want more information. Ask questions when you don't
  know the meaning of a word or when instructions
  aren't clear (e.g. does taking medicine with food mean
  before, during, or after a meal?). You might say,
  "Could you explain that a little further?" It may help to
  repeat what you think the doctor means back in your
  own words and ask, "Is this correct?" If you are worried about cost, say so.

- **Share your point of view**. Your doctor can't read
  your mind. Say if you feel rushed, worried, or uncomfortable. Try to voice your feelings in a positive way.
  For example, "I'm really worried about this. I'd feel
  much better if we could talk about it a little more." If
  necessary, you can offer to return for a second visit to
  discuss your concerns.

Getting Information from Your Doctor and Other Health Professionals

- **Take notes**. It can be difficult to remember what the doctor says, so take along a note pad and pen and write down the main points, or ask the doctor to write them down for you. If you can't write while the doctor is talking to you, make notes in the waiting room after the visit. You could even bring a tape recorder along, and (with the doctor's permission) record what is said. Recording is especially helpful if you want to share the details of the visit with others.

- **Get written or recorded information**. Whenever possible, have the doctor or staff provide written advice and instructions. Ask if your doctor has or can recommend any brochures, cassette tapes, videotapes, computer software, libraries or websites about your health conditions or treatments. For example, if your doctor says that your blood pressure is high, he or she may give you brochures explaining what causes high blood pressure and what you can do about it. Another possible source of information is a family medical encyclopaedia, available from most bookshops. Organisations such as the Irish Heart Foundation or the Irish Cancer Society provide a lot of information for free.

- **Evaluate health information on the web**. Many people are turning to the internet to look for information about medical problems and health issues. You can log your condition into www.google.ie and click on "search" for more information in Ireland or abroad. However, not all such health information is of equal quality. How do you find websites that are accurate and reliable? The following questions may be useful to consider when you look at a health-related website. And always remember to talk with your doctor about what you learn.

    o   What are the author's credentials? Is the author affiliated with any major medical institutions?

o   *Who is reviewing the material? Make sure a medical advisory board exists to read the medical content before it is made available to the public.*

o   *Is the purpose and goal of the sponsoring organisation clearly stated?*

o   *Is there a way to contact the sponsor for more information or to verify information presented?*

o   *Are advertisements separate from content?*

o   *Because health information becomes outdated quickly, does the website post the source and date for the information?*

o   *If you have to register, are you clear how your personal information will be used?*

o   *When medical data are given, are sources cited for the information? For example, it's easy enough to say "two out of five doctors agree . . ." but where did that statistic come from?*

- **Remember that doctors don't know everything.** *Even the best doctor may be unable to answer some questions. There is still much we don't know about the human body, the ageing process and disease. Most doctors will help you find the information you need or refer you to a specialist. If a doctor regularly brushes off your questions or symptoms as simply part of ageing, think about looking for another doctor.*

- **Talk to other health care workers.** *Today, health care is a team effort. Other professionals, including the practice nurse, public health nurse, hospital social workers, your pharmacist and occupational or physiotherapists play an active role in your health care. These professionals may be able to take more time with you.*

Talking about your health means sharing information about how you feel both physically and emotionally.

Knowing how to describe your symptoms, discuss treatments, and talk with specialists will help you become a partner in your health care.

Preventing Disease and Disability

Until recently, preventing disease in older people received little attention. But things are changing. It's never too late to stop smoking, improve your diet or start exercising. Getting regular checkups and seeing other health professionals such as dentists and eye specialists help promote good health. Even people who have chronic diseases like arthritis or diabetes, can prevent further disability and, in some cases, control the progress of the disease.

If a certain disease or health condition runs in your family, ask your doctor if there are steps you can take to help prevent it. If you have a chronic condition, ask how you can manage it and if there are ways of preventing it from getting worse. If you want to discuss health and disease prevention with your doctor, say so when you make your next appointment. This lets the doctor plan to spend more time with you and prepare for the discussion.

Learning More about Medical Tests

Sometimes doctors need to do blood tests, x-rays, or other procedures to find out what is wrong or to learn more about your medical condition. Some tests, such as cervical smears, mammograms, glaucoma tests, and screening for prostate and colorectal cancer, should be done as appropriate to check for hidden medical problems.

Before having a medical test, ask your doctor to explain why it is important and what it will cost. Ask what kind of things you need to do to prepare for the test. For example, you may need to have an empty stomach, or be asked to provide a urine sample. If possible, read up about the test. Ask how you will be notified of the results of the test and how long they will take to come in.

When the results are ready, make sure the doctor tells you what they are and explains what they mean. You may want to ask your doctor for a written copy of the test results. If the test is done by a specialist, ask to have the results sent to your primary doctor. Here are some questions to ask your doctor about medical tests:

- *What steps does the test involve? How should I get ready?*

- *Are there any dangers or side effects?*

- *How will I find out the results? How long will it take to get the results?*

- *What will we know after the test?*

Discussing Your Diagnosis and What You Can Expect

If you understand your medical condition, you can help make better decisions about treatment. If you know what to expect, it may be easier for you to deal with the condition.

Ask the doctor to tell you the name of the condition and why he or she thinks you have it. Ask how it may affect your body, and how long it might last. Some medical problems never go away completely. They can't be cured, but they can be treated or managed. Write down what the doctor says to help you remember.

It is not unusual to be surprised or upset by hearing you have a new medical problem. Questions may occur to you later. When they do, make a note of them for your next appointment.

Sometimes the doctor may want you to talk with other health professionals who can help you understand how to manage your condition. If you have the chance to work with other health professionals, take advantage of it. Also, find out how you can reach them if you have questions later. Here are some other questions to ask your doctor about the diagnosis:

- *What may have caused this condition? Will it be permanent?*

- *How is this condition treated or managed? What will be the long-term effects on my life?*

- *How can I learn more about it?*

Talking about Treatments

Although some medical conditions do not require treatment, most can be helped by medicine, surgery, changes in daily habits, or a combination of these. You will benefit most from treatment when you know what is happening and are involved in making decisions. If your doctor suggests a treatment, be sure you understand what it will and won't do and what it involves. Have the doctor give you directions in writing, and feel free to ask questions.

If your doctor suggests a treatment that makes you uncomfortable, ask if there are other treatments that might work. For example, if the doctor recommends medicine for your blood pressure, you may want to ask if you can try lowering it through diet and exercise first. The doctor can work with you to develop a treatment plan that meets your needs. Here are some other questions to ask your doctor about treatment:

- *Are there any risks associated with the treatment?*

- *How soon should treatment start? How long will it last?*

- *Are there other treatments available?*

- *How much will the treatment cost? Will insurance cover it?*

Making the Most of Medications

Your doctor may prescribe a drug for your condition. Make sure you know the name of the drug and understand why it has been prescribed for you. Have your doctor and/or pharmacist explain the written instructions on the medication. Make notes about any other special instructions such as foods or drinks you should avoid. If you are taking other medications, make sure your doctor knows, so he or she can prevent harmful drug interactions. You can also

*buy an encyclopaedia of drugs, which might help you un-
derstand more about the drugs you are prescribed.*

*Sometimes medicines affect older people differently
than younger people. Let the doctor know if your medicine
doesn't seem to be working or if it is causing problems. It
is best not to stop taking the medicine on your own. If you
do stop taking your medicine, let your doctor's office know
as soon as you can. If another doctor (e.g. a specialist)
prescribes a medication for you, you might like to check it
out with your GP. Also call to check with your doctor's office before taking any over-the-counter medications. You
may find it helpful to keep a chart of all the medicines you
take and when you take them.*

*The pharmacist is also a good source of information
about your medicines. In addition to answering questions
and helping you select over-the-counter medications, the
pharmacist keeps records of all the prescriptions you get
filled at that chemist. Because your pharmacist keeps
these records, it is helpful to use a regular chemist. At
your request, the pharmacist can fill your prescriptions in
easy-to-open containers and may be able to provide large-
print prescription labels.*

*If you have questions about your prescription or how
you should take it, ask your doctor or pharmacist. For example:*

- *Are there any side effects? What should I pay attention
  to?*

- *What should I do if I miss a dose?*

- *Are there foods, drugs, or activities I should avoid
  while taking this medicine?*

Seeing Specialists

*Your doctor may send you to a specialist for further
evaluation. You also may request to see one yourself.*

*Usually, your specialist will send information about
further diagnosis or treatment to your GP. This allows
your doctor to keep track of your medical care. You also*

should let your GP know at your next visit about any treatments or medications the specialist recommended.

A visit to the specialist may be short. Often, the specialist already has seen your medical records or test results and is familiar with your case. If you are unclear about what the specialist tells you, ask questions:

- *What is your diagnosis?*

- *Could you explain what the condition is and how it might affect me?*

- *What treatment do you recommend? How soon do I need to begin the new treatment?*

- *If the condition is painful, what can be done to prevent or manage the pain?*

- *Will you discuss my care with my primary doctor?*

Surgery

In some cases, surgery may be the best treatment for your condition. If so, your doctor will refer you to a surgeon. Knowing more about the operation will help you make an informed decision. It will also help you get ready for the surgery, which, in turn, makes for a better recovery. Ask the surgeon to explain what will be done during the operation and what reading material or videotapes you can look at before the operation. Find out if you will have to stay overnight in the hospital to have the surgery, or if it can be done on an outpatient basis. Questions to ask your surgeon about surgery:

- *What is the success rate of the operation? How many of these operations have you done successfully?*

- *What problems can occur with this surgery? What kind of pain and discomfort can I expect?*

- *Will I have to stay in the hospital overnight? How long is recovery expected to take? What does it involve?*

HOSPITALS AND NURSING HOMES

Admission to acute hospital care, including psychiatric hospital services is through Accident and Emergency Departments or by GP referral to a consultant physician.

Access to hospital outpatient services, including physio-therapy, phlebotomy (blood testing), day hospital assessments or other is usually by referral from a consultant physician.

Public Care in Hospitals and Nursing Homes

Access to public long-stay beds in hospitals or other residential care facilities that are funded by the health board or the Department of Health and Children is usually controlled by consultant geriatricians who assess people's need for long-term care and list them for public beds. Charges for services are usually calculated as a proportion of the person's income and savings and assets are not considered. Because of the scarcity of public beds in the context of increasing demand, as well as the relatively low cost of care in public hospitals and units, people are not as discriminating as they would be if they were paying for private care. You are advised to either visit the hospital/unit where a bed is offered or get a friend or relative to do so before agreeing to take up the bed. The standard of care in public hospitals and units is usually very high, although the standard of the physical facilities may be less than desirable.

There are some very high-standard, modern community nursing units which have been built in every health board in recent years, but demand far outstrips supply of beds in these units and applicants could spend a very long time on waiting lists for these facilities. Even in the new purpose-built units, single rooms are a rarity and residents may be expected to share a room with up to three other people. In some cases, the resident may have to give the nursing home access to their pension book, and their weekly allowance, in whole or in part, is taken as part payment for nursing home services.

Private Hospitals

Private hospital care is also available for those who can afford to pay, and many people take out health insurance to give themselves that option. While the medical standards of public and private may be similar (and most hospital consultants have public and private patients), paying for health care can put you ahead in the queue. Also, the level of comfort and privacy will be greater in a private hospital.

Private Nursing Homes

Private nursing homes take applications for beds and make their own decisions about who will be admitted, based on the level of need, services available, level of family contact/interest. Remember that, in the nature of the business, there will be turnover of beds in nursing homes. While there may be a waiting list today, beds will eventually free up and many of those on the waiting list may have found other places to go in the meantime. If you are really interested, keep in touch with the home and remind them that you are still interested. In the Dublin area, there is now a surplus of private nursing home beds, according to the nursing home providers' representative organisations, so you can afford to shop around and indeed, are advised to do so, given that charges range from €500 per week in some rural areas to over €1,000 per week, mainly in city areas.

Private Nursing Home Subvention

Older people now have the right to apply for funding to assist them in purchasing private nursing home care. The application process involves an assessment of income and assets (savings, property and other investments). Applicants with income over a certain threshold might be eligible but at a lower rate than someone with a lower income. The application process also involves an assessment of the applicant's level of dependency, usually by a consultant geriatrician or other doctor, and it must be demonstrated that the person needs 24-hour care.

Current payment levels range from €114 per week to €190 per week but some health boards (including all Dublin area boards) pay enhanced subventions on a discretionary basis, depending on individual circumstances.

To apply, contact the Private Nursing Home unit in your area health board and ask for a nursing home subvention application. People may apply from home or from hospital; in the latter case there are usually medical social workers to guide you and your family through the process. If you are at home, you must make an appointment to get a geriatrician's assessment in order to have the dependency assessment part of the form filled out. You may be asked to provide additional financial details such as bank statements as part of the means test.

Going into a Nursing Home

It can be very difficult to acknowledge that a person can no longer care for themselves and thus needs to go into a residential care setting: difficult for the person and sometimes even more difficult for family members or other carers. We all value our independence and like to have some control over our lives. The thought of relinquishing it by going into an institution is so unthinkable that we often deal with the possibility through absolute denial. Giving up our own home/space involves giving up part of who we are. Too often, we leave behind personal belongings, personal space, and the company of friends and family when we move into long-term care. A move into a hospital or nursing home involves living with complete strangers in a place where routine may be dictated by nursing needs rather than the needs of the individuals who live there. Individuals lose control over things as basic as bathing or going to the toilet, the choice of what to wear each day, what and when to eat.

It makes sense that, before someone moves permanently into residential care, some preparation be done to enable them to deal with it better. This should include discussion about the possible alternatives. Professional help to deal with this, in the form of counselling/social work/psychologist services, may be helpful in some situations. A visit to nursing homes in the area may help the older person to feel involved in decision-making and also familiarise them with the place where they may be spending the remainder of their lives.

"Eileen", who is a wonderful, independent, intelligent woman in her mid-80s, became increasingly frail over a period of two years and was no longer safe at home on her own. On the occasion of her third hospitalisation, her adult children talked with her about what she wanted to do. They openly discussed nursing home care as one possibility. They took their mother to visit local nursing homes and asked the questions that were important to them. They also took their mother back to her own home on a visit. It was she who eventually suggested that a nursing home was the best solution to her need for long-term care. Eileen was directly involved then in discussion around the disposition of her belongings and in preparations for the sale of the house. She also chose the nursing home. In this way, she retained control over what was happening to her. It didn't change the fact that she was unhappy about giving up her home and moving into a nursing home, but it did help to prepare her for this major change in her life. It also helped her children to deal with this very difficult situation. Eileen was fortunate that she and her family had the financial resources that gave her a choice of nursing home options. But allowing the older person to participate in discussions about their own future and involving her/him in the preparations around the move does not depend on finances and should be considered wherever possible.

Ideally, decisions about nursing homes should not be made in a hurry. If the older person is in an acute hospital, however, there may be extreme pressure exerted on family members to move the patient out immediately. Obviously, research done earlier rather than at crisis point is the best approach. But don't be bullied into making a hasty decision about long-term care.

When looking for a nursing home for yourself or a loved one, the following questions should be asked before any contracts are signed:

- What services are included in the charges quoted in the brochure or by the manager?

- What services are *not* included in the quoted charges? How much do additional services, like laundry, cost?

- What is the professional training of the staff? What is the staff–resident ratio?

- Is the home registered and inspected by the health board?

- What are the visiting hours? Are visitors welcome? Are children welcome?

- Can residents continue to use their own GPs?

- Can/do residents have access to the garden or other outdoor facilities?

- Can residents bring some of their own possessions into the home?

- Will residents have an opportunity to choose what they wear?

- What happens if a resident becomes ill and has to be admitted to hospital? Will their bed be held for them? Must residents continue to pay the full amount while in hospital?

- What activities are offered in the home and with what frequency? (Look for specific details and try to get an idea of what the schedule is like each day of the week.)

- Do residents have a choice of activities?

- Is physiotherapy or physical activity available?

- How often may residents take a bath or shower?

- Does the resident have any choice of food? Ask to see a sample menu.

- Must residents all get up at the same time and go to bed at the same time? If so, what time?

- Are any activities provided by outside staff/volunteers who come into the home?

- Is there a space where residents may be alone with visitors?

- Are pets allowed in the home?

- Does the home have public liability insurance?

This list is not exhaustive and there may be other things you wish to find out before committing yourself to a particular nursing home.

Some private nursing homes are developing apartment complexes adjacent to the main house. The idea is that people move into these apartments where they can live independently, but as they get older and if they need it, they can easily access the services available next door, including meals, nursing, day care and other support services. It is worth considering this and the above options when there is time to plan for the future, rather than just responding to a crisis at a stage in our lives when it is too late to do anything except move into full-time care.

HOSPICE CARE

Hospice care is the total, active care of patient and family at that stage of very serious illness when the focus has shifted from treatment aimed at cure to ensuring quality of life. The hospice philosophy takes as its starting point that death and dying is a natural and integral part of life, and in considering the leaving of life, gives equal value to the patient's physical, emotional, social and spiritual well-being. The hospice movement also realises that life-threatening illness affects not just the person who is ill, but also family and friends. Hospice care, therefore, seeks to include significant others in the scope of its support, both during the patient's illness and after death occurs.

While there are still only a small (but growing) number of hospices in Ireland, the hospice philosophy is having a positive influence in how patients with serious illness and their families are now viewed. It has led, for example, to the development of palliative care services in many hospitals. The word palliative means "alleviate without cure" and palliative care medicine seeks to offer physical relief from pain as well as psychological and emotional support for patient and family.

It has also encouraged the development of respite services where patients can come into care for short periods. The movement has been helped by advances in medicine which mean that symptom control can be more successful. Palliative care nurses who visit patients at home are a case in point. They are part-funded by the Irish Cancer Society (ICS) and trained in palliative care and cancer symptom control. Employed by a health board or hospice group, and based in hospital or health centre, these nurses work in patients' homes and in the hospital. Some thousands of families now avail of home palliative care each year. The ICS also provides a night nursing service as a support for home care teams. The night nurse is free of charge to families who might have difficulty paying her, although the service is not means-tested. For more information about availability in your area, contact your GP.

The headquarters of the Irish Hospice Foundation can be reached at Morrison Chambers, 32 Nassau St., Dublin 2; Tel: 01-67993189, E-mail: info@hospice-foundation.ie; Website: www.hospice-foundation.ie

HEALTH INSURANCE

Almost one in two of the Irish population now buy health insurance. However, premiums for such insurance have increased dramatically in recent years, and according to an EU report Ireland is the least competitive country in the EU for private health insurance. So, the entry of a new company into the health market in late 2004 could be good news. The long established VHI and the later entrant BUPA have now been joined by Vivas. The enhanced competition could mean better value for individuals and families, but the entry of a third insurer may also add to consumer confusion, as people try to work out which health plan offers them the best cover at the best price.

Health insurance is used to pay for private care in hospital or from various health professionals in hospitals or in their practices. There seems to be no way round the confusion other than getting as much information as you can and doing your homework as thoroughly as possible, taking the various plans offered by each company and seeing which one fits best with your needs at this time and for the projected future.

For more information contact:

- VHI, VHI House, Lower Abbey Street, Dublin 1; Tel: Call-Save 1850 444444. There are regional offices countrywide. E-mail: info@vhi.ie; Website: www.vhi.ie

- BUPA Ireland, Mill Island, Fermoy, County Cork; Tel: LoCall 1890 700890; E-mail: betteroff@bupaireland.ie; Website: www.bupaireland.ie

- Vivas Health, Paramont Court, Corrig Road, Sandyford Industrial Estate, Dublin 18; Tel: LoCall 1860 717717; E-mail: support@vivashealth.ie; Website: www.vivashealth.ie

Chapter 7

HOME SWEET HOME: LIVING INDEPENDENTLY

Janet Convery and Anne Dempsey

"Where we love is home — home that our feet may leave, but not our hearts." — Oliver Wendell Holmes

STAYING PUT

While society's image is that most older people will spend their last years in a nursing home, this picture is not accurate. Most older people live on in the family home, remaining a part of the community, with only a minority — indeed, only 5 per cent in 2001 according to the National Council on Ageing and Older People — moving into nursing home care.

To ensure that you can remain at home for as long as possible, it is a good idea to assess your living arrangements now, and make or plan any changes that may be needed. There may be steps you can take to make your life at home more comfortable, safer and more burglar-proof. In no particular order, you may want to consider some of the following:

- *Insulate*: improving attic insulation and installing double glazing will make your home cosier and save on heating bills.

- *Convert*: creating a ground floor toilet may be worthwhile.

- *Change*: while there's nothing like a real coal fire, it can be messy, laborious and time-consuming. Installing a coal-effect gas fire gives you heat at the click of a switch.

- *Outfit*: changing from soft low chairs to higher firmer chairs will give more support and accessibility.

- *Replace* faulty equipment such as kettles, toasters, heaters which may become dangerous and ineffective.

- *Landscape* the garden by replacing all or some of the grass with low maintenance gravel, stones or pebbles.

What else might need doing? Simple changes like converting to a duvet will make bed-making much easier. Installing fitted carpets will improve comfort, deaden noise and lessen risk of falls. Changing to a smaller fridge/freezer or cooker may also be a good idea if you are now catering for a smaller number. In assessing your own home, you may see more changes you can make now which will benefit you later.

 ## SAFETY AT HOME

Hundreds of people die at home every year as a result of accidents. Most common are falls, followed by accidental poisoning by drugs, fire or gas-related injuries or fatalities. Here is a safety checklist:

- Make sure doorways, halls, landings and stairs are well lit and free from clutter.

- Have a safety chain and peep-hole fitted to your front door.

- Apply non-slip backing to rugs, make sure rugs and carpets don't have tears or wrinkles.

- Get someone in to fit extra plugs if needed rather than overloading sockets with extra wires which could trip you up or become a fire hazard.

- Also check that plugs are properly wired and fused.

- Buy a fireguard if using an open fire, and don't dry clothes too close to an open fire.

- Buy a fire extinguisher, keep it serviced and know how to use it.

- Keep medicines clearly labelled, bring unfinished prescription pills back to the chemist.

- If taking a variety of medication, invest in a weekly pill dispenser with sections for morning, noon, evening and night. Fill at the beginning of each week.

- Assemble a small first aid kit — get your GP's advice on what it should contain for your particular situation — and keep it in a safe, accessible place.

- Have a list of emergency numbers beside the phone.

- Have a telephone installed beside your bed, or buy a cordless or mobile phone and bring it into the bedroom at night.

- Keep a torch near the bed in case of emergency

- Consider the following safety extras:

  o bathroom — grip rails by the bath and toilet, rubber mat or plastic non-slip strips in the bath

  o stairs — handrail on wall side

  o kitchen — fire blanket near at hand in case of fire.

Many older couples invest in a burglar alarm both for the practical and emotional protection it gives. These days some alarms are linked to the service provider and your local Garda station. For advice on alarm systems, contact the Crime Prevention Unit, Harcourt Square, Dublin 2; Tel: 01-6663362.

The National Safety Council has information and advice on all aspects of public, personal and domestic safety, including information on fire prevention. Contact them at 4 Northbrook Road, Ranelagh, Dublin 4; Tel: 01-4963422; LoCall: 1890-200844; E-mail: info@nsc.ie; Website: www.nsc.ie

Personal Alarms

Medical alarms, also referred to as medical alert devices, are most commonly small personal emergency alarms monitored 24 hours per day. Small enough to be worn as pendants, watches or key chains, they allow for people to live independently, while offering security and quick emergency response at the wearer's fingertips.

Personal medical alarms work anywhere there is a phone line. They are activated by pressing their emergency button. Once activated the signal will alert the emergency console to contact either the medical alarm company's 24-hour emergency response centre or will call family contacts in the order they have been programmed into the medical alert system. Wearing a medical alert pendant can offer a sense of security to an older person living alone and to family members. Discuss the installation of the device with your GP and public health nurse, and you will also receive helpful information about personal medical alarms from Age Action Ireland.

In Focus: Keeping you and your Home Safe from Crime[*]

Lucy is worried. She's lived in the old neighbourhood for 50 years but things seem to be changing. Last week her friend Rose was walking to the store when a young man ran by and pulled her purse right off her shoulder. Two weeks ago Joe, the man upstairs, said he put his grocery

---

[*] Reprinted and adapted with permission from the National Institute of Aging (US) — www.nia.hig.gov.

bags on the kerb while waiting for the bus, and before he knew it, someone had picked up his bags and run off. Lucy feels sad to think she might have to move. She wonders, is anywhere safe for older people anymore?

Older people and their families worry about crime. Though older people are less likely to be victims of crime than teenagers and young adults, the number of crimes against older people is hard to ignore. It is often highly publicised. Each year, hundreds of older people are victims of crime.

Older people are often targets for robbery, purse snatching, pocket picking, car theft or home repair scams. They are more likely than younger people to face attackers who are strangers. During a crime, an older person is more likely to be seriously hurt than someone who is younger.

But, even though there are risks, don't let a fear of crime stop you from enjoying life. Be careful and be aware of your surroundings. The following is a general overview of some of the areas of most concern to older people. These are common-sense tips that can help fight crime and protect your safety.

Stay Safe

There are a lot of things you can do to keep you, your money, and your property safe. These do's and don'ts give you a place to start:

Be Safe at Home

- Do try to make sure that your locks, doors, and windows are strong and cannot be broken easily. A good alarm system can help (see page 203 above).

- Do mark valuable property by engraving an identification number, such as your driver's licence number, on it.

- Do make a list of expensive belongings — you might even take pictures of the most valuable items. Store these details in a safe place.

- *Don't open your door before looking through the peep-hole or a safe window to see who's there. Ask any stranger to show proof that he or she is who they claim to be. Remember, you don't have to open the door if you feel uneasy.*

- *Don't keep large amounts of money in the house.*

- *Do get to know your neighbours — join a Neighbour-hood Watch Programme.*

Be Street Smart

- *Do try to stay alert. Walk with a friend. Stay away from unsafe places like dark car parks or lanes. If you drive, don't open your door or roll down your window for strangers. Park in well-lit areas.*

- *Do have your pension or social welfare cheques sent right to the bank for direct deposit. Try not to have a regular banking routine.*

- *Don't carry a lot of cash. Put your wallet, money or credit cards in an inside pocket. Carry your purse close to your body.*

- *Do not resist a robber; hand over your cash right away.*

- *Don't keep your chequebook and credit cards together. A thief who steals both could use the card to forge your signature on cheques.*

Fight Fraud

Older people may be victims of fraud, such as con games, insurance scams, home repair scams, and/or telephone and internet scams. Even trusted friends or family members can steal an older person's money or property. Trust what you feel. The following tips may help.

Be Smart with Your Money

- *Don't be afraid to hang up the phone on telephone salespeople. Remember, you can always say no to any* offer. You aren't being impolite — you are taking care of yourself!

- Don't give any personal information, including your credit card number or bank account, over the phone unless you have made the phone call. Be careful when returning a sales call.

- Don't take money from your bank account if a stranger tells you to. In one common swindle, a thief pretends to be a bank employee and asks you to take out money to "test" a bank teller. Banks do not check their employees this way.

- Don't be fooled by deals that are "too good to be true". They usually are. Beware of deals that ask for a lot of money up front and promise you success.

- Do be on guard about hiring people that come door-to-door looking for home repair work. They may over-charge you. You should try to check their references. Ask for two or three quotes from separate companies, or call the consumer advice office for advice on prices. Always spell out the details of the work you want done in writing. Never pay for the whole job in advance.

Avoid Identity Theft

How can someone steal your identity? Use of your name, PPS number, or credit card number without your go-ahead is called identity theft and it's a serious crime.

Protect Yourself:

- Do keep information about your bank accounts private — keep all new and cancelled cheques in a safe place; report any stolen cheques right away; carefully look at your monthly bank account statement.

- Do shred everything that has personal information about you written on it, especially anything with credit card numbers.

- *Do be very careful when buying things online. Websites without security may not protect your credit card or bank account information. Look for information saying that a website has a "secure server" before buying anything online. Preferably also buy from a well-known, reliable company.*

Elder Abuse — It's a Crime

Elder abuse can happen anywhere — at home by family or friends or in a nursing home by professional caregivers. In addition to physical harm, abuse can include taking financial advantage, neglecting, sexually abusing, or abandoning an older person. Most abuse involves verbal threats or hurtful words. It only rarely involves weapons or causes physical injury beyond minor cuts and bruises.

If someone you know is being abused, or if you need help, remember, you can help yourself and others by reporting the crimes to the Garda when they happen. If you do not report a crime because of embarrassment or fear, the criminal is allowed to continue.

However, you need to ensure that your whistle-blowing will not place the victim in further danger. It may be necessary, therefore, to ensure that the older person is in a place of safety or that they have someone they can rely on to protect them should charges of abuse become public.

If you suspect an older person is being abused but they deny it, due perhaps to fear of further retribution, you may need to gain their trust and assure them of protection — which you can deliver — before you go public with the information. A lawyer can assist you in any legal action that needs to be taken.

If an older person has been sexually abused, and particularly if charges are to be brought, you may be helped by contacting the Rape Crisis Centre (RCC). RCC counsellors can give you advice and information on the various options open to you, and they can offer counselling as appropriate to the person who has been attacked. Rape Cri-

sis Centre, 70 Leeson Street, Dublin 2; Tel: 01-6614911, Freephone 1800 778888.

If you have been hurt, go to a doctor as soon as possible. Even though you may not see anything wrong, there may be a possibility of internal damage.

WITH A LITTLE HELP FROM YOUR FRIENDS

As time goes on, some older people may need practical and emotional support to stay at home. They get by with a little help their friends, as The Beatles famously said — not forgetting family members who are often crucially involved. Sometimes it *is* just a little help — needing a lift to the shops, or asking the shop to deliver. Today, most supermarkets have a home delivery service and you can also order from them online. Sometimes it may be more, such as medical back-up, help with housework, or more personal help such as assistance in taking a bath or a shower. Very few people will need a day nurse in order to stay living at home.

So what's available? Below we list a range of services to help people manage the routine tasks of living.

Home Help Services

If you need help with ordinary household jobs or with your own personal care (including bathing, hair-washing, and dressing) in the short- or longer-term, home help services may be available to you directly from your local health board or from voluntary organisations funded by the health boards.

In recent years, the people who have been targeted by health board-funded home help services include disabled older people who live alone and have no social networks, older people recently discharged from hospital, those with a terminal illness, and people unable to stay at home without the provision of home care and personal care services. Those who may need only a periodic cleaning service would not be given priority for "public" services.

How to Access

Referral may be from the GP, public health nurse, other health professional or directly from the client, a neighbour or family member to local health centre.

Outside Dublin, there is rarely a charge imposed for home help services. In the Dublin area, charging practices vary. Some services are offered free while other organisations levy charges which may depend on income.

The home help organiser or public health nurse may be able to give information about private home help services available locally. Or consult bulletin boards in local shops, local newspapers or newsletters.

Meals on Wheels

Nutritious food is basic to good health, and voluntary meals on wheels services provide home-delivered meals to older people who experience difficulties in doing their own shopping and/or preparing their own meals.

How to Access

These services are widely available and can be accessed directly or through the public health nurse or other health professional at your local health centre. There may be a small charge for the service.

Personal Care Services (bathing/showering)

This service is obviously important to personal dignity and it can be difficult for family carers to do personal care of their loved one, through lack of training or because of problems around the intimacy of such work.

In the Dublin area, these services can be provided by the public health nursing department who employ home care attendants for this purpose. In other parts of the country, the service may be part of the home help service offered by the health board. As in the case of home help, there may also be private agencies or individuals offering this kind of service in your area.

How to Access

Referral to public health nurse department from GP, health professional or family member. Or direct referral to home help organisation. Contact local health centre for details.

There is no charge for services provided directly by the health boards. Those who can afford it may be advised to buy personal care services from private agencies which may be listed in your local telephone directory, in local newsletters, or who may be known to the home help organiser or public health nurse.

Rehabilitation Services Delivered in Your Own Home

If you have been in hospital and need help to get back to your normal routine, or need a "top-up" of services to get you active again, there may be rehabilitation teams in your health board available to help you do this.

Rehabilitation services are variously organised in each health board region. In Dublin, District Care Units are nurse-led community rehabilitation teams dedicated to providing short-term (six to eight weeks) intensive rehabilitation services tailored to your particular needs.

How to Access

Referrals from GPs, Medical Social Workers, public health nurses, family members or others to the Public Health Nursing Department in each Community Care area.

Enhanced Home Services

A range of enhanced home services funded by the health boards is currently being developed around the country. There are two main programmes. The Home Care Grant Scheme has been devised for older people at risk of having to go into nursing home, allowing families to apply for funding for services to keep the older person living at home. The second scheme is geared to helping an older person to return home from hospital rather than staying in hospital inappropriately or having to move from hospital to nursing home. Again its focus is on funding families to pay for additional services at home. There is growing enthusiasm for such schemes round the country. For more information about the programmes, see "In Focus: Staying at Home with Support" below.

How to Access

Applicants for the Home Care Grant are assessed usually by the public health nurse on level of physical dependency, income and savings. Contact your local health board to see if a Home Care Grant Scheme is available and to get details regarding the application process. If it is not available, ask why.

Families interested in the home from hospital support programme should approach the public health nursing department in the local health board to see if such services are available. Referrals are via public health nurse, GP, Medical Social Worker or other health professional. A formal application process may be in place.

In Focus: Staying at Home with Support: Home Care Grants*

Like all good ideas, the emerging enhanced home support programmes are simple, obvious and long overdue. While government-stated policy on services for older people accepts that the best place for most of them is at home, funding for services has been strongly biased towards their leaving it.

This is partly because nursing home beds have traditionally been identified as the key response to the needs of older people with funding for such beds growing in spite of spiralling costs and quality concerns about kind of care provided in some residential care settings.

So while families may apply for state subvention towards private nursing home costs, there has been no funding entitlement to maintain a relative in the family home. The effect, says Janet Convery, Director of Services for Older People at the East Coast Area Health Board, has been a "perverse incentive", encouraging people into nursing homes and hospitals, although repeated policy documents recommend that they be supported to remain in the community for as long as possible. According to the Health and Social Services for Older People Report commissioned by the National Council on Ageing and Older People in 2001, in terms of long-term care, most older people expressed the preference of staying at home with local service support. But, until relatively recently, that has not been a real option. Now, since 2002, a number of schemes are progressively being put in place, some on a pilot basis, to keep older people happily and safely at home and to facilitate a speedier and sustained good quality return home from hospital.

---

* Adapted with kind permission from *The Irish Times*.

The Home Care Grant Project was initiated in August 2002 in the East Coast Area Health Board. Open to people aged 65 and over who want to stay at home but can't manage it, a growing number of families avail of a grant to purchase much-needed services. Each applicant's dependency needs and financial circumstances are individually assessed and it is often found that families are already contributing hugely both financially and emotionally. The current average maximum payment is between €150 and €190 per week, which buys up to 20 hours of extra care and service, though some families apply for and receive greater funding.

There is a flexible approach. So, for example, an older person receiving intermittent respite — that is, spending regular periods in residential care — may still qualify for the time they are at home and avail of community services, such as meals on wheels, home help, day care. The scheme is making a positive difference in people's lives.

In 1986 Alison's parents came to live with her in a newly built apartment attached to her family home, and for many years they were completely independent. But gradually their dependency increased and the family paid for a day carer, with Alison taking over on her return from work. Weekend care was shared between family members. Even so, they were at full stretch and wondered how they could continue. Today, the family still pays the daily carer but the extra Home Care funding has allowed them to buy early evening and some weekend cover.

The second type of programme facilitates a patient's return home from hospital. Care packages usually provide a combination of intensive home help/personal care services with occupational therapy, physiotherapy and/or nursing services at home. The effort is on development of a package which is responsive to the individual's needs, while the availability of extra home help/personal care services in the evening and at weekends is often critical to the project's success.

In the North Western Health Board (NWHB), this scheme is called the Choice programme. Serving Sligo, Lei-

trim and Donegal with a population of 29,395 over-65s, the NWHB has been a pioneer in overturning a blinkered view of older people. "We knew we needed to change from being service-driven to needs-led," says Bridget Smith, Service Manager for Older People. In other words, to see services designed for people rather than the other way around. In 2001 they surveyed a cross-section of older urban and rural residents about their needs. "At the very top of the list, 97 per cent wanted to stay at home. Out of this was born an approach to care based on the wishes and needs of older people."

Under the Choice programme successful applicants receive payments of up to €150 a week to buy services to enable an older relative stay at home. Typical services would include helping an older person to get up, and leaving the house comfortable and warm and a meal prepared, or giving a carer some time off by sitting with the older person, or providing day cover to a carer who works full time.

Some people need a relatively short visit three times a day each day, others may need fewer, longer visits. The family sources carers themselves, which can be a friend or neighbour, and pay for it out of the grant. The public health nurse ensures that the person has the necessary skills and continues to monitor the scheme. Already they have seen positive results in reduced admissions to hospital, but stress that caring for older people is more than cutting down on hospital bed use and ideally involves a collaborative approach with older people and their families.

In the East Coast Area Health Board area, the home from hospital programme called Slán Abhaile (Safe Home) aims to reduce the time an older person spends in hospital and/or avoid the need to move to a nursing home by providing services at home. A total of €1.3 million was allocated to the scheme in its first year. Again, the health board is responding to each family's individual needs. For example, one recipient needs only 14 hours extra care a week, because he spends two days a week at a day centre. Another recipient needs someone to take her to church *on Sunday. A third person needs a number of short visits each day, totalling 30 hours a week. A somewhat similar project, Home First, is available in parts of North Dublin administered by the Northern Area Health Board.*

Public Health Nurse as Resource

If you have questions about a health problem, need information about services that might be available to you, nursing assistance to deal with medication or other issues, the public health nurse is the most important source of information and advice for older people and their carers. Public health nurses can be of help to people with chronic and complex problems, including those who are terminally ill; they also visit older people who have been discharged from hospital and so can be critical to a successful convalescence or rehabilitation after a serious illness. They are the single biggest source of referral to home help services and also make referrals for day care/day centre services, meals on wheels, respite care and other available community services. They are a fund of useful, practical information for older people and their carers and are usually very approachable. They also deliver valuable services like wound treatment, catheter care and medication monitoring.

There are specialist incontinence nurses in each health board who provide information and advice to individuals and families and also to nursing homes.

How to Access

Contact your local health centre or telephone your health board headquarters to find out which public health nurse is working in your geographic area.

Palliative Care Services

All health boards now employ palliative care nurses in the community to give assistance to people with terminal illness and their families. Services include regular home visits, personal care, information and advice. People living in areas lucky enough to have a hospice may also be able to access in-patient respite and long-term care as well as outpatient pain control and home nursing services. Referrals to hospice services are through the public health nurses, GP, consultant physician or by application to the local hospice. (See also "Hospice Care" in Chapter 6, page 198–9.)

How to Access

Contact the Public Health Nursing department in your local health board.

CARING FOR OTHERS

There are tens of thousands of people over age 50 caring for other people in their families throughout Ireland. It should go without saying that carers need to look after their own health and do whatever is necessary to minimise stress in their lives. But it's often easier said than done.

Your role as a carer may begin when a spouse, parent or family member is discharged from hospital or becomes progressively more frail.

Home from Hospital

If someone is being discharged from hospital into your care, you should find out in advance:

- How much care will they need?
- Who can give it in the family?

- How do you access professional care in the community? Ask the hospital social worker, your GP or public health nurse what services are available.

- What medicines are needed and how often?

- Do the medicines or treatments have any side effects?

- What is the ongoing relationship with the hospital? Are there future outpatient appointments?

- Who can you turn to in an emergency?

- Will the home need adaptation?

These are just some of the questions families may have.

Staying in Touch

Keeping the channels of communication open between yourself and the person you are caring for will help you both:

- Include the other in conversations, plans and arrangements as much as possible rather than making arbitrary decisions; this will make them feel less dependent and you less isolated.

- For their sake and yours, do only as much as they need, for as long as you need. Without being cruel or irresponsible, encourage the other person to help themselves too. You may need some guidance from GP or public health nurse on this.

- If the person you're caring for is developing hearing problems, speak audibly and while facing them. Would a hearing aid help?

- If the person has developed speech difficulties, as in post-stroke, for example, try to be patient and devise ways together of communicating (as well as checking out speech therapy support; see Chapter 6, pages 158–159).

Safe Handling

You may need to learn how to handle someone safely to avoid injuring them or yourself:

- When moving someone, straighten your back and bend your knees where necessary.

- Reassure and tell the person what you are planning to do in terms of movement.

- Allow them to help you if possible.

- Use moving and handling equipment only when it has been fully demonstrated to you.

- Do not move someone if you have a back injury; try to organise some regular support.

Easing the Pressure

When someone has to spend long periods in bed or chair they may be vulnerable to developing pressure sores. Taking the following precautions can help:

- Encourage the person to move regularly and to get out of bed as much as possible, again explaining why this will help them.

- Make sure bedding is not irritating the skin. Change bedding regularly.

- Avoid if possible the person lying in wet or damp conditions.

- Don't drag the person up or down the bed.

- Apply to health board for any special bed materials or ointments that may be available.

Caring for the Carer

To fulfil your role as carer you need to be able to maintain your own physical and emotional health as best you can:

- Don't turn into a martyr — this helps nobody.

- Find out, if things are getting tough, what extra services might be available, including respite care.

- Enlist the help of your adult children, siblings, other family and friends. Get into the habit of asking and be specific about what you need and when.

- Try to have some regular time out for yourself.

- Give yourself credit for what you do well.

- Don't be ashamed if you feel angry, or sad, or hurt or deprived. This can be a very normal response to what you're going through. Would some counselling help?

- Realise that the person you're caring for may be going through the same emotions. If you can talk to each other about how you both feel, so much the better.

How to Access

The situation regarding availability of services or supports to carers in Ireland is complex and confusing. There is rarely one point of contact which will give you the information you may require to find out what supports are available to you or to your loved one, and this can be extremely frustrating. However, here are some ideas of what is available.

- **Health board support services to carers** typically include advice and information, home help services, and personal care services to complement services undertaken by the carer. Access by contacting the public health nurse.

- **Day care:** this provides services to the person being cared for but also gives relief to carers. The health boards offer day care in a variety of settings, including purpose-built premises, day centres in hospitals and residential units. Health board day care is usually nurse-led and services may include: chiropody, physiotherapy, hairdressing, personal care, monitoring of medications, a hot dinner and social activities. To access, contact the public health nurse.

  Voluntary organisations also provide day care in many communities, offering services similar to those of health board day centres with programmes focusing more on social activities than on care services.

- **Home respite** involves a worker coming into the home to allow the carer to go out for a short period of time. This service may be offered by the health board or by a voluntary organisation, and again the public health nurse is a good point of contact.

- **Away from home respite.** This usually involves placement of the person being cared for in a residential setting for one to two weeks. The health boards offer respite care in their own public units/hospitals and sometimes in private nursing homes. Access by contacting the public health nurse or other health professional in your local health board.

  Respite may also be offered by a voluntary organisation like the Alzheimer Society, Western Alzheimer's Society, the MS Society or other. Contact the organisations directly. Respite care can also be purchased from private nursing homes directly on a weekly basis; charges vary. In the Dublin area, they can be as high as €800 a week or higher, depending on the nursing home or the amount of care required.

- **Intermittent respite** has developed in response to the complexity of needs of many older people now living in the community and in acknowledgement of the tremendous pressure on carers, many of whom are elderly themselves. Intermittent respite involves placement of the person being cared for in residential care on a regular basis, e.g. one week per month or two weeks out of every four or six weeks. This service is usually offered in health board long-stay hospitals or units and may also be available in voluntary hospital settings. Access is through the consultant geriatrician or the GP or public health nurse. Charges vary within and between health boards and some services are free.

Advocacy

The Carers Association of Ireland is dedicated to lobbying for improvements in public support for carers and also to provision of carer support services including: advice and information, home respite, carer training and carer support groups. Its client group are the carers for whom services are developed.

Helpful Contacts in Summary

- The Carers Association, Dublin HQ, 26 Wesley Road, Rathgar, Dublin 6, Tel: 01-4904554; Freefone; 1800 24 07 24; E-mail carersrathgar@eircom.net. National Office: The Carers Association, Prior's Orchard, John's Quay, Kilkenny; Tel: 056-7721424; E-mail: carerskilkenny@eircom.net; Website: www.carersireland.com. There are branches in Clondalkin, Blanchardstown and Harold's Cross in Dublin and elsewhere around the country.

- Public health nurses have already been mentioned as good sources of information.

- Most GP practices will have information useful to carers.

- Citizens Information Centres have a national network of centres working to give information on a range of health-related topics, including the needs of carers.

- A number of voluntary organisations include carers' needs in their brief.

- Organisations representing older people such as Age Action, the National Council on Ageing and Older People, the Irish Association of Older People and the Senior Citizens Parliament may offer advice and information that is useful to people caring for others (see Appendix 2).

Occupational Therapy

Following accidents, acute illnesses like a stroke or heart attack, or the progression of an existing condition like arthritis, Parkinson's disease or osteoporosis, it may become difficult for people to continue to carry out normal activities at home. The occupational therapist's focus is on developing strategies to compensate for any such difficulties. Part of the therapist's professional brief is to advise people how best to organise and re-arrange the home to cope with a disability. They can also advise on suggested strategies, aids and appliances (including handrails, bath seats and rails, kitchen aids, walking aids, wheelchairs, utensils and so on) to make everyday life easier.

While equipment like stair-rails, bath rails, raised toilet seats or walking sticks are available on the open market, it is advisable to consult a professional where possible to get advice on correct positioning/height/fit to get maximum benefit.

Occupational therapists are practical and resourceful people and the available technology is improving all the time. They also do the assessments required for the Disabled Person's Grants which give funding for home adaptation (such as the provision of a ground floor bathroom) in the case of serious disability. Occupational therapy services may help you manage and enjoy life more.

How to Access

- **Hospital services (in-patient):** referral from consultant physician.

- **Day hospital:** referral from consultant physician.

- **Community services:** referral from GPs, public health nurses, medical social workers, consultant physicians and other health physicians or directly from clients and/or their families.

- **Disabled Person's Grants:** application to local authority in your area.

- **Private occupational therapy services** may be found in the Golden Pages or through the Association of Occupational Therapists at 29 Gardiner Place, Dublin 1.

MOVING HOUSE

Even with improvements and safety precautions, the family home may become less manageable as you grow older, depending on its size and accommodation. Here are some questions to ask while you still have time to make any changes or repairs needed:

- Has it become too big? Are you using only a few rooms now that the family has gone?

- What kind of repair is it in? If you can no longer manage to maintain yourself, can you afford to pay for services?

- How about the garden? Can you manage to look after it, or has it, too, become a bit of a chore?

- What about location? How accessible are you to shops, buses, doctor, church, post office?

Moving house and leaving a long-term family home can be a very big wrench, but moving in time to a smaller more manageable home can make good sense as retirement approaches, particularly if you can stay in the same area where you have friends and are known. Also, moving from a larger to a smaller home could provide a nest egg which could buy extra comforts and enjoyment in retirement.

Other options include local authority housing, sheltered housing, retirement development schemes where people live independently in a development with a caretaker and a doctor and other services on call. Other schemes offer more facilities such as communal dining areas. Your local authority will have information on such schemes in your area, and there are a growing number of community voluntary organisations who become involved in solving the housing needs for older people. A typical example in rural Ireland is Mulrany Day Centre Housing Ltd., which created St Brendan's Village overlooking the Atlantic in Mulrany, County Mayo.

There are a number of voluntary national organisations also working in this field. The charity Respond is a housing organisation with thousands of properties to rent, which responds to requests from individuals and families countrywide. The many schemes are connected or affiliated to the umbrella body, the Irish Council for Social Housing, which should be the first point of contact for anyone needing help to find affordable accommodation, or information on sheltered schemes.

Threshold Housing Advice and Research Centre, founded in 1978, is a not-for-profit organisation whose aim is to secure a right to housing, particularly for households experiencing the problems of poverty and exclusion. Threshold has a number of advice centres, advocates on behalf of clients and advises clients on various housing options. Social housing options include local authority housing, shared ownership, and joining a housing association as a means towards achieving one's own home.

Threshold campaigns for suitable housing delivered on a rights-base approach, analyses existing problems, seeks innovative approaches and solutions through quality research, and works in collaboration with other peer organisations.

- Threshold, 21 Stoneybatter, Dublin 7; Advice Office Tel: 01-6786096; Head Office, 01-6786310; Access Housing Unit Tel: 01-6786094; E-mail: advice@threshold.ie; Website: www.threshold.ie

- Respond Housing Association, High Park, Gracepark Road, Drumcondra, Dublin 9; Tel: 01-8572020; E-mail: info@respond.ie; Website: www.respond.ie

- Irish Council for Social Housing, 50 Merrion Square, Dublin 2; Tel: 01-6618334, info@icsh.ie; Website: www.isch.ie.

Other families come to individual arrangements. Some families pool resources and buy a large home which provides independent living accommodation for older parents. The granny flat idea is still alive and kicking; many people are now getting planning permission to build in their gardens, and there is a growing trend for married sons or daughters with family to move into the main house while the parents or parent build a smaller house in the grounds.

Chapter 8

LIFE AND DEATH

Anne Dempsey

*"He left a paper sealed up, wherein were found three
articles as his last will: 'I owe much; I have nothing;
I give the rest to the poor'."* — François Rabelais

One thing we all have in common is that, eventually, we all die.
The idea of preparing for one's own death, or for the death of a
spouse/partner, is not one we like to face up to until we have to.
Chapter 10 looks at the spiritual side of old age, death and bereavement. But it is also useful to take a practical approach to
matters that will inevitably arise when you or your loved ones
die — and it is best to look at these practical matters while you
are still healthy enough to do so without undue distress.

PUTTING YOUR FINANCIAL AFFAIRS IN ORDER

Financial matters flow more smoothly after a death when a couple have a joint bank account. This allows the surviving spouse/
partner to have access to money as needed. Failing this, being
open with each other regarding financial details and/or keeping
a check list of relevant documentation will minimise problems at
an already stressful time. These are more likely to be avoided
when people keep a check list of relevant documentation, with

all papers, including the will, in a safe secure place known to the family. Some families keep the will with their solicitor.

The Institute of Chartered Accountants in Ireland has produced a check list called "The Personal Affairs Check List" to help you keep track. This provides headings for everything from family valuables to share certificates to credit cards, including insurance policies, investment certificates, house deeds, mortgage details and bank accounts. Filling in the relevant details will leave a full record of your affairs, facilitating executors and family alike. The Check List is available free from the Institute at CA House, 87/89 Pembroke Road, Dublin 4, Tel: 01-6377200; E-mail: ca@icai.ie. The document can also be downloaded from www.icai.ie/documents/Personal%20Affairs.pdf.

*In Focus: The Paper Trail**

Eighty-year-old Louise who lives alone fell in her kitchen one evening and broke her hip. She spent one week in the hospital. After two months in an assisted living facility, she returned to her apartment. Her son lives one hundred miles away, but was able to take over paying her bills and handling the insurance questions.

Seventy-five-year-old Ben has been married for 50 years and has always handled all the family matters involving money. He suffered a stroke one afternoon. He cannot walk; his speech is very slurred. His wife is feeling overwhelmed. She is worried about his health and has no idea what bills need to be paid and when. She doesn't even know where Ben's life insurance policy is.

---

* Reprinted and adapted with permission from the National Institute of Aging (US) — www.nia.hig.gov.

Plan for the Future

No one plans on being sick or disabled. The difference between these two families is that Louise had gathered together all papers related to her spending, savings, investments and insurance in her desk. She had told her son where they were. In addition, she put her son's name on her bank account, so that he could write cheques for her. She also gave her health insurer permission to discuss her insurance claims with her son.

Ben was always prompt and accurate paying the couple's bills, but never showed his wife how to do it. His life insurance policy is in a box in the wardrobe, along with the car title and deed to the house. Information on their savings is in a drawer in his dresser. He knows where they are, but no one else does.

We all need to prepare for the uncertainties of the future. Making decisions and arrangements before they are needed simplifies caring for an older person or planning for your own old age. Complete personal and financial records will have most of the details you need to plan for any changes that might come up in the years ahead — such as retirement, a move or a death in the family.

The first step is to assemble as much information as possible about you and your income and savings. A spouse or partner, trusted family member or friend should know where you keep all these records and documents, including your will. It is not necessary to tell them what's in your will, but they should know where you keep it. If you don't have a relative or friend you trust, ask a lawyer to help. One day, you might need help managing your money or be unable to make important decisions. Helping you is much simpler for the person who steps in if all your papers are already in order.

Everyone's life history is different. So are their income, savings, debts and investments. Still, some general suggestions may help you begin to organise your important papers. You might wish to set up a file, assemble everything in a desk or dresser drawer, or just list the informa-

tion and the location of documents in a notebook. Alternatively, use "The Personal Affairs Check List" from the Institute of Chartered Accountants (see page 228). Review these records regularly to make sure they are up-to-date.

Personal Records

Personal records are facts, dates, names, and documents that are part of your history. A personal records file should include the following information:

- *Full legal name*

- *PPS number (formerly PRSI number)*

- *VAT number (if relevant)*

- *Legal address*

- *Date and place of birth*

- *Names and addresses of spouse and children (or location of death certificate if any are deceased)*

- *Location of "living will" or other advance directive if one exists*

- *Location of birth certificate and certificates of marriage or divorce*

- *Location of property deeds, vehicle registrations, etc.*

- *List of employers and dates of employment*

- *Education records*

- *Religious affiliation, name of church and names of clergy*

- *Memberships in organisations and awards received*

- *Names and addresses of close friends, relatives, doctors, and lawyers or financial advisers*

- *Requests, preferences or prearrangements for burial.*

Financial Records

A financial records file is a place to list information about insurance policies, bank accounts, deeds, investments, and other valuables. Here are some suggestions:

- *Sources of income and assets (pension funds, interest income, etc.)*

- *Personal Public Service (PPS) number and life, health, property and other insurance information, with policy numbers and agents' names*

- *Investment income (stocks, shares, bonds, property, and any brokers' names and addresses)*

- *Bank account names and numbers (e.g. deposit, savings, credit card, post office, building societies and credit union) Remember to keep PIN numbers and other such security codes secret and separate from bank cards*

- *Location of safe deposit boxes*

- *Copy of most recent P60*

- *Liabilities: what is owed to whom and when payments are due*

- *Mortgages and debts — how and when paid*

- *Property taxes*

- *Location of all personal items such as jewellery or family treasures.*

Sometimes the person helping you may have questions about a bill or a health insurance claim. They may need to talk directly with the people involved. The law does not allow this without your consent. You might consider giving permission to your health insurance company, a credit card company, or your bank, for example, to discuss your affairs with this person. You can give signed permission in writing for such questions to be asked on your behalf.

Legal Documents

When people think of legal documents associated with ageing, they probably think of a will. Another way to do that is a trust. Sometimes, before death, older people need other legal documents. Perhaps, someone has to take over an older person's affairs. A standard power of attorney or a durable power of attorney can give one person the right to handle personal or financial matters for another. A standard power of attorney is not useful, however, if the person being cared for cannot make their own decisions. A durable power of attorney may be a better choice because it is effective even if a person becomes unable to make decisions for themselves.

MAKING A WILL

Making a will allows you to dispose of your possessions as you wish rather than having the state divide them according to the Succession Act of 1965. If you do not make a will, or it is invalid, you are described as dying intestate. Under the Succession Act, your spouse, if any, will automatically receive your entire estate, or if you have children, your spouse will receive two-thirds of your estate, and your children will divide the remaining one-third between them.

This may sound like a fair arrangement, but many families have circumstances, needs and wishes unmet by the state response. There may, for example, be a sibling who by reason of disability or illness needs more care than the others. Someone who has been married more than once may wish to make particular arrangements for an ex-spouse and for stepchildren if any. You may wish to leave something to a charity, or money or possessions to an old friend or much loved grandchild. You may also wish to set up a trust which would release monies at certain regular periods or cover specific events in the lives of individuals or organisations you care about. Discuss this with your solicitor.

Secondly, by making a will you may choose your executors, preferably more than one, who will look after your affairs after your death. Thirdly, by taking legal advice at the time of making your will, you may be able to legally mitigate the amount of inheritance tax payable by your family.

A valid will must be in writing and demonstrably the wishes of someone of sound mind. A set format is not necessary, though many wills open by stating the testator's (will-maker's) name and address, followed by a sentence stating that this is their last will and testament, revoking all earlier wills and codicils (additions to wills). The executors would be named, and their addresses given.

The will then sets out how the property should be disposed of. You may also set out how property not effectively dealt with in the will should be allocated, in the form of specific gifts and bequests, for example.

The will should then be dated and signed by the testator. This signature must take place in the presence of two witnesses, who in turn sign the will, with their address, in the presence of the testator. The evidence of this mutual witnessing should be expressed in a sentence such as "signed by the testator in our presence, and signed by us in the presence of the testator". While this attestation clause is not a formal requirement, it is recommended, as it indicates that proceedings have been validly executed and can head off future problems should the will, for example, be contested.

There is one very important point to remember when making a will and that is that your executor, the person(s) who will carry out your wishes after your death, cannot be a witness. Lack of understanding of this point can be cause of invalid wills and cause much distress.

So while you may make a will yourself, it will be obvious from the potential pitfalls involved that getting professional help from a solicitor is probably a safer idea. Solicitors will also help with phraseology; that is, they can set out your wishes in precise and legal language to ensure that what you want to happen will happen without any ambiguity.

ADVANCE DIRECTIVES AND LIVING WILLS

An **advance directive** is a formal written document which tells your doctor what kind of care you would like to have if you become unable to make decisions.

In the UK, for example, provided that a patient is deemed competent to give consent to a treatment (by understanding the nature and purpose of the treatment) then any refusal of consent is valid. The doctors must accept their desire not to be treated. If you arrive in hospital conscious, coherent and able to make your wishes heard, then enforcing this should not be a problem. Otherwise, you will be deemed incompetent to give consent and the doctors will, in general, be free to act in what they see as your best interests, as well as consulting your next-of-kin. In that case, the only way to ensure that you get the sort of care you would want should you be unable to make medical decisions is by having made an advance directive.

Advance directives can take many forms. A good one describes the sort of treatment you would want for different levels of illness, such as if you have a critical illness, a terminal illness, permanent unconsciousness or dementia. Advance directives usually tell the doctors that you don't want certain types of treatment if you are ill (such as to be put on a ventilator if you are in a coma).

A **living will** is one type of an advance directive. It only comes into effect when you are terminally ill (which generally is held to mean that you have less than six months to live). A living will does not let you select someone to make decisions for you (you would need to appoint a proxy in this case).

Unfortunately, according to the Irish government's website, there is no legislation in Ireland in relation to advance directives or living wills. A person wishing to draw up an advance directive or living will should get legal advice, including any instructions for the care of dependants.

FUNERALS

Making it Personal

In Ireland 28,500 people die each year, and for the families concerned, each is probably a deeply emotional rite of passage. A well-managed funeral will hopefully offer solace by allowing you pay tribute to the person who has died in the way you want to. The range of services offered by funeral companies includes offering support and advice, laying out the body, looking after the grave and discussing the rite of service. Most families still opt for burial, with about 2,000 cremations each year.

Many people would like the funeral service to express their feelings and capture the spirit of the person who has died. This has led to an increasing number of funerals becoming quite personalised. Recently some dioceses have issued guidelines on what is acceptable for a Catholic funeral mass — and what is not. The aim is to preserve the integrity of the liturgy, while being sensitive to family needs — a difficult balancing act.

However, family involvement can happen in various ways. In many religious ceremonies, different family members can participate in the readings, in general prayers and where gifts are taken to the altar. Many funerals now have the option for a member of the family or a friend can speak about the person who has died in a meaningful way.

Non-religious ceremonies have more leeway. The Humanist Association publishes an Irish guide to non-religious ceremonies, and helps families by providing someone to officiate at the funeral or by mentoring a family member in how to do it. The ceremony tends to take place in the crematorium or in the funeral director's, may begin with music, favourite songs, poetry, a short biography of the person's life, followed by tributes from family and friends, including a quiet time for reflection, allowing those present with a religious faith to say a silent prayer if they wish. *The Humanist Philosophy: Irish Guide to Non-Religious Ceremonies* is available at a cost of €15 from the Humanist Association, 47 Sugarloaf Crescent, Bray, County Wicklow, Tel: 01-2869870; or directly from www.irish-humanist.org.

Burial

The burial site often remains a most significant place in the life of a family after someone has died and its ornamentation can be part of the grieving process. Victorians had a fashion for porcelain angels and cherubs on the grave. These days people bring flowers, photographs, mementos, plaques, windmills and — a new trend — solar lights which softly illuminate the grave at night. Some newer cemeteries today are lawn cemeteries, characterised by an open plan where graves are marked by a headstone, but no longer defined by a kerbed perimeter delineating the area in front of the headstone. A woodland cemetery is another option, not yet available in Ireland. The idea, which originated in Scandinavia, takes an area and creates a natural burial ground with no statutory or visible memorials whatever. Headstones are replaced by bulbs and flower seeds scattered over the grave, with small trees planted nearby. There are plans to create a woodland cemetery, initially for cremated remains, on one to two acres in Dublin, planting the area with birch, oak and bluebells. There is something appealing about the dead being transfigured literally into new bud and new life each year.

Funeral Costs

It may seem inappropriate to think about money when someone dies. But a funeral can be expensive. You will be served best if you opt for the services of a member company of the Irish Association of Funeral Directors. (IAFD, Meghan House, Riverside Way, Middleton, County Cork; Tel: 021-4631155.)

IAFD members are obliged by their code of practice to give you an estimate from the start. The minimum cost of a Dublin funeral is approximately €2,750 with the average as much as €5,000. Rural funerals generally cost less.

Grave purchase and opening costs are set by county councils and local authorities and buying a plot in Dublin can cost €1,000. Coffins range from about €400 up to €2,500 for a casket. Then there are additional fees called disbursements paid out to third parties on your behalf, and these cover opening the grave, church offerings and death notices. Optional extras include flowers, music, personalised rite of service, limousines, and catering. Funeral directors will try to work to your budget. If, for example, they have the leeway to organise the ceremony at a time that suits them, they can pass on any savings to the client.

Cremation

Cremation is a personal choice. Some people choose it because they feel they don't want to give the family the trouble of visiting a grave, while others would opt for burial precisely because they want a grave as a final resting place which can be visited. An increasing number now decide on cremation for environmental and ecological reasons, realising that land is a finite resource. Cremation is accepted by all Christian churches. Some choose cremation for economic reasons. It costs much less than burial because you are not paying for a plot or headstone, however if ashes are interred in the family plot, grave opening fees are incurred. Generally speaking, a cremation costs around €320, and the standard urn to receive the ashes costs €55.

Someone choosing cremation should make their wishes known in advance by mentioning it to their solicitor, doctor, a family member, friend or in their will. After a death, the paper work is detailed and precise, extra layers of caution needed because after a cremation there can be no possibility of exhumation.

Cemeteries are increasingly acknowledging the growth in cremations. Glasnevin Cemetery in Dublin has a Columbarium, a special wall with niches in which to place the urn. The ashes can also be buried in Glasnevin's Garden of Remembrance or buried in the existing family plot. Many families take the ashes for private disposal, and scatter them, or some of them, over a favourite place or places of significance to the deceased.

Prepaid Funerals

It is possible to pay for your funeral many years in advance. Established in Ireland in 2001, Golden Charter (Ireland) Limited operates a national prepaid funeral service in co-operation with local funeral directors countrywide. The costs range from €2,565 to €5,100 based on the style of the funeral and range of services requested.

The money goes into a trust fund which pays out when the time comes, as the fund will have accumulated to cover standard current costs, including plot purchase and grave opening, public notices and church fees. There may be a shortfall if families want extra services and disbursements, but every effort is made to tailor each plan in advance to client needs and it is unusual that families have to pay any extra.

There is growing interest in prepaid funerals, and they have their place. You may not want the family to be burdened with funeral costs, or you may be concerned about rising costs. For some people making the prepaid decision can be therapeutic and take a weight off their mind.

Further information about Golden Charter is available from local funeral directors. The company can also be contacted at Golden Charter Ireland Ltd., PO Box 9480, Freepost Dublin 2; Tel: 1800-777800.

Bereavement Grant

A once-off payment to help towards funeral expenses, based on PRSI contributions, is payable on the death of an insured person/contributory pensioner, their spouse, or certain dependents. Contact Social Welfare Services Office, Government Buildings, Ballinalee Road, Longford; Tel: 043-45211/01-7043487.

Last Wishes

A growing number of people now carry an organ donor card. If you carry a donor card, make sure this is known to your executor or close family members before your death. If you are interested in carrying a donor card and what it entails, contact the Irish Kidney Association, Block 43a, Donor House, Parkwest, Dublin 12, Tel: 01-6689788; E-mail: info@ika.ie; Website: www.ika.ie.

Chapter 5

CHANGING AGEIST ATTITUDES?

Paul Murray

> Nobody grows old merely by living a number of years.
> We grow old by deserting our ideals. Years may wrinkle
> the skin, but to give up enthusiasm wrinkles the soul.
> —Samuel Ullman

ATTITUDE

It's all about attitude. Change attitudes, and the legislation changes too, yet you could add change the legislation and the attitude changes. If anything it more obvious in social policy over the last ten years it is that attitude, particularly public attitude, and others legislators to bring in new laws and that law, however, inculcates ideas and plays a new way of thinking; it must also be said that England, attitudes and discussions have led us to set us a way in the well of established attitudes and law. Some way. We owe much thanks to the Equality Authority for helping to shape the Irish equality agenda, for relentlessly pinpointing the nine areas of our life we wish need to be free of prejudice and discrimination, among them race, gender, sexuality and our main issues, age.

So many married people today have little fire of the marriage bar, that arcane tradition which obliged women on marriage to de-

Chapter 9

CHANGING AGEIST ATTITUDES?

Paul Murray

> *"Nobody grows old merely by living a number of years.*
> *We grow old by deserting out ideals. Years may wrinkle*
> *the skin, but to give up enthusiasm wrinkles the soul."*
> — Samuel Ullman

ATTITUDE

It's all about attitude. Change attitudes, and the legislation changes. But, you could add, change the legislation, and the attitude changes. If anything is more obvious in social policy over the last ten years, it is that attitude, particularly public attitude, emboldens legislators to bring in new law, and that law, however unwillingly, leads our citizens to new ways of thinking. It might also be said that European attitudes and directions have led us in some way to the well of enlightened attitudes and law. Some way. We owe much thanks to the Equality Authority for helping to shape the Irish equality agenda, for relentlessly pinpointing the nine areas of our life which need to be free of prejudice and discrimination, among them race, gender, sexuality and, our main focus, age.

Young married people today know little of the marriage bar, that arcane tradition which obliged women on marriage to defect from the public service and state bodies, with a few bob in hand to help the arrival of the first child. Hearth and home, and the livelihoods of the husband would have been endangered it seems if young sexually awakened women were to be let loose on the labour force! Even allowing for the then job scarcity, it was a practice tolerated by all, until fuelled by foreign ideas and feminist endeavours, the sheer daftness of denying wives the right to work hit the body politic.

So, Ireland, or some of it, was about to change, as "isms" began to be attacked. Racism became socially unacceptable, sexism the refuge of the lumpen lad, and homophobia a badge of the sexually insecure. Ageism? Well, it came near last on the "ism" list, surprisingly enough because it is the one ism that faces us all, unless we have an early death.

Older people, and the discriminatory attitudes they faced, were largely invisible. Old age was really part of the spiritual dispensation, a time of personal reflection. There was a "reward in heaven" mindset which regarded ageing as a time of weakening bladders and dickey hearts.

This was reflected pertinently in the dogma that we should necessarily retire at 65 years of age, when apparently our batteries dimmed and we most needed a golden handshake and a watch. It was seen in fashion as clothing became increasingly geared to the under-thirties, even the under-twenties. As someone once said, "Do you see all those young people walking down Grafton Street? Well, they don't see you."

Sexuality was an arena only for the young, never mind that older people felt, dreamed and acted out their sexual drives just like anyone else, although perhaps with less intensity. Did anyone think that at least some people in a nursing home might appreciate the option of a double bed?

A Polish delegation in Dublin described how some elderly women in their country were ashamed of going out, because of their ageing looks. Poor self-image is not just the prerogative of adolescents. In France, we were told that the main concern of older people was that they were seen, and perhaps saw themselves, as a burden. Forty-one per cent believed their experience was undervalued. Ten per cent said the young equated being old with being unhappy. Indeed, in Ireland, in a southside Dublin school, Transition Year students, when asked for words describing older people, offered eight to ten negative words about senior citizens before one of them came up with a positive, wisdom.

With hardly a glance towards the wishes of older people, packaging became more complicated and difficult to unravel. Yes, preserve food, and make products safe for children, but how about considering older people also? Older people would say, of course, that their greatest irritant was being ignored. As one man put it, "I wouldn't mind is they deliberately didn't ask me if I wanted to travel, it's just that they never thought I'd be interested."

And when older people are asked for their views, their response can puncture many common assumptions. For example, the typical picture of an "elderly" holiday is of packaged tours; but not all older people like holidaying in touring buses and stopping endlessly for cups of tea. Another example: there has been an increasing push by the government towards providing inter-generational housing, so the generations can mix, but this is not always what older people want.

Older people were often seen as one grey amorphous mass, not as individuals who happened to be elderly. Old age became the badge, regardless of precise years lived, income, mental or physical health, skills or expertise. The older job seeker faced narrowing eyes and nods from the interview panel as its chairman promised to "let you know".

Options for civilised living began to narrow, despite the freedoms offered after rearing children and paying off the mortgage. As child care and house costs rose, grandparents, dutifully, if a little wearily, minded their children's offspring.

As one, now deceased, social activist once said, "I have raised my children, loved them, housed them, sent them to good schools, why should I perpetuate poverty by leaving them any money?" The impetus arises from a belief that parents have rights, and many parents are older people.

In Focus: Senior Citizens Parliament

Beginning in November 1993, the European Parliament held its first Senior Citizens Parliament in Luxembourg. Irish delegates returned full of enthusiasm and, recognising the need for a strong national voice for older people, they founded the Irish Senior Citizens Parliament in 1994.

Today the Parliament has 300 affiliated organisations with a total membership of 80,000. Unlike its national counterpart, this one is non-party political. Membership is open to organisations who wish to work with the Parliament on mutually relevant issues and are fully supportive of its ethos. All affiliated organisations have equal status, with the right to nominate three delegates, regardless of their size. The Parliament recognises the autonomy of each affiliate and a provision to give effect to this is contained in the Constitution, though frequently there is common cause among member bodies in terms of advocacy for policy change.

While the Parliament meets in plenary session once a year, the Senior Cabinet meet once a month in Dublin, where its 21 elected members present and debate issues, pass motions and adopt policies. Also, perhaps unlike some government ministers, these representatives are very accessible to their constituents. "People are in constant communication with us, bringing up a range of issues for our attention," says chief executive Michael O'Halloran.

Aims

The Parliament's objectives are to:

- *Be a strong voice representing older people and their needs at international, national and local level;*

- *Promote inter-generational solidarity;*

- *Work through the existing affiliated organisations to ensure better co-ordination of policies and activities;*

- *Develop solidarity with organisations working to improve the quality of life of older people;*

- *Promote improvement in the quality of life of older people.*

Issues

The Parliament seeks to achieve those objectives by identifying issues of concern to older people, and bring these to the attention of government and relevant agencies. Such issues include integrated health care delivery for older people; access to local life which impacts on public transport; elder abuse; insurance costs; and more. Given that many of the factors which impact on the well-being of older people are interlinked, how does the Parliament prioritise?

"Our overall aim is to improve the quality of life for older people. In terms of human need, the first issue is income, because without adequate income it's hard to have any quality of life. Those on a basic state pension do not have adequate resources and do not move on relative to others in the community," says Michael O'Halloran.

"The government has given a commitment to a basic pension of €200 by 2007 but our proposals are much more radical. We would say that pension should be a reflection of the general state of the economy, to be paid out in a structured way as a percentage of average industrial earnings. There should be a system similar to that existing for public service employees who have parity, who keep pace with their employed colleague in terms of per-

centage increases. The same system should apply to state pensions in relation to the average industrial wage.

"The next issue is the ability to live independently as part of the community. Many older people now find themselves having to look for long-term care, but this should be a last resort. We need a change in policy so that supporting people to remain at home is a first priority. This is not a cheap option and would need more of the services we already have such as home helps, day care centres, sheltered housing.

"The ability to live independently is obviously allied to health and health care. I don't believe that older people are being discriminated against in the health systems. I have no evidence of this. I would trust that the vast majority of health professionals are equable in their dealing with older people. We would like to see health care improved for everyone, but because older people have more health problems than the average, you may need to put in a health infrastructure to help older people remain in their community, so improving community care services."

The Parliament is also campaigning to find out the basis of insurance actuarial tables which impose a higher risk on older people, leading to higher premiums and less access to cover. They want disability parking to be respected by able-bodied people. They want the reinstatement of community employment schemes on which many services providers for older people depend. Public transport in rural Ireland is a hot issue among a number of organisations, and the Senior Parliament has recently been invited to join a government Transport Forum which is discussing such issues.

Success?

The Parliament works by conveying its views to relevant government departments, making budget submissions, and lobbying politicians in local, national and European elections.

Michael O'Halloran believes the message is getting through, and the voice of older people is increasingly being heard. The Parliament is now recognised as a Social Partner in the Voluntary & Community Pillar, thereby enhancing its opportunity to have a place at the decision-making table. Michael O'Halloran has been appointed to the Pensions Board, and feels he will bring a necessary insight from his fellow pensioners and retirees with whom he consults broadly.

"We have had a number of successes. We did raise the profile of older people with regard to income. We asked for free travel to be extended to older people in Northern Ireland and this was granted. It's a small gesture of reconciliation. It means that older people who have lived through the troubles can now travel free in the south. The other thing I am proud of achieving is asking for €1 million to promote leisure activities for older people. As a result €500,000 was granted to the organisation Go for Life, a big increase in what they had been receiving which allowed them greatly improve their infrastructure."

Inclusivity

Finally, what does he feel is distinctive about the older voice. "Nothing. There is nothing distinctive about the older voice, and we would bring an inter-generational philosophy to what we do. Many of us who are old are parents or grandparents, and we cannot ignore the future needs of our children and our grandchildren in taking a political view of the world we live in. If we have that spirit, we are responsive not only to the needs of older people but we also articulate through our age and experience that we want to give something back."

Irish Senior Citizens Parliament, 90 Fairview Street, Dublin 3; Tel: 01-8561243/4; Website: www.seniors.ie

PIVOT OF CAMPAIGNING

Rights are the pivot of Age Action Ireland's campaigning. Political lobbying, years of building media relations, daily briefings, all tumble down if not fuelled by a rights-based philosophy. As much as any other age cohort, older people are entitled to proper housing, medical care, employment, sporting and cultural activity. As one activist said, "Chronological age is no more than a date on a birth certificate. It does not say how old you are".

We used to laugh at the story of the elderly man who moaned that he was refused a job "just because he was 85". But campaigners for older people's rights ask the question, "Why should an old person not be allowed to work?" — and before rushing off to berate the relevant government minister, let us clarify their view. It goes something like this: people of any age are entitled to live fully human lives. They have rights to love and to be loved and, in Dylan Thomas's words, to "rage against the dying of the light". They are entitled to lifelong learning, because life is long. Decent housing is a prerequisite, because, as all the charters say, it is a basic human right. Adequate health care is a must for civilised living. Employment, to be active, to feel and be useful, is a need for all ages, one which can mean different things in different societies. Unfortunately, when we think of employment, jobs and careers, we focus on paid work, with the concomitant feeling that unpaid activity is a somewhat lesser thing.

We allow ourselves to be trapped into the idea of careers that rise rapidly, with earnings in line, until we are pushed into retirement. Why should we want our salaries to peak in the autumn of our lives, and not in the summer, when near adult children and mortgages are emptying our pockets? The good campaigner, therefore, begs the question, "What do we really mean by employment, retirement and career structure?"

It is, indeed, by asking "why?" that we come nearer the truth for the reasons older people are held down. In Age Action Ireland we continually seek rational responses. Why is it that the retiring age is 65? Who invented this arbitrary figure? It seems it was Bismarck or our former British rulers who were delighted to dole out pensions to those who managed to reach 65. Why? Because there were so few of them. But now the demographics have changed. Twelve or so per cent of us are over 65, and rising, although not at the pace of other European countries which have greater population imbalances then ourselves.

Pensions have been a catalyst for much of the recent change in attitudes both privately and politically. Older people are now finding that their pensions, based largely on equities, have been losing value. This older generation, however, are lucky that by and large they have defined benefit pensions — in other words, pensions that have known precise payments. For younger people, however, such pensions will become uncommon, and younger workers are being required to get involved with defined contribution pensions. (See Chapter 1 for more on the different types of pension.) Indeed, it is suggested that young people should be putting aside 15 per cent of their incomes if they are to be covered for their old age. An allied problem is that not much over 50 per cent of the working population have occupational pensions, a matter the government is trying to address with the new Personal Retirement Savings Accounts (PRSAs).

Within the last few years the Tánaiste, Mary Harney, was criticised for her seeming suggestion that adult children do not care for their old parents. Some children, of course, ignore their parents' plight, leave them at the mercy of the state, and then go on to inherit. But they are a minority and we can forget how heroic so many adult children and carers are in protecting the health and happiness of their older relatives.

Ms Harney clarified her position later and recognised the role of many such family members. The public, particularly carers and charitable agencies, watched fascinated as they saw ageing come onto the political agenda, for perhaps the first time. Fuelled by widespread worries of a pension "time bomb", and the price of nursing homes and caring, the political vacuum began to be fuelled. At least there were ideas being knocked around, attitudes shifting.

No longer was the public going to be content with the annual ritual dance about the size of the old age pension. Did it go up by more, or the same, as the rate of inflation? Oh, it went up by more. Great. Only for it to dawn on all older people, for instance, that widows and widowers were going to lose the half-rate unemployment, disability and injury benefits they would have received, if they were new claimants, the theory being that no one should receive two benefits. So a widow who had received a pension on her late husband's stamps would not have been eligible also to receive half-rate unemployment benefit, as had been the practice. A hapless Mary Coughlan, then Minister for Social and Family Affairs, who attempted to introduce such cuts, was castigated. Thanks to RTÉ's "Liveline", the National Association of Widows, and other groups, this little bit of cruelty headed off into the horizon. She brought back memories of the attempted tax on children's shoes by a Fine Gael/Labour coalition, Ernest Blythe reducing the old age pension, and even James (Rasher) Dillon telling the citizenry that they should eat the streaky while the back rashers were exported. No one likes to be called the minister "who robbed the widows", as Mary Coughlan was dubbed, and at the time pending local elections also concentrated the political mind.

The media has a huge role in changing attitudes, but the print, broadcast and electronic outlets have first to be briefed, to know the issues. They need to have confidence that their briefer is conversant with ageing and all its ramifications.

Journalists can only feel confidence, too, if the briefing arises from an organisation's experience. Age Action Ireland can have a view on older people's education, for example, because, through the University of the Third Age (U3A), it has built up a portfolio of experience (see Chapter 3, pages 87–91). On the health front, Age Action runs an advice, training and support service for carers. *Ageing Matters in Ireland* is Age Action Ireland's monthly magazine which is distributed through its charity shops, and to the media, Oireachtas members and inquirers.

Like other organisations, Age Action Ireland endeavours through the print and electronic media, and through lobbying, to articulate what is happening to the nation's carers, to make government realise that because a person has a family carer, that does not mean he or she is able to cope. (See the section on Carers in Chapter 7, pages 217–224.) Through press statements, radio interviews, seminars and talks with schools, colleges, meetings of older people, in day care centres, and during Positive Ageing Week, we continually stress that no one has the right to deny older people their due.

POSITIVE AGEING WEEK

Positive Ageing Week was initiated in 2003 by AAI to highlight ageing issues and build on the UN Day of Older Persons on 1 October each year. The Week aims to highlight issues of discrimination against older people in travel insurance, jobs and education as well as in other areas, and to stress that older age can be a positive time of one's life. The 2003 Week involved religious services, cross-border seminars on best practice in care of older people, a Dublin seminar on Fourth Age education, an anti-discrimination phone-in, a seminar on relationships between the generations, coffee mornings in Age Action shops, the launch of essay and photo bank competitions for Transition Year students and a billboard campaign on discrimination against older people.

The first Positive Ageing Week succeeded perhaps because it did not seek to be too ambitious. It sought to bring ageing as an issue to the general public, and in the process change many negative attitudes. In campaign terms it was a "dry run", a learning experience.

Small communities around the country were asked to indicate what they might do during the first week of October, and over 100 groups and communities told us they were going to walk, sing, dance, climb, pray, drink coffee, paint, read and visit, among other things. It was an amazing array of activity. In various churches, there were interdenominational prayerful interludes to mark the week.

The phone-in invited older people to ring up and tell us about any discriminations visited on them. A lively seminar addressed the need for intergenerational solidarity and focused on the tensions that can exist between different age groups; a second seminar discussed opportunities for education for older people in long-stay settings. A third seminar at Farmleigh House, a forum for consultation on older people's needs, was hosted by Ivor Callely, Minister of State for Older People at the Department of Health and Children.

Coffee mornings were held in Age Action's charity shops which many older people seemed to enjoy. Indeed, the intention was, and is in the future, to make Positive Ageing Week a celebration of growing old, a week which could take hold as much as the UN Day on Ageing, first on an all-Ireland basis and later across the rest of Europe.

All organisations and individuals are invited to become involved in their own way and under their own banner. It is hoped that this week, which grew even more in 2004, will involve the whole island and other countries over the next few years.

OTHER ISSUES AND ACTIVITIES

Older people are now standing up for their rights, judging by the calls to Age Action Ireland. Many queries involve discrimination in travel insurance, people over 65 being obliged to pay two or three times the going rate. There are complaints about ageism in jobs, in promotion and hiring, but complainants often have difficulty in proving age discrimination. Angry women ring to object that they have been refused by the national Breast-Check screening programme, because they are over 64. The Back to Education initiative, aimed at encouraging people who missed out on early education, does not apply to most older people, nor do FÁS courses. Why, older people ask, should I lose out on opportunities because of my chronological age?

Nor have we had any luck with our lobbying campaign with the Voluntary Health Insurance Board, which used the "underwriters" as its reasoning for a decision to charge over-65s €179 for holiday insurance, while those under 65 were only charged €49. While it might be reasonable to expect that travel insurance costs might rise with age, the refusal to gradually raise the price didn't please the older people who rang Age Action.

But there have been victories. Age Action awareness-raising can take some credit for the government decision to end the Civil Service rule that retirement is at 65 years of age. It applies only to new entrants, and has been opposed by some in the public service, but it is a step in the right direction, towards the view that workers should not be judged merely by their chronological age. The only measure should be ability, character and personality. The cost of pensions will be the main reason for the government decision, but for the first time there might also be a hint of a belief that all workers, including older ones, have rights. We can soon wave goodbye to the daft situation in which over-65s were denied jobs as heritage centre guides, on the basis that 65 was the Civil Service retirement age.

Indeed, when people ring the Information Service, particularly older people, the staff are delighted, because it indicates that there is a preparedness to challenge attitudes that unfairly undermine older people. Why is my car insurance suddenly higher? Is that advertisement for a paint product not ageist (as Age & Opportunity highlighted)? Did we see the story about the two civil servants who did not get promotion because of their age? (We did and we followed it up in the media.) I'm over 65, why can I not be part of the Back to Education programme? (We asked that too!) Why are the widows losing out on their right to half-rate unemployment benefit? Age Action raised this issue, as did the National Association of Widows, and the Irish Senior Citizens Parliament.

WORKING WITH THE MEDIA

Another way of changing attitudes is through media skills training, a successful Age Action activity. Why should older people not be involved with the media, particularly as it is so forceful in changing attitudes? By teaching media skills, Age Action is indirectly helping to change views on ageing and older people's interests. People can feel disenfranchised, particularly if they are isolated, and it was enlightening during some courses in the southeast how many participants felt they had been dismissed by the metropolitan media, that their voice, basically that of Middle Ireland, was not being given a platform.

We suggested how that might be changed. The first secret is to "know your journalist" and persevere with him or her. Meet for coffee when there is no story to tell, so there will be an existing relationship when the journalist is being sought to get across a particular view. The reporter/feature writer may be junior, but today's junior is tomorrow's senior who will be more than useful when lobbying or attempting to change local attitudes.

How do you write a press release to publicise an event, announce an initiative or highlight an injustice? Ideally, keep it simple, with the salient facts in the first few paragraphs, followed by a short background. It must have a contact name, address and phone number, including one for outside business hours if possible, as many journalists look for additional comment and clarifications. If there is no one available after 5.00 pm, the press release will go to the nearest bin, or spike, where most of them go anyway.

The first paragraph should interest the journalist who hopefully will then go on to ensure that the reader will be equally or even more interested. It will do this by including short, snappy facts, the who, what, when and where.

The news editor has to be enticed to take an interest. Similarly with radio and television, Age Action Ireland teaches the skills of being interviewed, suggesting to organisations, particularly charitable or community ones, that they allocate their best person for the interview. Mary Bloggs may have been a founder member and is still revered, but this is not necessarily a qualification for being interviewed by an intrepid reporter. A less experienced member who is relaxed, humorous and speaks concisely may be far better.

A confident educated group of older people willing to take to the airwaves does more for the ageing cause than any number of commentators or spokespersons. The newer media, whose brief is often to talk to the consumers of a service rather than merely its administrators, are a welcome and emerging arena which can be utilised by older people. Local radio has become very powerful, sometimes taking 50 per cent of listeners in local areas.

People are realising that with services such as INN Independent Network which provides stories for many local radio stations, they can keep up with the national news, while retaining their grip on happenings in their local area. The local radio can focus on a local issue in a concentrated way not available to the national media. It can allow for longer and more in-depth interviews with the bonus of local knowledge.

AGE EQUALITY TRAINING*

Another organisation, Age & Opportunity, offers workshops and training programmes on age equality to organisations dealing with older people and older people's issues. They deliver a workshop, entitled *AgeWise: Age, Equality and You*, lasting two-and-a-half hours to public sector organisations, including employees in government departments and local authorities. Organisations availing of this workshop cover the cost of the venue and catering costs only. Age & Opportunity can also work with organisations in the public and the private sector to tailor a training programme to suit their specific needs. They sometimes make a presentation on age equality at the request of an organisation, rather than delivering a full workshop.

Age & Opportunity developed age equality training to tackle the underlying attitudes that lead to ageism and age discrimination. The Age Equality Training workshops are aimed at:

- Raising age awareness amongst participants;

- Challenging myths and stereotypes about ageing and older people;

- Demonstrating the personal, cultural and structural effects of ageism;

- Encouraging participants to reflect on how ageism might be countered in their organisation or workplace.

Organisations who have attended Age Equality Training include local authority and public sector organisations, staff and board members of a number of local partnership companies and some active retirement associations.

---

* The section on age equality training is adapted from the Age & Opportunity website, www.olderinireland.ie. For more information, e-mail info@olderinireland.ie or contact Paul Maher at 01-8057709.

THE POWER OF NUMBERS

In the southeast, another arm in the battle against ageism has been in the lobbying courses organised by Age Action Ireland. Here older people are encouraged to see their way through the maze in their lobbying of local and national government and politicians. In other words, it is emerging that older people have to do it for themselves. The national organisations with their networks and expertise can only do so much.

With one million people over 50, 500,000 over 65, and 100,000 over 80, figures which are rising all the time (although our demographic imbalance is nothing like in some other countries), older people can be an unstoppable political lobby. It is sometimes forgotten that politics, which is the arena where real decisions are made, is about the distribution of resources.

Older people need to assert that they want their fair share, no more or no less. Little rumblings in Germany from a small group which intimated that older people were getting too much (and this despite cutbacks by a Social Democrat government), suggest that without reasonable debate an intergenerational row could emerge. It is the job of the grey organisations, and their members, to lead this debate responsibly, with the facts, hinged on the ultimate fact that younger people are also facing old age. They, too, will become beneficiaries of pensions, community care, decent health care services and education, if they fight for it now for today's older people.

As a society, in our efforts to be truly human, at different times in our lives, we focus on the varying areas of life that we believe need reform. Certain categories of social deprivation become trendy; we are moved by the plight of this or that suffering, abused children, the Third World, or whatever. But we are only now focusing as a community on one of the last "isms" to be condemned, ageism. Yet ageing is something that will affect us all, unlike racism or sexism.

UN Secretary General Kofi Annan says that the ageing population will be the defining issue of the twenty-first century, with the world's older population rising from 600 million to two billion by 2050. In Ireland, the population percentage of over-65s is moving from 12 to 24 per cent. Is there the collective will to change perspectives so we can deal with these changing demographics? And we say deal with, not cope with, so as not to regard older people as a burden, but to include them as an intrinsic unit in society, when so often they are excluded.

Simone de Beauvoir, in her book *Old Age*, speaks of the need to "break the conspiracy of silence" which she perceived treated older people as outcasts. She says, "Let us recognise ourselves in this old man or in that old woman. It must be done if we are to take upon ourselves the entirety of our human state. And when it is done we will no longer acquiesce in the misery of the last age; we will no longer be indifferent, because we will feel concerned, as indeed we are."

"Old age is particularly difficult to assume because we have always regarded it as something alien, a foreign species," she says. In other words, for many people, it is another country, but it is a country to which, if we have not arrived, we are all going. And unless something is done, the journey will be increasingly difficult for everyone.

There is an assumption that once we reach a certain age we do not want certain things. Not true. Theodore Green, an 87-year-old US senator, puts it another way: "Many people say that as you grow old you have to give up things; I think you get old because you give things up". Do not discriminate against us just because we are here longer. The only difference between a young person at the height of their exuberance and the very old . . . is time.

Chapter 10

THE SPIRITUAL DIMENSION

Catherine McCann

"Age puzzles me. I thought it was a quiet time. My seventies were interesting and fairly serene, but my eighties are passionate. I grow more intense as I age. To my own surprise I burst out with hot conviction." — Florida Scott-Maxwell

Florida Scott-Maxwell's words may not immediately appear to relate to the spiritual dimension of our lives, yet what is the source of this woman's passion? I suggest her deep spirituality, and as her comment suggests, a spirituality that grew stronger as she moved on in years.

We largely create our own ageing by the choices we make and the attitudes we adopt. For many the last third of life does become a time when people flourish by discovering greater depths in living human existence to the full.[1] This could show itself in becoming passionate about life at personal, family, local or global levels. Living in this full way is supported and en-

---

[1] This chapter's assumption is that the older years are the 60+ period of life. This author has just entered her seventies.

ergised by developing our spiritual lives — a dimension present in everyone, be they a religious believer or not.[2]

The physical, mental and psychosocial dimensions of the person are taken into account within social and health care systems. But apart from palliative care the relevance of the spiritual dimension, an essential element to becoming fully human, has held a Cinderella place. Recognition and attention to the interaction of the psychosocial and spiritual dimensions is necessary if the health status of individuals and societies is to be balanced. Leaving this core dimension of human living at the margins leads to an incompleteness, to something missing yet not always consciously missed. Symptoms of ignoring the spiritual dimension might include inner restlessness, apathy, sadness, feelings of uselessness or purposelessness, confidence and self-worth dipping, a lack of a general sense of wellbeing. Two significant indicators of such a state are an absence of joy and an awareness of meaninglessness within everyday living.

DESCRIBING THE SPIRITUAL DIMENSION

How would one describe the spiritual dimension of the human person? It is generally accepted that the inner dimension, the deepest core of who we are, has a spiritual quality about it. A way of getting in touch with our spirituality is to ask the question, "What do I ache for?" In our daily lives, our spiritual self lies quietly in the background, orienting and prompting, eliciting inspirations, desires and longings. Sometimes our "spirit-self" forces itself into consciousness, enabling us to appreciate,

---

[2] In *Falling in Love with Life: An Understanding of Ageing* (McCann, 1997), I looked positively at the ageing process, taking into account the physical, intellectual, emotional and spiritual dimensions of our person. It examined the first three areas in some depth, leaving the spiritual aspect largely hidden except for the chapter "Living with Wisdom, Hope and Joy" (pp. 92-106). I am pleased now to have the opportunity to look at the spiritual aspect of our lives in a more explicit and integrated way.

delight in, and above all search for and discover more truth, goodness, beauty, love and inner freedom. One of the blessings of the older years is the opportunity afforded to allow this spirit-self to flourish. With the responsibilities of rearing children and formal work receding, everyday living has the possibility of becoming less functionally oriented. As a result, opportunities for listening to the inner promptings that well up from within can more easily be noticed. Some act on these promptings and allow them take precedence in a way that was not possible earlier in life.

Spirituality permeates our lives whether we are conscious of it or not. It is the source that enlivens our ability to appreciate, long for greater inner freedom, want to do good, search for truth, including ultimate truth, and above all ache for love. Within the last two decades it is acceptable to use the word spirituality, although a haziness about its meaning abounds.

EXPRESSIONS OF SPIRITUALITY

Creativity and Appreciation

One expression of spirituality is our aesthetic sense — our ability to appreciate and as well as be creators in a wide range of fields. In the older years there is more time — if we make it — "to stand and stare", to delight in the world of nature and the arts. Music, painting, sculpture, theatre, dance, literature and other art forms are highly spiritual activities where appreciation, delight and wonder can grow by exposing ourselves to new expressions of art as well as returning to old favourites. We can also become creators ourselves, maybe for the first time, in areas such as writing, painting, acting, gardening . . . the opportunities are limitless.

Freedom

Developing an explorer spirit is part of spirituality. This may manifest itself in a hunger for learning — by study, joining reading groups, travel or by heightening awareness of the environment as we notice and delight in its treasures. Alternatively, the exploration could manifest itself in expanding and deepening our relationships — grandchildren, new friends or maybe even falling in love for the first or umpteenth time! It could also take the form of an inward exploration, a movement to interiority that possibly has largely been unexcavated. There is a saying: "We only grow old when we lose our sense of adventure." This is supported by Eliot's words:

> "Old men [and women] ought to be explorers. Here or there does not matter. We must be still and still moving. Into another intensity. For a further union, a deeper communion. . . . In my end is my beginning.[3]

Truth: The Search for Meaning

According to Viktor Frankl, freedom of spirit makes life meaningful.[4] In *Man's Search for Meaning* is found his famous dictum: "People today [in the West] have enough to *live by* but not enough to *live for*." Finding worthwhile levels of meaning is intensely pertinent when work and parenting roles are no longer there to give a *raison d'être* to "who I am" and "what I do". Society itself has no clear ideas around what this "for" might be in the older years. This is largely because the extended period of life following retirement is such a recent phenomenon. Personally discovering what one's "for" might be is essential. Knowing and living out that "for" gives the motivation that sustains us

---

[3] Eliot, 1944.

[4] Frankl, 1946, page 87. Victor Frankl was a psychiatrist and a concentration camp survivor.

in the present as well as providing a realistic yet positive outlook towards the future. Being comfortable with yet at the same time challenged by "what my life is for" is a key issue of the older years. It is a new form of responsibility and one that needs constant reappraisal as further life changes occur over subsequent decades. It is salutary to be reminded of Eliot's words: "we had the experience but missed the meaning"[5] in order that this occurrence does not happen.

While discerning meaning was part and parcel of the middle years, those meanings are unlikely to be sufficient in the last third of life. Creating and adopting newly framed meanings, and especially those that enhance self-worth, form the bedrock of "successful" ageing. Self-esteem can easily drop in the transition to the older years and also later in the frailer older years unless noticed and attended to. A loss of worthwhile systems of meaning is serious. An effect of this situation is shown in the raised suicide rates of older people.

A central task is to make sense of life and our part in it. It is also about realising what becoming more fully human entails. This includes accepting vulnerabilities and limitations as well as personal strengths. Owning and making sense of one's life story, delighting and being absorbed in the present and, in an ongoing way, affirming life while acknowledging death, are all part of human living. Personally satisfying levels of meaning are more likely to emerge from being open and welcoming as we live the present while at the same time facing the future with hope. Clinging to the past or to the inessentials of the present can prevent one's inner spirit from soaring! It is a time to explore issues and questions; face uncertainties as questions outweigh answers; and remain interested in making the world a better place.

---

[5] Eliot, 1944, page 39.

Truth: The Search for Ultimate Meaning

Ultimate meaning arises from the core of one's being. This inner core or spirit is enlivened by openness, questioning, honesty. We get in touch with this inner spirit through realising and accepting that there is something further in life that goes beyond oneself and the here and now. There is always more to our loving, questioning, appreciating. For some, this self-transcending movement is open to a further transcendence — namely it is open to receiving the Divine as a reality in personal living. While science, and those solely influenced by the present-day cultural influences of materialism and individualism, focus on "how" questions, religion wrestles with the "why" variety and in particular with questions that are concerned with origins and destiny. People adopt varying systems of meaning — both religious and other — and these demand respect when such choices are authentically made and lived in a way that enhances human living. It is desirable that ultimate meaning questions are faced with open as opposed to closed minds and hearts and allow for the possibility of wonder at the mystery element in life being aroused. This can happen within both the ordinary and extraordinary events of life as one looks at a flower or a newborn grandchild, receiving a key insight, meeting a significant person.

Many older people in this country draw energy and meaning from their religious faith. Spirituality and religion are not identical but feed into each other. The link between spirituality and religion can be particularly close in experiences of love, beauty and freedom. Other forms of depth experiencing such as in crises or other suffering moments can lead to a "crying out" to the mystery element within human living and maybe to Ultimate Mystery/God. It is also true that the ordinary, familiar happenings of our everyday lives can put us in touch with mystery, which for the Christian is known as Loving Mystery, since God is revealed as a God who is love.[6]

Love

At the heart of all our spiritual capacities lies love. The love in question is not so much love of self, although a healthy love of self is essential, but a love that leads beyond ourselves to others; a love that extends to the entire cosmos. Concern for others' wellbeing at local and global levels flows from sharing a common humanity. Personal love has the inventiveness to expresses itself in new and ancient ways. Communal love expresses itself through respect for human rights and democratic processes. Inclusive loving is the hallmark of Christian love as well as the more demanding forms of love shown through acts of forgiveness and self-sacrifice.

Due to varying limitations of fatigue and disability, the outward reaches of love can wane. However this does not excuse from remaining a contributor to society. The latter is a value that assists personal flourishing as well as benefiting others. Carrying out tasks for others may no longer be possible but offering personal presence to those one comes in contact with, even giving a smile, can be a wonderful way of contributing to the good of others as well as to our own good. Remaining open to receive gestures of love from others is also important.

ISSUES RELATED TO SPIRITUALITY

Spiritual Development

Spiritual development is achieved by the explicit choices we make around ourselves and our world. According to some authors, spiritual development commences largely in mid-life as

---

[6] I find the word "God" difficult to use because of the limitations and "hangups" that can surround this term. Holy Mystery if my preferred option.

people approach the maturity of being a self-responsible person while at the same time desiring further authenticity and integration. Helminiak outlines four stages in spiritual development, a process that integrates spiritual issues within the structures of human development.[7]

The baseline stage is termed the *conformist stage* where an individual unquestioningly accepts their inherited worldview. Development begins when stirrings are felt as one begins to learn that it is up to oneself to decide for oneself what one will make of oneself. The second *conscientious stage* is seen as the actual commencement of spiritual growth. It is characterised by structuring one's life according to personally chosen understandings and commitments. This is followed by the mellower *compassionate stage*. At this stage one's commitments become more realistic and nuanced, with gentleness towards oneself and others becoming more prominent. In addition there is a letting-go of some previously chosen world-views. Finally there is the *cosmic stage* where "one would be fully open to all that is, ever willing to change and adjust as circumstances demand, alive always to the present moment, responding as one ought in every situation, in touch with the depths of one's own self, aware of the furthest implications of one's spiritual nature, in harmony with oneself and with all else, and all this, not as a momentary passing experience but as a perduring [enduring] way of being."[8]

Grieving/Acceptance/Receptivity Issues

Times of loss draw deeply from and can be helped by one's spirituality. Over the span of the older years, many losses will be undergone. Familiarising oneself with the grieving process along Kubler-Ross's five stages of denial, anger, bargaining,

---

[7] Helminiak, 1987, page 84.

[8] Helminiak, 1987, page 89.

depression and acceptance is helpful, since it will require implementation around many issues. The obvious one is the loss
experienced when someone close dies. There is also the loss
that comes from ill-health or fatigue, especially when this de-
prives us of carrying out functional or favourite tasks, like driving the car or being involved in particular leisure pursuits.
Maybe it becomes necessary to give up one's home because of
a need for a more suitable dwelling. There is the painful loss in
the early stages of Alzheimer's when intimations depriving one
of the ability to think and love freely appear. There is also the
acute loss of a sense of God in later years. It seems from recent
writings about Mother Teresa that she lived through this loss
right up to the time of her death.

Making the grieving journey with some degree of adequacy
can, from a spirituality perspective, have positive effects. Sur-
rendering to life as it unfolds and accepting this with courage
and willingness can prove beneficial. This does not mean ignoring the physical, mental or emotional pain involved. But in
some mysterious way by positively entering the flow of *un-
avoidable* suffering, a path to inner peace can open up that
maybe was never conceived possible before. If these difficult
times have a meaningful "for" attached to them, then inner
peace is more likely to become a reality.

Letting go of what we hold dear calls not only for the ability
to surrender, a profoundly spiritual process, but in some in-
stances there is the added requirement of becoming a good receiver. When independence around personal tasks has to be
relinquished, the art of receiving is called for. It is easier to
give than to receive. However, by learning to be a gracious receiver, we enhance not only the quality of our own lives but
also enrich the giver in the tasks they perform for us.

The Preciousness of Life

Valuing life's preciousness can surface as the years proceed. If this is accompanied by a greater ability to enter the riches of each "now" moment, then life is more likely to be experienced as fulfilling. Ideally as we age we allow quality to take precedence over quantity, being over doing; hope to conquer despondency. Groucho Marx said the following: "I, not events, have the power to make me happy or unhappy today. I can chose which it shall be. Yesterday is dead, tomorrow hasn't arrived yet. I have just one day, today, and I'm going to be happy in it."

Groucho Marx was a wonderfully humorous person. Humour has been described by Nouwen as "knowledge with a soft smile".[9] Humour is also an element in spirituality, since it is largely connected with perspective and as such has a way of unveiling what is genuine. It relativises without ridiculing. Remaining fun-loving and not becoming overly serious can be expressions of a joyous spirituality.

Death and Dying

The link between humour and death is not far-fetched in Irish culture. Jewish and Christian people (especially the Irish) joke easily about death, a fact that tends to reveal a healthy attitude towards the end of life. Normally after turning 50 thoughts of personal mortality enter awareness. A medical diagnosis that could shorten life span heightens that awareness, as does, naturally, terminal illness. Some fear death in a phobic way, like phobias around other human issues. Fear tends to surround the dying process rather then death itself. No matter what ideas or feelings one has, death is the great human mystery that confronts everyone. Our attitude towards death is coloured by beliefs, culture, personal experiences. Many people with an alive

---

[9] Nouwen, 1976, page 74.

spirituality draw on it in an attempt to make some sense of death's awesomeness, while others have difficulty in attaching any meaning to this great unknown. Spirituality usually but not necessarily proves helpful in looking at the reality of death or in helping people in the process of preparing for it. A deep spirituality can positively enable people let go into death's eventuality as the moment approaches. It is particularly stressful for those who struggle with imminent death, as well as for family members who watch this struggle.

Life is full of little "dyings".[10] Many "death rehearsals" are undergone in life as we let go of things dear to us. Each time we cross these mini-thresholds we enter an unknown world — a world without that person or thing. Awareness of the finiteness in living constantly comes to us through experiencing our own physical, intellectual or emotional limitations. At times one feels the environment "letting us down" in some way. Feelings of disappointment also arouse an inward-dying type of experience. The perishable nature of reality such as perceived in nature or human relationships also alerts us to life's fragility.

Death faces us with the ultimate question, which in turn calls everything else into question. It challenges our "for" in the most profound way of all. In some strange way our earthly life needs to be "rounded off". Two days before his death, Donald Nicholl wrote in his dairy *Testing unto Death* of his "rounding off" his life by letting go of everything except gratitude. "When you are full of gratitude there isn't room for anything else; . . . My gratitude . . . has in a way transformed my life in the way I look back on my life. I am full of gratitude."[11]

Death is more than a biological event. (It is possible to be biologically alive while clinically dead.) It is an event that chal-

---

[10] McCann, 1998; see a fuller exposition on thoughts around death and dying in the chapter on death, pages 101–109. See also Dowling Singh, 1999.

[11] Nicholl, 1998.

lenges anyone who claims some form of spirituality around a "Beyond", a "Higher Power",[12] an "Ultimate" dimension to life. In death, that element takes on an incomprehensible form. Thoughts around the possibility of "life after death" are extremely difficult because of our problem in letting go of concepts around time and space. But death is not about a "place" or a "forever". For a Christian, death is the happening that brings about a state of completion, where each one retains their own uniqueness and is welcomed to enter the presence of Loving Mystery as opposed to falling into nothingness, or becoming part of some amorphous spirit-life with personal identity lost.

REFLECTIONS ON THE RELIGIOUS DIMENSION OF SPIRITUALITY

Religion — A Significant Reality within Human History

While the word "spirituality" has re-emerged as acceptable, the term "religion" has dwindled in favour. This is partially due to Western culture appearing "religionless". Defining the word religion is accepted as difficult. The Latin word "relegere" contains the notion of "constantly turning to", insinuating that the object of one's turning demands attention.

Each religion struggles in its own way with ultimate questions in an effort to explain the universe's existence and this has led to particular religions establishing different meanings and practices. Significant today is the movement towards inter-religious dialogue among the world religions. Religion's core — religious experience — is more and more perceived today as having similar traits among all the religions.

Central to the three monotheistic faiths, Islam, Judaism and Christianity, is the notion and experiencing of a personal God. This God reveals the God-self to humankind by establishing a

---

[12] The term used in the rich spirituality of Alcoholics Anonymous.

relationship with a people. The identity of the Jewish people emerged from their knowing they were a people of God. The emphasis in this chapter is on the Judeo-Christian tradition and especially the Christian religion since Christianity has formed the bedrock of Irish society and its spirituality since the fifth century. Christian values still permeate modern Ireland despite the fact that some describe Irish society as post-Christian.

People may enter their older years with a lost or wavering religious faith that seems unable to adequately sustain them in those older years. Faith is and always remains gift. An important reality, as previously mentioned, is to remain open in one's search for truth to the end of life. Sadly, narrowness, emptiness and even bitterness can ensue when the ongoing search for truth and meaning is absent.

Christianity

Christianity is unique among world religions in that it believes God became a member of the human family. This astonishing "Good News" dramatically broke all conceivable boundaries in relation to humanity's limited ideas about who God is. God enters human history in the person of Jesus, who through his life and death became like us in all things except sin and in doing so became vulnerable as we are. Through Jesus we learn that God is now to be addressed as a loving parent who has sent his Son to show how much we are loved as well as to liberate humanity from its inherent selfishness. By his life and teaching, Jesus continuously portrayed the depth and intimacy of divine love in human form by simple homely stories and parables, shared meals, acts of forgiveness and through his sensitive encounters with people from all walks of life. He was particularly drawn to frequenting the company of sinners and those marginalised as a result of gender, religion, race or illness. He clearly wished his followers/disciples to adopt these values.

Life-giving is central to who Jesus is and affirming life was what Jesus' coming was all about. He came first of all to share Divine life with humanity. "The Father who is the source of life has made the Son the source of life" (Jn. 5:26). He also came as giver of life at all levels of our being. "I have come that they may have life and have it to the full" (Jn. 10:10). He spoke of himself using image-laden titles: "I am life" (Jn. 11:25), "I am the bread of life" (Jn. 6:35), "I am the vine" (Jn. 15:1), of his words as "spirit and life" (Jn. 6:63), and refers to his Spirit as "living water" (Jn. 4:10). Life, both divine and human, was and is his greatest gift to every human being.

This offer of a loving relationship that is utterly life-giving is available to all who accept this gift. The gift of faith which contains within it the ability to surrender to such lavish gift-giving has been for many older people in Ireland an important reality since early childhood. Others may have fallen away for a variety of reasons, some may wish to come back, still more may want to discover the richness of Christian faith for the first time, while still more may yearn to deepen an existing faith. It matters little to the "God of Jesus Christ" where one exists on that spectrum. God's offer of Love is unconditional and ready to embrace those who return or who wish to deepen their response, as shown in the striking story of the Prodigal Son (Lk. 15: 11-32).

Religious Development within the Christian Tradition

In the older years, religious faith can become more alive and meaningful. One's present level of religious development plus the desire for further growth influences the part religion plays in the older years. For some, religion becomes an increasingly important part of life.

It is helpful to return to Helminiak's four stages of spiritual development and apply these to our religious story. In category one — the conformist stage — a person may still be living with inherited beliefs as learnt and understood in childhood. This could result in an individual living with possibly the same image of God, having the same ideas around Church, giving the same weight to rules and practices, living with a knowledge of Jesus, that they had in their teens. In category two — the conscientious stage — a person will have looked at basic beliefs and made them their own in a way that is relevant to their life situation. New understandings may have come through contact with the teachings and subsequent insights that have emerged from Vatican II. Listening to the lived voice of Christian memory (another word for tradition), having contact with scripture, practising more meaningful forms of prayer and participation in sacramental celebrations may also prove helpful to growth. The third category — the compassionate stage — will be familiar to many people in their older years. Mellowness, realism and gentleness, as well as the letting-go of the non-essentials in regard to religious living can lead to a more integrated self. Seeing the value of the Christian faith's core elements and the realisation that God is infinitely more unlike than like any images we might hold, are possible factors that make up this stage. At the fourth category — the cosmic stage — the central message of Christian love takes on cosmic proportions. To possess a greater ability to live in the present, to be adaptable to change, to live in harmony with oneself and the world, and yet remain open to the more of truth, love and beauty while endeavouring to offer one's personal contribution, is truly a form of cosmic living.

Faith is a human experience. It is a gift that brings with it the knowledge that one is profoundly loved by God. It is a relational entity and therefore calls for a personal response of knowing and loving. Like all relationships, if it is not nourished it may wane or even die. This can happen at any stage of life, including the older years. Possible practical suggestions that nourish faith life might include:

- Seeking further understanding of one's faith through reading, study, or in small faith-sharing groups.

- Prayer in its personal form and, for some, communal prayer such as devotions, shared or charismatic prayer groups.

- Worship and especially the Eucharist. This action acknowledges dependence on and gratitude to God. It brings about not only communion with God but also with the entire Christian community, as well as enabling "this community realise that it is truly and intimately linked with mankind and its history".[13]

- Reading scripture and especially the gospels.

- Charity that particularly works for justice, in whatever form that takes.

- Keeping alive faith, hope and love.

- Living a lifestyle in accordance with the Beatitudes.

Hope may need to be brought to the fore as we age and particularly for those with terminal illness or who are close to death. Christ's death, and particularly his resurrection, without which Christian faith, as Paul says, would be in vain, sustains the hope that death has been conquered through the Easter event.

CONCLUSION

The power of a story is an effective way of opening us to profound human truths. An Anthony de Mello story offers an apt and, I hope, delightful conclusion to a chapter on spirituality.

> The Master was in an expansive mood so his disciples sought to learn from him the stages he had passed through

---

[13] The Documents of Vatican II, *Pastoral Constitution on the Church in the Modern World*, par. 1.

in his quest for the divine. "God first led me by the hand," he said, "into the Land of Action and there I dwelt for several years. Then he returned and led me to the Land of Sorrows; there I lived until my heart was purged of every inordinate attachment. That is when I found myself in the Land of Love whose burning flames consumed whatever was left in me of self. This brought me to the Land of Silence where the mysteries of life and death were bared before my wondering eyes." "Was that the final stage of your quest?" they asked. "No," the Master said. "One day God said, 'Today I shall take you to the innermost sanctuary of the Temple, to the heart of God himself.' And I was led to the Land of Laughter."

Bibliography

de Mello, Anthony (1984), *The Song of the Bird*, New York: Image Books.

de Mello, Anthony (1988), *Prayer of the Frog*, Anand: Gujarat Sahitya Prakash.

Dowling Singh, Kathleen (1999), *The Grace in Dying: How we are Transformed Spiritually as we Die*, Dublin: Newleaf.

Eliot, T.S. (1944), *Four Quartets*, London: Faber and Faber.

Frankl, Victor (1946), *Man's Search for Meaning*, New York: Washington Square Press.

Jerusalem Bible (1968), London: Darton Longman and Todd.

Hanh, Thich Nhat (1975), *The Miracle of Mindfulness*, London: Rider.

Helminiak, Daniel (1987), *Spiritual Development: An Interdisciplinary Study*, Chicago: Loyola University Press.

Helminiak, Daniel (1996), *The Human Core of Spirituality: Mind as Psyche and Spirit*, New York: Albany Press.

Luke, Helen (1987), *Old Age: Journey into Simplicity*, New York: Parabola Books.

Hillman, James (1999), *The Force of Character and the Lasting Life*, New York: Ballantine Books.

MacKinlay, Elizabeth (2001), *The Spiritual Dimensions of Ageing*, London: Jessica Kingsley Publishers.

McCann, Catherine (1996), *Falling in Love with Life: An Understanding of Ageing*, Dublin: Columba Press/Eleona Books.

McCann, Catherine (1998), *Time-Out in Shekina: The Value of Symbols in our Search for Meaning*, Dublin: Eleona Books.

McCann, Catherine (2001), *Diary of a Hippie: Journeying through Surgery*, Dublin: Eleona Books.

McCann, Catherine (2002), *Saying Yes to Life: A Way to Wisdom*, Dublin: Eleona Books.

Nicholl, D. (1998), *The Testing of Hearts, A Pilgrim's Journey*, London: Darton Longman & Todd.

Nouwen, Henri and Walter Gaffney (1974), *Aging: The Fulfilment of Life*, New York: Image Books.

Whitehead, E. and J. Whitehead (1982), *Christian Life Patterns: The Psychological Challenges and Religious Invitations of Adult Life*, New York: Image Books.

Appendix 1

UNITED NATIONS PRINCIPLES FOR OLDER PERSONS

The General Assembly:

Appreciating the contribution that older persons make to their societies,

Recognising that, in the Charter of the United Nations, the peoples of the United Nations declare, inter alia, their determination to reaffirm faith in fundamental human rights, in the dignity and worth of the human person, in the equal rights of men and women and of nations large and small and to promote social progress and better standards of life in larger freedom,

Noting the elaboration of those rights in the Universal Declaration of Human Rights, the International Covenant on Economic, Social and Cultural Rights and the International Covenant on Civil and Political Rights and other declarations to ensure the application of universal standards to particular groups,

In pursuance of the International Plan of Action on Ageing, adopted by the World Assembly on Ageing and endorsed by the General Assembly in its resolution 37/51 of 3 December 1982,

Appreciating the tremendous diversity in the situation of older persons, not only between countries but within countries and between individuals, which requires a variety of policy responses,

Aware that in all countries, individuals are reaching an advanced age in greater numbers and in better health than ever before,

Aware of the scientific research disproving many stereotypes about inevitable and irreversible declines with age,

Convinced that in a world characterised by an increasing number and proportion of older persons, opportunities must be provided for willing and capable older persons to participate in and contribute to the ongoing activities of society,

Mindful that the strains on family life in both developed and developing countries require support for those providing care to frail older persons,

Bearing in mind the standards already set by the International Plan of Action on Ageing and the conventions, recommendations and resolutions of the International Labour Organisation, the World Health Organisation and other United Nations entities,

Encourages Governments to incorporate the following principles into their national programmes whenever possible: . . .

Independence

1. Older persons should have access to adequate food, water, shelter, clothing and health care through the provision of income, family and community support and self-help.

2. Older persons should have the opportunity to work or to have access to other income-generating opportunities.

3. Older persons should be able to participate in determining when and at what pace withdrawal from the labour force takes place.

4. Older persons should have access to appropriate educational and training programmes.

5. Older persons should be able to live in environments that are safe and adaptable to personal preferences and changing capacities.

6. Older persons should be able to reside at home for as long as possible.

Participation

7. Older persons should remain integrated in society, participate actively in the formulation and implementation of policies that directly affect their well-being and share their knowledge and skills with younger generations.

8. Older persons should be able to seek and develop opportunities for service to the community and to serve as volunteers in positions appropriate to their interests and capabilities.

9. Older persons should be able to form movements or associations of older persons.

Care ˙

10. Older persons should benefit from family and community care and protection in accordance with each society's system of cultural values.

11. Older persons should have access to health care to help them to maintain or regain the optimum level of physical, mental and emotional well-being and to prevent or delay the onset of illness.

12. Older persons should have access to social and legal services to enhance their autonomy, protection and care.

13. Older persons should be able to utilise appropriate levels of institutional care providing protection, rehabilitation and social and mental stimulation in a humane and secure environment.

14. Older persons should be able to enjoy human rights and fundamental freedoms when residing in any shelter, care or treatment facility, including full respect for their dignity, beliefs, needs and privacy and for the right to make decisions about their care and the quality of their lives.

Self-fulfilment

15. Older persons should be able to pursue opportunities for the full development of their potential.

16. Older persons should have access to the educational, cultural, spiritual and recreational resources of society.

Dignity

17. Older persons should be able to live in dignity and security and be free of exploitation and physical or mental abuse.

18. Older persons should be treated fairly regardless of age, gender, racial or ethnic background, disability or other status, and be valued independently of their economic contribution.

Appendix 2

LIST OF ORGANISATIONS

Age & Opportunity
Marino Institute of Education, Griffith Avenue, Dublin 9
Telephone: 01-8057709
E-mail: ageandop@mie.ie
Website: www.olderinireland.ie

Age & Opportunity is the Irish national agency working to challenge negative attitudes to ageing, and to promote greater participation by older people in society. Age & Opportunity's initiatives include *Bealtaine*, the national arts festival celebrating creativity in older age; *Go for Life*, the national programme for sport and physical activity for older people; and *AgeWise*, Age Equality Training, which raises awareness of attitudes to ageing, available free of charge to organisations working with older people.

Age Action Ireland
30–31 Lower Camden Street, Dublin 2
Telephone: 01-4756989
Fax: 01-4756011
E-mail: info@ageaction.ie
Website: www.ageaction.ie

Age Action Ireland is the national network on ageing and older people. Age Action promotes better policies and services for all older people and an ageing society. Its main aim is to improve the quality of life of all older people, especially those who are most disadvantaged and vulnerable, by enabling them to live full, independent and satisfying lives for as long as they wish in their own homes, or in other appropriate accommodation. Age Action Ireland, through its information service, library devoted to ageing matters, publications website, caring advice, support and training, co-operative learning for older people, research and development work, seminars and lobbying aims to make life better for older people. Age Action is a network that includes individual, statutory, voluntary and corporate membership. It is an independent, non-governmental body.

ALONE

1 Willie Bermingham Place, Kilmainham Lane, Dublin 8
Telephone: 01-6791032
E-mail: alone@iol.ie

ALONE (A Little Offering Never Ends), an independent voluntary organisation, attempts to protect the old and lonely from disease, hunger and neglect; helps to expose and alleviate the suffering of elderly people; and encourages neighbours of the isolated old to take direct action in relieving their distress. ALONE provides food, clothing and fuel to those who are over 60 years of age who are unable to provide for themselves. ALONE also provides accommodation on a temporary or permanent basis.

Alzheimer Society of Ireland

43 Northumberland Avenue, Dun Laoghaire, Co Dublin
Telephone: 01-2846616
E-mail: info@alzheimer.ie
Website: www.alzheimer.ie

The Alzheimer Society of Ireland is a national voluntary organisation providing a range of services and supports to people with dementia and their carers. It also campaigns for improved access to and better quality services for people with dementia and their families.

AONTAS

2nd Floor, 83-87, Main Street, Ranelagh, Dublin 6
Telephone:01-4068220
E-mail: mail@aontas.com
Website: www.aontas.com

AONTAS is the Irish National Association of Adult Education, a voluntary membership organisation. It exists to promote the development of a learning society through the provision of a quality and comprehensive system of adult learning and education which is accessible to and inclusive to all.

Care Alliance Ireland

30–31 Lower Camden Street, Dublin 2
Telephone: 01-4756989
E-mail: cai@ageaction.ie

A network of family carers and voluntary organisations providing a forum for the promotion, development and implementation of policies to meet carers' needs.

Care Local

Carmichael House, North Brunswick Street, Dublin 7
Telephone: 01-8782358

Assists older people stay in their own homes for as long as possible and to enjoy a better way of life, forging friendships and long-term relationships with clients. Volunteers visit and befriend older people at home or in hospital, help to provide beds, bed linen, clothing, food, fuel, wheelchairs, help with electricity, gas and telephone bills, redecorate homes, assist with shopping and provide entertainment in homes and community centres.

Caring and Sharing Association

Carmichael House, North Brunswick Street, Dublin 7
Telephone: 01-8725370

Organisation of voluntary helpers and handicapped people. Aims to develop an awareness of the spiritual, social and personal needs of members, organises holidays, pilgrimages and social events. Respite provided in family setting.

Centre for Independent Living

Carmichael House, North Brunswick Street, Dublin 7
Telephone: 01-8730986
E-mail: info@dubcil.org
Website: www.dubcil.org

Founded by people with significant disabilities to address the existing ongoing difficulties and discriminations they face. CIL promotes self-determination and civil rights by developing appropriate programmes that uphold the right to independent living. There are 27 centres round the country.

Disability Federation of Ireland (DFI)

Fumbally Court, Fumbally Lane, Dublin 8
Telephone: 01-4547978
E-mail: info@disability-federation.ie
Website: www.disability-federation.ie

A support organisation for voluntary organisations covering all areas of disability. DFI's central mission is to act as advocate for this sector and to support member organisations.

Energy Action Ltd

IDA Unit 14, Newmarket, Dublin 8
Telephone: 01-45454664
E-mail: info@energyaction.ie

Energy Action is a Dublin-based charity that provides home insulation (attic insulation, draught-proofing of doors and windows, lagging jackets and low energy light bulbs) free of charge to eligible householders. Criteria for eligibility are that recipients must be in privately owned or rented accommodation and must be in receipt of either an old age, blind or disability pension. Home security devices are also provided in the houses of old age pensioners living alone.

Equality Authority

2 Clonmel Street, Dublin 2
Telephone: 01-4173333
LoCall Information Line: 1890 245545
E-mail: info@equality.ie
Website: www.equality.ie

The Equality Authority is an independent body working to monitor and eliminate discrimination in employment, vocational training, advertising, collective agreements, the provision of goods and services on nine distinct grounds: gender; marital status, family status, age, disability, race, sexual orientation, religious belief and being a Traveller. The Equality Authority is available to give advice on legislation and can refer complaints to the Director of Equality Investigation. The Equality has produced reports on "Implementing Equality for Older People" and "Ageism and Labour Market Participation".

Federation of Active Retirement Associations

1–2 Eustace Street, Dublin 2
Telephone: 01-6792142
E-mail: fara@eircom.net

The Federation was constituted in 1985 when representatives from 16 Dublin-based active retirement groups came together and decided to set up a formal structure to oversee and guide the expansion of active retirement groups throughout Ireland. The movement has grown substantially with over 300 affiliated associations with a membership approaching 20,000 people. In addition, five regional councils have been established, each with their own training and development structures.

Forum of People with Disabilities

21 Hill Street, Dublin 1
Telephone: 01-8786077
E-mail: inforum@indigo.ie
Website: www.inforum.ie

Ireland's only organisation wholly controlled by people with disabilities. The Forum is rights-based, promoting civil rights among members and others.

Friends of the Elderly

25 Bolton Street, Dublin 1
Telephone: 01-8731855
E-mail: info@friendsoftheelderly.ie

Aims to combat loneliness in older people by providing friendship, social contact and opportunities for involvement in communities activities. Services include social contact, home and hospital visiting, transport, minor home improvements, holidays, outings and parties.

GROW Community Mental Health
National Office, Ormonde Home, Barrack Street, Kilkenny
Telephone 056-7761624

A community mental health organisation with branches country-wide whose aim is to help members recover from all forms of mental breakdown or to prevent such happening through mutual help groups in a caring and sharing community. GROW emphasises a self-help/mutual help approach to mental health and the development of personal coping responses.

Health Boards
There are eight health boards in the Republic of Ireland, the largest of which, the Eastern Regional Health Authority, is divided into three autonomous areas. While the types of services for older people vary across the different health boards, all offer a broad range of services in community, hospital and residential settings. An important point of contact is the Public Health Nurse for a specific area within each Health Board Region. Contact your local public health clinic for details. Also, see Chapter 6 for contacts relating to specific health issues. You should also find out what your community care area is, as well as your local hospital. This and other information should be available from the main Health Boards, whose contact details are listed below. Remember, you may not get the information you require directly from these contacts, but they should be able to point you in the right direction.

Eastern Regional Health Authority:
Customer Service Freephone: 1800-520520

East Coast Area Health Board,
Southern Cross House, Boghall Road, Bray, County Wicklow
Telephone: 01-2014200
The ECAHB ranges from Ringsend in the north to Carnew in the south, and from the east coast of Wicklow to the borders of West Wicklow and Carlow.

Northern Area Health Board
Swords Business Campus, Balheary Road, Swords, County Dublin
Telephone: 01-8131800
E-mail: nahb@nahb.ie
Website: www.nahb.ie
The NAHB covers Dublin city and county north of the River Liffey.

South Western Area Health Board
Oak House, Limetree Avenue, Millennium Park, Naas, County Kildare
LoCall: 1890-737343
Telephone: 045-800400
The SWAHB covers Dublin South City, Dublin South West, Dublin West, Kildare and West Wicklow.

Midland Health Board
Central Office, Arden Road, Tullamore, County Offaly
Telephone: 0506-21868
E-mail: comments@mhb.ie
Website: www.mhb.ie
The Midland Health Board has responsibility for health services in counties Laois, Offaly, Longford and Westmeath.

Mid-Western Health Board
31–33 Catherine Street, Limerick
Telephone: 061-316655
Website: www.mwhb.ie
The Mid-Western Health Board has responsibility for health services in counties Limerick, Clare and Tipperary North Riding.

North-Eastern Health Board
Administrative Head Office, Navan Road, Kells, County Meath
Telephone: 046-9280500
E-mail: info@nehb.ie
Website: www.nehb.ie
The North-Eastern Health Board has responsibility for health services in counties Louth, Meath, Cavan and Monaghan.

North-Western Health Board

Head Office, Manorhamilton, County Leitrim
Telephone: 071-9820400
Customer Information Line: 1850-636313
Website: www.nwhb.ie

The North-Western Health Board has responsibility for health services in counties Donegal, Sligo and Leitrim.

South-Eastern Health Board

Lacken, Dublin Road, Kilkenny
Telephone: 056-7784100
Website: www.sehb.ie

The South-Eastern Health Board has responsibility for health services in counties Carlow, Kilkenny, Tipperary South Riding, Waterford, and Wexford.

Southern Health Board

Aras Slainte, Wilton Road, Cork
LoCall Customer Service Line: 1850-742000
Telephone: 021-4545011
E-mail: feedback@shb.ie
Website: www.shb.ie

The Southern Health Board has responsibility for health services in counties Cork and Kerry.

Western Health Board

Merlin Park Regional Hospital, Galway.
Telephone: (091) 751131
E-mail: eservices@whb.ie
Website: www.whb.ie

The Western Health Board has responsibility for health services in counties Galway, Mayo, and Roscommon.

Irish Association of Older People

Room G02, UCD, Earlsfort Terrace, Dublin 2
Telephone: 01-4750071
E-mail: iaop@oceanfree.net

Aims to serve as the direct voice of older people, representing their interests, campaigning on their behalf, promoting independence, dignity and purpose. Also to serve as an information centre.

Irish Hospice Foundation

Morrison Chambers, 32 Nassau Street, Dublin 2.
Telephone: 01-6793188.
E-mail: info@hospice-foundation.ie
Website: www.hospice-foundation.ie

A voluntary body which provides advocacy in the provision and development of hospices services, and a supportive role for the voluntary hospice movement.

Irish Osteoporosis Society

P O Box 8134, Cardiff Lane, Dublin 2
Telephone: 01-6774267

Aims to prevent the growing prevalence of osteoporosis, increase awareness of the disease, offer advice and information to sufferers, establish a network of local support groups, disseminate information to health professionals on current methods of treatment and prevention.

Irish Wheelchair Association

Blackheath Drive, Clontarf, Dublin 3
Telephone: 01-8186400
E-mail: info@iwa.ie
Website: www.iwa.ie

Dedicated to the full integration of people with disabilities as equal, independent members of the community. Provides national programmes covering personal assistant/care attendant services, driving assessment/tuition, peer counselling, holiday breaks, wheelchair sales/loan/repair, sports, day programmes, lobbying and access.

Mental Health Ireland

6 Adelaide Street, Dun Laoghaire, County Dublin
Telephone: 01-2841166
E-mail: info@mentalhealthireland.ie
Website: www.mentalhealthireland.ie

Aims to promote positive mental health, and support those with a mental illness, their families and carers by identifying their needs and advocating for their rights.

Money Advice and Budgeting Services (MABS)

Offices throughout the country
E-mail: info@mabs.ie

MABS is a free and confidential service for people with debt and money management problems. There are 62 MABS offices in Ireland with professional money advisers who will help people deal with their debts and make out a budget; make sure people are getting their full entitlements; contact creditors if so desired; and help people decide on the best way to make payments.

National Association for Deaf People

35 North Federick Street, Dublin 1
Telephone: 01-8723800

Since 1963 the National Association for Deaf People has campaigned for full equality in all aspects of life for deaf and hearing-impaired people, as well as for parents of deaf children to have all appropriate supports and services for their children's development.

National Council for the Blind of Ireland

Whitworth Road, Drumcondra, Dublin 9
Telephone: 01-8307033
E-mail: info@ncbi.ie
Website: www.ncbi.ie

The National Council for the Blind of Ireland was established to promote the full independence of people with impaired vision and to minimise the disabling effect of vision impairment.

National Council on Ageing and Older People

22 Clanwilliam Square, Grand Canal Quay, Dublin 2
Telephone: 01-6768484
E-mail: info@ncaop.ie

The aim of the Council is to develop a comprehensive understanding of ageing and of the older population of this country, with a view to providing the best possible advice to the Minister for Health and Children and others concerned with the health and well-being of older people. The Council undertakes and commission research, and has published 83 studies on a wide range of subjects relating to the welfare of older people in Ireland.

National Federation of Pensioners Associations

c/o Irish Congress of Trade Unions, 31 Parnell Square, Dublin 1
Telephone: 01-8897777
Website: www.ictu.ie

National umbrella organisation which protects and promotes the interests of pensioners and co-ordinates the work of affiliated associations.

National Safety Council

4 Northbrook Road, Ranelagh, Dublin 6
Telephone: 01-4963422
E-mail: info@nsc.ie
Website: www.nsc.ie

Established in December 1987 under the Local Government Services (Corporate Bodies) Act, 1971, its function is to promote road safety and fire prevention through education, promotions and publicity campaigns.

Office of the Pensions Ombudsman

36 Upper Mount Street, Dublin 2
Telephone: 01-6471650
E-mail: info@pensionsombudsman.ie
Website: www.pensionsombudsman.ie

The Pensions Ombudsman investigates complaints of injustice due to maladministration, and disputes of fact or law, in Occupational Pension Schemes and Personal Retirement Savings Accounts (PRSAs). The Ombudsman is completely independent and acts as an impartial adjudicator.

Recovery Inc

PO Box 2210, Dublin 13
Telephone 01-6260775

A community mental health organisation offering a self-help method for controlling temperamental behaviour and changing attitudes towards nervous symptoms and fears through a training and leadership programme.

Retirement Planning Council of Ireland

27/29 Lower Pembroke Street, Dublin 2
Telephone: 01-6613139
E-mail: info@rpc.ie
Website: www.rpc.ie

The Retirement Planning Council of Ireland Ltd. (RPC) has charitable status supported by almost 300 private and semi-state bodies. RPC has over 30 years experience of conducting planning for retirement courses. We offer three different types of courses as well as talks covering all aspects of planning for the future. All of the courses are led by an RPC professional with each specialist subject being delivered by an approved expert.

Safe Home Programme

St Brendan's Village, Mulrany, County Mayo
Telephone: 098-36036
E-mail: safehome@rural-health.net

The Safe Home Programme seeks to assist older Irish-born emigrants to return to their homeland in situations where they lack the financial means to do so without help. Applicants must be 60 or older, living abroad in rented accommodation and seeking to return to the city or county of origin. They also need to be unable to provide accommodation for themselves from their own resources.

Senior Help Line

Third Age Centre, Summerhill, County Meath
Telephone: 1850-440444
E-mail: info@thirdage-ireland.com

Aimed at older people who are feeling lonely, are worried about something or just want someone to talk to, the Senior Help Line provides a friendly, helpful and confidential services for the price of a local call from anywhere in Ireland. Over 300 volunteers in nine centres are available from 10.00 am to 1.00 pm and from 7.00 pm to 10.00 pm every day.

Society of St Vincent de Paul

8 New Cabra Road, Dublin 7
Telephone: 01-8384164
E-mail: info@svp.ie

Services for older people by the Society of St Vincent de Paul include housing support, visitation to elderly in homes and hospitals, holiday centres and day care centres.

Threshold

21 Stoneybatter, Dublin 7
Telephone: 01-6786096
E-mail: advice@threshold.ie
Website: www.threshold.ie

Threshold is a not-for-profit organisation whose aim is to secure a right to housing. Threshold provides a free, confidential, professional advisory and advocacy service. The Eastern Regional Advice Centre is open Monday to Friday, 9.30 am to 5.00 pm, and from 5.30 to 7.30 pm every Thursday.

University of the Third Age (U3A)

c/o Age Action Ireland, 30–31 Lower Camden Street, Dublin 2
Telephone: 01-4756989
E-mail: development@ageaction.ie

U3A is a learning co-operative. There are a number of groups around Ireland that share the U3A philosophy. Contact Mary Colclough, Age Action Development Officer, Education, for further details. See also "In Focus: University of the Third Age" on pages 87–91.

Victim Support

Haliday House, 32 Arran Quay, Dublin 7
Telephone: 01-8780870
E-mail: info@victimsupport.ie
Website: www.victimsupport.ie

Victim Support is a community-based organisation of trained volunteers who provide emotional and practical support to those affected by crime. Services include court witness service support, tourist victim support and families of murder victims support.

Volunteering Ireland

Coleraine House, Coleraine Street, Dublin 7.
Telephone: 01-8722622.
E-mail: info@volunteeringireland.com

Volunteering Ireland, the national resource for volunteering in the Republic of Ireland, promotes, supports and facilitates volunteering. A placement service matches volunteers and organisations in Dublin, and throughout Ireland Volunteering Ireland provides support, advice, training, consultancy and information to individuals and organisations.

Volunteer Stroke Scheme

249 Crumlin Road, Dublin 12.
Telephone: 01-4559036.
E-mail: info@strokescheme.ie
Website: www.strokescheme.ie

Caters for stroke patients and their families by running weekly clubs, information and support, newsletter, holidays, outings, support meetings for carers, plus home visits to help with speech programmes. Operates a Technical Aids Loan Scheme.

Widows Association of Ireland

29 Gardiner Place, Dublin 1
Telephone: 01-8728814
E-mail: natwid@eircom.net
Website: www.nawi.ie

Aims to help widows readjust to their new role through advice and counselling and to seek reform in social conditions. Legal, financial and bereavement support. Organises social events, there are 30 branches throughout the country.

INDEX

Abbey Theatre, 102
Abbeyquarter Arts, 104
accidents, 154, 201–3
    preventing, 201–3
Active Age Week, 10
active ageing, 80, 117–18, 123–6,
    143; *see also* exercise and
    fitness
active retirement associations,
    44–8, 98, 170
activism, 1, 6–7, 14–15, 244–58
acupuncture, 179
adult children, 5
adult education; *see* AONTAS;
    education
adult literacy, 78–9
advance directives, 234, 235
Aeschylus, 75
Age Action Ireland, 10, 68, 86,
    87, 89–90, 91, 166, 223, 248–55,
    281–2
    information service, 253–4
Age & Opportunity, 57, 100, 105–
    6, 107, 115–16, 117, 140, 142,
    254, 256, 281
age equality training, 12, 256
Age Matters in Ireland, 251
*Ageing and Labour Market
    Participation*, 83

ageism, 6–14, 76–8, 241–58
    behaviour, attitudes and
        language, 7–8, 76–8, 241–4
    changing stereotypes, 6, 8–9,
        13–14
    discrimination, 14
    government strategy, 11–13
    prevalence of, 6–8
    tackling, 10–14, 241–58
alarms,
    burglar, 203–4
    personal, 204
allergies, 149
ALONE, 282
alternative therapy, 179–80
Alzheimer's disease, 173, 178,
    267
Alzheimer Society of Ireland,
    178, 221, 282
American Association of Retired
    Persons (AARP), 15
Amnesty International, 68
anaemia, 149
Annan, Kofi, 258
antidepressants, 176–7
AONTAS (National Association
    for Adult Education), 75–8, 79,
    83, 86, 87, 282
arthritis, 159

arts and older people, 95–116,
     261
   health benefits, 97–100
   in care settings, 99–100
   organisations, 98, 102–5
   programmes, 96–8
   see also Bealtaine
arts centres, 101, 102–4, 105
Association of Optometrists
     Ireland, 157
Aware, 171, 172

Back to Education, 253, 254
bank accounts, 231; *see also*
   financial records
Barnardos, 68
Bealtaine, 98, 100–2, 106
   resources, 101
   types of events, 100–1
bereavement grant, 239
Bethany Group, 171
Bewick, Pauline, 96
Binchy, Maeve, 2
Blake, Eubie (James Herbert), 143
blindness, 158
blood pressure, 135, 149, 152;
   see also heart disease
Blythe, Ernest, 250
Bowling Alone, 51
Brady, Berni, 75
BreastCheck, 7, 165–6, 253
Brown, Robert McAfee, 53
Browning, Robert, 1
Buchan, William, 117
budgeting, 24
BUPA Ireland, 200
Bygren, Lars, 97

Callely, Ivor, 252
Camphill Communities of
     Ireland, 71

cancer, 160–2, 165–7
   bowel (colorectal), 132, 160,
     162
   breast, 165–6
   cervical, 166–7
   lip, 161
   lung, 160, 161
   prostate, 160, 161–2
   skin, 144, 145, 160, 161, 165
   testicular, 162
   womb/ovaries, 167
Care Alliance Ireland, 283
Care Local, 283
carers, 178, 217–23, 251
   home from hospital, 217–18
   importance of communication,
     218
   safe handling, 219
   supports for, 220–3
     day care, 221
     health boards, 220–1
     respite, 221–2
Carers Association, 222
Caring and Sharing Association,
     283
Cashman, Seamus, 109
cataracts, 7, 158
Centre for Independent Living,
     283
Chinese medicine, 179
chiropody, 155–6
Christianity, 265, 270–4
   nourishing faith, 273–4
   religious development within,
     272–4
Churchill, Winston, 117
Citizens Information Centres, 44,
     67, 68, 170, 171, 223
coeliac, 149
Coeliac Society of Ireland, 150
Cohen, Gene, 97

Colclough, Mary, 89, 91
Collier, Jim, 45, 47
Comhairle, 40, 68, 69
community health services, 155,
  159, 178, 208–12, 224
complementary medicine, 151,
  168, 179–80
computers, 84–5, 90, 113–15
Conservation Volunteers Ireland,
  68
constipation, 149
consumers, older people as, 15
Convery, Janet, 143, 201, 213
Coughlan, Mary, 250
counselling and psychotherapy,
  63–6, 171, 175, 176
creativity, 95–7, 261; *see also* arts
  and older people
crime, protecting against, 204–9
  do's and don'ts, 205–6
  elder abuse, 208–9, 245
  fraud, 206–7
  identity theft, 207–8
Cronin, Kevin, 63–6
cycling, 132

de Beauvoir, Simone, 258
de Mello, Anthony, 274–5
deafness, 157
death and bereavement, 17, 171,
  227, 232–9, 266–70
  acceptance of, 17, 268–70
  fear of, 268
  grieving process, 266–7
  practical matters relating to,
    227–39; *see also* advance
    directives; funerals; living
    wills; putting personal affairs
    in order; will, writing a
  sense of mortality, 268–70
Debra Ireland, 72

debt, handling, 42–3
dementia, 178
"demographic time bomb",
  9–10, 14, 19–20, 257
Dempsey, Anne, 1, 115, 117, 143,
  201, 227
Dennehy, Brian, 96
dental benefits, 39
Department of Education and
  Science, 75
Department of Health and
  Children, 118, 150, 193, 252
Department of Social and Family
  Affairs, 40, 250
depression, 7, 170–7
  accessing help for, 171–2, 175
  causes, 170–1, 173
  diagnosing, 173, 175
  preventing, 177–8
  support from family and
    friends, 177
  symptoms of, 174–5
  treating, 175–6
diabetes, 132, 133, 149, 182
diarrhoea, 149
Dillon, James, 250
disability, 39, 211
  benefits/grants, 39, 224
Disability Federation of Ireland
  (DFI), 284
Divine, sense of the, 264–5; *see*
  also God; spirituality
doctor/GP
  and medical cards, 180–1
  importance of regular visits
    to, 144–5, 151–2
  referrals from, 154, 155, 156,
    157, 159, 161, 162, 163, 165,
    167, 171, 178, 180, 182, 210
  services; *see* general
    practitioner (GP) services

doctor/GP (cont'd)
  talking with, 183–92
    diagnosis, 189–90
    getting information, 186–8
    medical tests, 188–9
    medications, 190–1
    preparing for visit, 183–5
    seeing specialists, 191–2
    sharing information, 185
    surgery, 192
    treatments, 190
  see also health
Doing Local History, 113
Donnelly, Eamon, 19
Draíocht Arts Centre, 103
drug refund scheme, 181
Dublin City University (DCU),
  131
Dublin Literacy Scheme, 92
Dublin's Evening Classes, 86

education, 75–93
  accessing, 84–7, 253
  changing attitudes to, 76–8
  choices in, 84–7
  lifelong learning, 79–81
  nonformal and community,
    81–2
  overcoming barriers, 83–4
  see also adult literacy;
    University of the Third Age
Egan, Pat, 107
EIL Intercultural Learning, 72–3
e-libraries, 113–15
Eliot, T.S., 262
employment, older people in, 12,
  14, 40–1, 83, 248–9
Employment Equality Act 1998, 7
Energy Action Ltd., 284
entitlements, state, 38–40
Entitlements for the Over-Sixties,
  40

Equal Status Act 2000, 7
Equality Authority, 11, 12, 83,
  241, 284
Erikson, Erik, 16–17
evening classes; see education
exercise and fitness, 13, 117–42
  barriers to, 125–6
  benefits, 123–5
  endurance/stamina, 131, 132–3
    improving, 132
    safety, 133
    time and effort, 132–3
  flexibility, 136–7
    improving, 137
    safety, 137
    time and effort, 137
  levels of fitness, 118–19
  managing change and getting
    fit, stages in, 119–23
      1. precontemplation, 120–1
      2. contemplation, 121
      3. preparation, 121–2
      4. action, 122
      5. maintenance, 122
      6. relapse, 123
  muscle strength and balance,
    131, 133–6
    improving, 134–5
    safety, 135–6
    time and effort, 135
  safety, 126–30
  see also Go for Life
    programme
eye problems, 157–8

Falling in Love with Life, 260
family
  changes in patterns, 5–6
FÁS, 67, 253
Federation of Active Retirement
  Associations (FARA), 44–8, 131,
  285

FETAC (Further Education and Training Awards Council), 99
Financial Information Service Centres (FISC), 44
financial records, 227–8, 231
fitness; *see* exercise and fitness
fluid retention, 130, 149
food; *see* nutrition
foot care, 155–6
Forum of People with Disabilities, 285
"fourth age", 3, 16, 90
Frances, Fi, 95
Frankl, Viktor, 262
Friel, Brian, 81
Friends of the Elderly, 58, 71, 285
funerals, 235–9
    bereavement grant, 239 1
    burial options, 236
    costs, 237, 239
    cremation, 237–80
    humanist, 235–6
    personalising, 235–6
    prepaid, 238–9
    religious, 235

gardening, 118, 119, 132, 261
general practitioner (GP) services, 181–3
    Cardiac Daiagnosis Programme, 183
    Diabetes Shared Care Programme, 182
    Heartwatch, 182
    out-of-hours services, 182
    Primary Care Implementation Project, 183
Glasnevin Cemetery, 238
glaucoma, 158
Glencree Centre for Reconciliation, 71–2

Go for Life programme, 117, 118, 128–30, 139–42, 246
    Get Active Challenge, 140
    Get Walking Challenge, 141
    National Grant Scheme, 141–2
    publications, 142
    training, 141
    warming up, 128
        keeping warm, cool and hydrated, 130
        mobilisers, 128–9
        pulse, breathing and temperature, 129–30
GOAL, 73
God, 264–5, 267, 270–4
    Christian view of, 271–2; *see also* Christianity
    loss of a sense of, 267, 271
    loving relationship with, 272
    religious notions of, 270–1
    see also meaning, search for; religion; spirituality
Golden Charter (Ireland) Ltd., 238–9
Golman, C., 95
grandparenthood, 5–6, 262
Green, Theodore, 258
"grey power", 14–15, 241–58; *see also* activism
GROW Community Mental Health, 286

Harkin, Mary, 117
Harney, Mary, 249
health, 3, 7, 13, 14, 143–200, 245
    arts and, 97–100
    disease prevention, 144–5, 151–2, 188
    exercise and, 126–7, 144; *see also* exercise and fitness
    lifestyle and, 144
    men and, 159–63

health (cont'd)
    mental and emotional, 169–79;
        see also Alzheimer's
        disease; counselling and
        psychotherapy; dementia;
        depression; loneliness
    physical problems, conditions
        and diseases, 151–69; see
        also entries for specific
        conditions
    promotion, 145–51; see also
        nutrition; smoking
    women and, 164–9
Health and Safety Authority, 161
Health Board Executive, 12
Health Boards, 140, 286–8
    Eastern Regional Health
        Authority, 286
        East Coast Area, 131, 213,
            286
            Northern Area, 287
            South Western Area, 287
    health promotion, 150, 151
    Midland, 99, 100, 287
    Mid-Western, 287
    North-Eastern, 287
    North-Western, 288
    payments from, 39, 40
    South-Eastern, 288
    Southern, 288
    Western, 288
health insurance, 200
hearing aids, 39, 156–7
hearing problems, 156–7
heart attack, 154, 182
heart disease, 135, 144, 149, 152,
    160, 164–5, 182
Helminiak, Daniel, 266, 272
hernia, 163
hip replacement, 7, 127, 136, 137
Holmes, Oliver Wendell, 201
Home Care Grant Scheme, 212–16

home support, 12, 178, 209–16;
    see also independent living
homeopathy, 168, 179
hormone replacement therapy
    (HRT), 168
hospice care, 198–9, 217
hospital services, 154, 159, 172,
    193–4, 224
    private, 194, 200
    public, 193
Household Budget Scheme, 43
houses and housing, 3, 5
    adapting for older age, 201–2
    moving, 224–6
    right to, 248
    safety, 202–8
    see also independent living
Humanist Association, 235, 236
hygiene, 155

I'm Not Finished Yet, 90
Implementing Equality for Older
    People, 11
impotence, 163
incontinence, 153, 216
independent living, 201–26, 246
    campaigning for, 246
    Home Care Grant Scheme,
        212, 213–16
    home from hospital scheme
        (Slán Abhaile), 212, 215–16,
        217–18
    home help services, 209–10
    meals on wheels, 210
    personal care services, 210–
        11
    rehabilitation at home, 211–12
    staying at home vs. nursing
        home, 201, 195–8
Inquiry into the Third Age
    (Carnegie UK Trust), 2
insurance, 200, 231, 245

Institute of Chartered
Accountants, 44, 228, 230
integrity, 16–17
*International Adult Literacy
Survey*, 78
International Federation on
Ageing, 55
internet, 15, 87, 113–15
in libraries, 113–15
medical information, 186–7
shopping, 15
investments, 35–8
lump sum, 36–7
property, 37–8
Irish Association for Speech and
Language Therapists, 159
Irish Association of Counselling
and Psychotherapy, 172, 176
Irish Association of Funeral
Directors, 237
Irish Association of Older People,
223, 288
Irish Cancer Society, 150, 151,
160, 165, 166, 186, 199
Irish Council for Social Housing,
226
Irish Film Institute, 103
Irish Financial Services
Regulatory Authority (IFSRA), 37
Irish Heart Foundation, 149–50,
186
Irish Hospice Foundation, 199,
289
Irish Medicines Board, 179
Irish Museum of Modern Art, 98,
103
Irish Osteoporosis Society, 169,
289
Irish Universities Nutrition
Alliance (IUNA), 118
Irish Wheelchair Association, 289
Islam, 270

James, PD, 96
Jesus, 271–2, 273; *see also*
Christianity; God; religion;
spirituality
Johnson, Samuel, 19
Judaism, 270, 271

Kelly, Anne Marie, 114
Kennelly, Brendan, 2
"kipper" generation, 5
Knowles, Sonny, 2
Kubler-Ross, Elisabeth, 266

L'Arche Communities Ireland, 71
le Brocquy, Louis, 96
Leahy, Ann, 95
Learning for Life (White Paper on
Adult Education), 79–81
libraries, 67, 86–7, 101–2, 106–9
computers and, 113–15
gramophone circles, 108
other activities, 115–16
reading groups, 107–8, 115
research, 109
life expectancy/longevity, 2,
9–10, 19–20, 144
life stages, 16–17
lifelong learning; *see* education
Living Alone Allowance, 39
living wills, 234–5
local authority arts officers, 99,
101, 104–5
local history, researching, 109–13
Local Sports Partnerships (LSPs),
140
loneliness, 169–70
loss, sense of, 266–7
love, 265
LV Book Club (Cork), 107

macular degeneration, 158
Maher, Paul, 256

male menopause, 162–3
Manahan, Anna, 1
Man's Search for Meaning, 262
marginalisation, 8
marriage, 5
Marx, Groucho, 268
mature students, 75–6
Maugherow Project, 104
Mayo County Council Arts Office,
    99, 104
McCann, Catherine, 259
McCrea, Elly, 100
McGovern, Gabriel, 100
McGowan, Emer, 103
McGuinness, Clare, 53
meaning, search for, 262–5
    personal, 262–3
    ultimate, 264–5
media, 250–1, 254–5
medical cards, 180–1
    benefits of, 156, 157, 180–1
    entitlement to, 180, 181
medical services, 159
medicines, taking, 176–7, 179,
    190–1
melanoma, 145
*Memorandum on Lifelong
    Learning*, 80
memory loss, 171
menopause, 167–7
Men's Cancer Action Week, 160
Mental Health Association of
    Ireland, 172, 289
Mimnagh, Lorraine, 105
mobility problems, 153–5, 159
Money Advice and Budgeting
    Service (MABS), 42–3, 290
Moreau, Jeanne, 96
MS Society, 221
Murray, Paul, 241
music, 95, 261

National Adult Literary Agency
    (NALA), 69, 79
National Association for Deaf
    People, 157, 290
National Association of Widows,
    250, 254
National Council for the Blind in
    Ireland, 158, 290
National Council on Ageing and
    Older People, 12, 201, 213, 223,
    290
National Economic and Social
    Forum (NESF), 12
National Federation of
    Pensioners Associations, 291
National Institute of Aging (US),
    172, 183, 228
National Programme for Sport
    and Physical Activity for Older
    People; *see* Go for Life
    programme
National Safety Council, 291
National Survey of Involvement in
    Sport and Physical Activity, 117
Nelligan, Maurice, 1–2
Never Too Old to Learn, 77
Nicholl, Donald, 269
Nouwen, Henri, 268
nursing homes, 12–13, 193, 194–8
    decision to enter, 195–8; *see
    also* independent living
    private, 194–8
        costs/subventions, 194–5
    public, 193
nutrition, 13, 146–50, 152
    balanced diet, 146–8
    food pyramid, 146–7
    medical conditions and, 149–
        50
    tips for older people, 148

obesity, 126, 133, 149
occupational therapy, 223–4
OECD, 78, 79
O'Halloran, Michael, 244, 245, 247
Old Age, 258
O'Mahony, Andy, 2
O'Neill, Desmond, 11
Opportunity Knocks, 68
optical benefits, 39, 157
O'Reilly, Anthony, 2
organ donation, 239
O'Rourke, Mary, 2
O'Shea, Eamon, 144
osteoporosis, 133, 149, 153, 168–9
Oxfam Ireland, 69

painting, 95, 96, 102, 103, 105,
    261
palliative care, 199, 217
parenthood, 5–6
Peck, Robert, 17
pensions, 4, 20, 21, 23, 25–35,
    249–50
    additional voluntary
        contributions (AVCs), 21, 25,
        26
    approved retirement fund
        (ARF), 25
    death benefit, 30–1
    defined benefit scheme, 26–7,
        34
    defined contribution scheme,
        26, 28–31, 34
    investment funds, 29–30
    how they work, 25–31
    lump sum, 30, 31, 34, 35–7
    on retirement, 30–1
    personal pension plans, 35
    Personal Retirement Savings
        Accounts (PRSAs), 4, 26,
        31–3, 251

    rights regarding, 14, 251–2
    risks, 31
    self-employment and, 35
    shortfall, 21, 42–4
    state ("old age"), 40
    tax treatment, 34
Pensions Board, 33, 246
Pensions Ombudsman, 291
Personal Public Service (PPS)
    number, 230, 231
physiotherapy, 154–5
    accessing, 154–5
policy-making, 11–12
positive ageing, 16
Positive Ageing Week, 251–2
Psychiatry of Old Age services,
    172, 178
public health nurse, 204, 216,
    217, 222
public transport, 245
Putnam, Robert, 51
putting personal affairs in order,
    227–32
    Personal Affairs Checklist,
        228, 230
    financial records, 231
    legal documents, 232
    personal records, 230

Rabelais, François, 227
racism, 242
Rape Crisis Centre, 208–9
reading groups; *see* libraries
Recovery Inc., 291
religion, 264, 270–4; *see also*
    Christianity; God; meaning,
    search for; spirituality
rent/mortgage assistance, 39
Report on Healthy Ageing, 144
respiratory illnesses, 144
Respond, 225, 226

retirement, 19–51
    adjusting to, 20–5
    age, 19–20, 83
    changes in patterns, 4, 19–20
    marriage and, 49
    money and, 20–1, 23–5
    pensions; *see* pensions
    relationships and, 20–2, 48–50
    social life, 44–8, 50–1
    use of time in, 22–3, 48
Retirement Planning Council of
    Ireland, 20, 292
rights, 248–51

Safe Home Programme, 292
Samaritans, 63–6
Schizophrenia Ireland, 172
Scott-Maxwell, Florida, 259
seasonal affective disorder
    (SAD), 179
self-esteem, 263
Senior Citizens Parliament, 223,
    244–7, 254
    aims, 245
    inclusivity, 247
    issues, 245–6
    success, 246–7
Senior Helpline, 70, 292
Senior Singers Chorale
    (Washington DC), 97
sexism, 242
sexuality, 242
Sharing a Personal Pleasure, 115
skills, 3
Slán Abhaile; *see* independent
    living
Slán Survey (2003), 118
Sligo County Council Arts Office,
    104–5
smoking, 126, 150–1, 161, 182
    cancer and, 160, 161
    Cessation Officers, 150, 151

social contacts, maintaining, 44–8,
    50–1, 169–70
social insurance, 38–9
Social Mentor Project, 69
social welfare, 39
Society of St Vincent de Paul, 54,
    69, 293
Special Olympics, 54
speech and language difficulties,
    158–9
    therapists, 158–9
spiritual dimension, 51, 259–76
    death and dying, 268–70; *see
        also* death and bereavement
    describing, 260–1
    development, 265–6, 272–4
        compassionate stage, 266,
            273
        conformist stage, 266, 272
        conscientious stage, 266,
            273
        cosmic stage, 266, 273
        within the Christian
            tradition, 272–4
    expressions of, 261–5
        creativity and
            appreciation, 261
        freedom, 262
        truth and personal
            meaning, 262–3
        truth and ultimate
            meaning, 264–5
    grieving/acceptance/
        receptivity, 266–7
    preciousness of life, 268
    religion and, 270; *see also*
        Christianity; religion
sport and physical activity, 117–
    19; *see also* exercise and fitness
St Anne's (Sligo), 104–5
St Brendan's Village, Mulrany,
    225

St John's Wort, 179
St Michael's Parish Active
  Retirement Group, 98
starting a business, 41–2
Stephenson, Sam, 2
stroke, 132, 152–3, 154, 158
Succession Act 1965, 232
suicide, 63–6, 174
surgery, 192
swimming, 132, 137

t'ai chi, 130–1
Taylor, Judy, 63–6
TEFL (Teaching English as a
  Foreign Language), 77, 83–4
terminal illness, 198–9, 268
Testing unto Death, 269
theatre, 95, 261
"third age", 2–4, 9, 16, 20, 87
  definition of, 3–4, 87
Thomas, Dylan, 248
Threshold Housing Advice and
  Research Centre, 225–6, 293
tinnitus, 156
Translations, 81
treatment benefits, 39, 156, 157
Trevor, William, 96
Trocaire, 72
truth, 262–5
  ultimate, 264–5; *see also* God

Ullman, Samuel, 241
United Nations
  Day of Older Persons, 251
  Principles for Older Persons,
    277–80
university, going to, 75–6, 77, 86
University College Cork (UCC),
  11
University College Dublin (UCD),
  75

University of the Third Age
  (U3A), 86, 87–91, 251, 293
  activities, 90–1
  founding of, 87–8
  in Ireland, 86, 89–91
  principles, 88–9
Ustinov, Peter, 96

Viatores Christi, 73
Victim Support, 293
Vivas Health, 200
Vocational Education Committee
  (VEC), 69, 85–6, 114
Voluntary Health Insurance
  (VHI), 200, 253
Voluntary Service International
  (VSI), 73
volunteer bureaux, 67, 70
Volunteer Organisers Linking
  Together (VOLT), 70
Volunteer Stroke Scheme, 294
volunteering, 6, 51, 53–74
  contacts for, 67–74
  definition of, 53–4
  do's and don'ts, 61–2
  holidays, 72
  is it for you?, 58–61
  overseas opportunities, 72–4
  reasons for, 55–6
  residential opportunities, 70–2
  skills for, 59
  time available for, 60–1
  what older people can bring
    to, 56–8
Volunteering Ireland, 54, 56, 60,
  67, 68, 70, 72, 294

walking, 118, 119, 126, 136, 138–
  9, 141; *see also* exercise and
  fitness
Walsh, Deirdre, 99, 104

Webster, Robin, 10
weight loss, 127, 149
West Cork Arts Centre, 105
Western Alzheimer's Society, 221
Westmeath County Council Arts
    Office, 105
Whittaker, Pamela, 90
Widows Association of Ireland,
    294; *see also* National
    Association of Widows in
    Ireland
widows/widowers pension, 39,
    250
will, making a, 232–4

Willoughby, Lillian, 1
Wisdom of the Ages, 90
*Wolfhound Guide to Evening
    Classes*, 86
World Health Organisation, 144
worker types, examples of, 20–2
writing, 261
Wwoof (Willing Workers on
    Organic Farms), 74

Yeats, William Butler, 95, 96
"young-old" and "old-old", 3–4,
    12, 16